NO ORDINARY LIFE
Awakenings in the Final Days of Apartheid

Mary Ann Byron
with Lori Windsor Mohr

Copyright © 2018 Mary Ann Byron

All rights reserved. Except as permitted under the U.S. Copyright Act of 1976 and all subsequent amendments. No part of this publication may be reproduced, distributed, or transmitted in any form or by any means, or stored in a database or retrieval system, without the prior written permission of the author.

Cover Design by Mountain High Publishing

Cover Photography by Barichivich Vitoria

Interior Photography provided by Mary Ann Byron

ISBN: 978-0578431031

Published by © Mountain High Publishing
www.MountainHighPublishing.com

For Patrick, to whom I am enormously grateful for our adventure in South Africa, its incomparable land, wildlife and people. Your loving support and encouragement in my telling this story is a gift.

Mary

TABLE OF CONTENTS

PROLOGUE
CHAPTER 1   My Side of the Mountain   1
CHAPTER 2   White Beaches   15
CHAPTER 3   Uninvited Guests   30
CHAPTER 4   Town and Country   46
CHAPTER 5   I Become My Mother   58
CHAPTER 6   The Diplomat's Wife   69
CHAPTER 7   Woman of Desire   82
CHAPTER 8   Freed from Domesticity   93
CHAPTER 9   Relief and Warlords   106
CHAPTER 10   Other Side of the Mountain   121
CHAPTER 11   Lost and Found   134
CHAPTER 12   A Rose by Any Other Name   147
CHAPTER 13   Revelations to a Friend   160
CHAPTER 14   Deadly Spring   172
CHAPTER 15   Closer to Home   193
CHAPTER 16   Mothers, Fathers, Sisters, Brothers   206
CHAPTER 17   Rhinos Bearing Gifts   222
CHAPTER 18   New Assignment   232
CHAPTER 19   White Flight   247
CHAPTER 20   Countdown   262
CHAPTER 21   Bittersweet Parting   273
BIOGRAPHIES
ACKNOWLEDGEMENTS
DISCUSSION QUESTIONS

FOREWORD

In writing a memoir, the inevitable question arises about how much of the story actually happened and how much is purely imagined. It all happened. I met Mary five years ago, but she was not yet ready to tell her story to the world. When her husband Patrick retired from the State Department as a special agent in diplomatic security, she was free to share that part of her life.

Over the last two years, Mary and I have collaborated by way of personal visits, tape recordings, phone conversations and email. Those conversations, along with her written journals, allowed me to recreate her experience in this memoir. The scenes and conversations are drawn from real events. The history is factually accurate.

But journals by nature are self-censored at the time of writing. The emotional truths can only be found between the lines. The South Africa assignment generated by Patrick's job would seem to make him the key person, but this is very much Mary's narrative. While it is a story about their marriage, I wanted to explore Mary's inner life for the emotional truths. In reading her journals, what I discovered was an intelligent and courageous woman whose resilience was borne of a deep, core strength. It had been there all along, but looking at one's life through someone else's eyes in storytelling reveals new layers. Sharing the personal aspects of her life in South Africa was not easy. Her willingness to do so reflects that courage and strength. Mary has spent a lifetime confiding in a handful of trusted girlfriends. In telling her story, she has elevated every reader to that status.

Mary's inner journey is not an unfamiliar one, but where most women take decades to find their voice, Mary navigates the difficult terrain of early marriage in a foreign land without benefit of family and friends from home. The woman who emerges from that crucible is the Mary I know today. It is the events of that journey that make her life extraordinary, a story very much worth telling.

Lori Windsor Mohr

Arriving at each new city the traveler finds a past he did not know he had—the foreignness of what you no longer are or no longer possess lies in wait for you to discover in foreign, unpossessed places.

~ Italo Calvino, *Invisible Cities*

PROLOGUE

For me that afternoon in August of 1992 was a beginning. I was stepping into a new world, a world I never knew existed. At 29, I was newly married, and ready for something. I wasn't quite sure what. My memories of that time in South Africa remain vivid as the start of my awakening.

Two decades later I am still captivated by all that happened, with a deep yearning to recount it. The further away in time, the more precious, the more fragile those memories become. My experience in South Africa and the work in Foreign Service, the struggle to find my footing in a strange new land, the terrible violence, the stress on our marriage, the election of Nelson Mandela as president, all of it—has been sequestered from the life I've lived since, tucked away as a separate reality. At midlife I feel driven to reconcile the two, and pay homage to forces that shaped me into the woman I am today.

As I look back on my marriage and the historical event in which we participated, I realize how much I have come to love the country—its people, their sorrows, their triumphs.

For I am part of South Africa. South Africa is a part of me.

One

My Side of the Mountain

August 1992

Patrick kissed me awake before our plane touched down in Johannesburg on a cloudless afternoon in August of 1992.

"You're going to love South Africa." I opened my eyes to kiss him back, then remembered we were no longer on our honeymoon. Just twelve hours earlier we had departed London after two weeks of romance traveling the British Isles. We could barely keep our hands off each other.

He handed me a glass of champagne, then put his face next to mine, squished against the window for my first view. The sky was a brilliant blue, the color of clean air and hope.

"Didn't I tell you it was beautiful?"

"The perfect vacation destination," that's how Patrick had described South Africa—a wildly diverse land with virgin beaches, majestic mountains, wide-open deserts and big game reserves. It was a world away from Minnesota, my world, where everything was white—the landscape, the people, the customs, the attitudes.

One of eight children, I was raised by parents who wanted nothing more than to be together, to work hard and die of old age surrounded by those they loved.

I had a different plan.

Like millions of girls born during the 1970's Women's Movement, Mary Richards was my role model, the character played by Mary Tyler Moore in the sitcom bearing her name. Like Mary Richards, I would go to college, find a job in the city, and thrive as a single woman in a man's world with a Mr. Grant and Rhoda as surrogate family. I had created a facsimile of that life in Minneapolis having worked my way up to Director of Public Relations at a luxury hotel. Life was all about work, friends, boyfriends, fun. Politics was a distant bleep on the radar. South Africa meant Meryl Streep in *Out of Africa*. That was before I met Patrick.

When we landed in Johannesburg that afternoon, I knew as much about South Africa as most Americans—that it was a country torn apart by racial tension, unfathomable inequality between the races. Apartheid had been exposed as the brutal, racist brainchild of a white minority government desperate to stay in power. By the time we arrived, Nelson Mandela had been released from prison under the same international pressure that convinced President F.W. de Klerk's white National Party to negotiate an end to the apartheid regime. The writing on the wall—apartheid was unsustainable even through the use of brutal force. President de Klerk could either deal with anarchy at home or face global isolation.

The president and Nelson Mandela had already begun negotiations for a new government—both a president and new parliament—determined by vote in which all South Africans would have a say for the first time in three hundred years of white minority rule. But it wasn't just President de Klerk and Nelson Mandela at the negotiating table. Zulu Chief Buthelezi was a major player. Like Mandela, he wanted to end white rule. But Chief Buthelezi had no interest in a united, democratic South Africa—he wanted his own sovereign nation in the Zulu homeland.

Change was in the air.

But change brought uncertainty fueled by fear, racist stereotyping on both sides. The entire world held its collective breath waiting for the country either to devolve into civil war or keep it together through the negotiation process long enough to get to a "one-person-one-vote" election. Patrick's mission, our mission, was to protect the entire American community in the Western Cape Province during the transition to democracy.

I say our mission because marriage to a Special Agent meant marriage to the State Department. Like the second sister-wife in a polygamous union, time with my husband would be whatever was left over after the State took its share.

That was okay. I was thrilled to join my husband on assignment. A stint in public relations at one of Cape Town's high-end hotels would certainly add to my resume. No one would ever refer to me as a "trailing spouse."

Patrick's mission to protect the American community in Cape Town had not seemed so daunting with President de Klerk and Nelson Mandela already well into negotiations. Then Boipatong happened. That changed everything. Two months before we arrived I was packing dishes to go into storage when CNN broke news of the killings.

> "...one of the bloodiest and most brutal massacres in South Africa has taken place in Boipatong with forty-five killed."

I ran to our wall map. My finger stopped over Eastern South Africa. Cape Town was in the West. It was the first of countless moments of guilt-followed-by-relief that would wash over me in the next two years.

Boipatong was a township near Johannesburg, one of ten areas designated for blacks under apartheid law. The day of the massacre supporters of Mandela's African National Congress, the party of most South Africans, had staged a peaceful march in a bid for votes in the township. Three hundred armed men affiliated with Chief Buthelezi's Inkatha Freedom Party attacked the marchers. Political pundits suspected the attack was aimed at undermining the delicate negotiations between Mandela's ANC and President de Klerk's National Party.

It worked. The violence disrupted the talks as Mandela fought Buthelezi for control of the KwaZulu Natal homeland. Mandela wanted all blacks to support a united South Africa. Buthelezi didn't. The two men were at loggerheads, a political battle that would plague the negotiation process and threaten the election into the eleventh hour.

Black-on-black violence in the townships was endemic. Mandela blamed de Klerk's heavy-handed state police for instigating it to prolong instability, delay an election.

De Klerk blamed Buthelezi with his demand for a separate Zulu nation. Buthelezi blamed Mandela for forcing people to choose allegiance between tribal homelands and a united country. It was political chaos.

By the time we arrived, negotiations were still at an impasse. Violence continued to escalate. U.S. Ambassador Princeton Lyman's safety and that of his family were paramount after threats from right wing radicals who had a vested interest in continued minority rule.

As we taxied down the runway Patrick pointed to a billboard—*A World within One Country*. South Africa, on the southern tip of the continent, is twice the size of Texas, but unlike the desert southwest, this country had mountains, forests, plains, tropics, jungles, all reflected in the billboard image. It also had gold and diamond mines. Rich in natural resources, impoverished in humanity, it was a clash of first and third worlds. Dependent on cheap labor for its economy, the white minority had used legalized racism in apartheid rule to sustain it. That was about to end.

The African sun was bright when we deplaned at Johannesburg International Airport. Warm wind whipped my skirt. Heat was welcome after the air-conditioned cabin. Patrick stood behind me in the customs line, nuzzling my neck as I pulled my hair into a ponytail. A short two-hour flight to Cape Town and we could resume our honeymoon, at least until Monday, when Patrick had to report for work at the American Embassy.

We crossed the tarmac to board the smaller plane. Flying at low altitude gave me a glimpse of the countryside, the prairies and deserts between Johannesburg and the Atlantic coast. My spine tingled. Located in the coastal neighborhood of Sea Point, our new residence was near a beach. I couldn't wait for the big reveal.

Cape Town came into focus. My stomach tightened. Army tanks patrolled the streets downtown. I flashed on the Rodney King riots at home a few months earlier when four white police officers had been acquitted of the videotaped beating.

Now it was déjà vu with racial tension roiling beneath the surface in Cape Town. A vague sense of apprehension took hold. It had been a recurring feeling, nascent but there. The wedding, the honeymoon, a condo to pack, a new Director of Public Relations to orient, friends and family to part with—there had been plenty of reason to avoid worries about the political climate in South Africa.

"Not exactly *Out of Africa*, is it?"

"No."

"How 'bout I order a safari outfit from Abercrombie and Fitch?"

I smirked. "It didn't look all that convincing on Robert Redford." Patrick's body was made for the three-piece suits he had worn as a trial lawyer, the suits he now wore as a Special Agent in the Bureau of Diplomatic Security. After commercial salmon fishing in Bristol Bay, Alaska, in the summers during law school, Patrick was convinced that he was better suited for real life action than courtroom drama. After winning his first and only trial, he concluded the stress of litigation wasn't worth it. Foreign Service would be a better way to appease his adventure bug.

He looked over my shoulder at the scene on the streets. "Things have heated up since Boipatong." He caressed my neck. "You're tense." I closed my eyes as he rolled my neck side-to-side.

This was the pressure cooker we walked into that August afternoon in 1992.

Patrick and I had commuter dated for a year before moving in together. Every big city has luxury hotels. His job was based in D.C. I got the transfer to my hotel corporation's sister city in the capital so we could be together.

It hadn't been love at first sight, but almost. I had organized the VIP logistics for the Chinese vice-premier's stay at my hotel. From the entrance I watched Patrick step out of the first limo, his long lean body packed with muscular authority.

Sexy, sophisticated in his dark suit and mirrored sunglasses, he reminded me of a contemporary James Bond. Patrick glanced in my direction but didn't notice me. At least that's what I thought at the time.

The deeper we fell in love, the more tentative Patrick became about marriage. It wasn't his heavy schedule as a federal agent. It was the career itself, a line of work which included big chunks of time apart with little or no communication. It had taken me a long time to understand his job in the Bureau of Diplomatic Security, the U.S. State Department's lead law enforcement and security organization abroad responsible for the protection of all our diplomatic missions. An agent assigned to a high-risk environment somewhere around the globe created and administered security programs, advised U.S. ambassadors and other officers on security matters, and implemented and managed programs to protect American officials.

How that translated into a job description was another matter. Patrick wasn't in the Secret Service. He wasn't a private bodyguard. He wasn't in the military. He wasn't an intelligence officer. Yet his job encompassed all four. Tasked with protecting the ambassador and the diplomatic staff as well as the community on foreign soil, Patrick traveled with the ambassador on high risk details within the mission, dealt with intelligence and counterintelligence, and worked with the military to implement security programs. I still wasn't sure what all that meant. "High risk details" sounded vaguely dangerous. But all I ever saw him wear to work was a three-piece suit, so whatever he did on a mission was cloaked in mystery, devoid of context under well-tailored clothes.

What *was* perfectly clear in our first year of dating was that Patrick was gone a lot, couldn't tell me much and was probably exposed to considerable danger. Professionally, we lived completely separate lives. My worries about his safety were abstract since it was hard to imagine exactly what he was doing. But I didn't understand how gaps of time apart along with secrecy about his job fed into reservations about marriage.

On my own for a decade since leaving home, I was comfortable with time alone, time with friends, long hours at work. A full time man was the last thing I needed. In fact, it suited me to have time on my own, as if I hadn't really given up my single life.

The first year we lived together I had been tested. Patrick traveled with Secretary of State Shultz for the better part of that time. No email. No phone. We had minimal contact as he and the secretary moved from one hotspot to another, Patrick gathering intelligence to secure the secretary and his staff. That year was my boot camp. I had perfected the art of waiting. As would any single woman proud of her independence, I carried on with my own life with plenty of friends to stave off loneliness. Things changed with his next assignment. We had talked about my joining him abroad. But girlfriend status wouldn't do for the State Department. We had to make a decision. One month before our arrival in Johannesburg we tied the knot. As far as I was concerned the South African mission would be bliss compared with his previous assignment. Here, we were together, madly in love, about to be part of history. I had no reason to worry about civil unrest in Cape Town or the impact of a high-risk post on our marriage.

I did have reason to wonder what else Patrick hadn't told me or what I hadn't wanted to hear. The Boipatong Massacre happened on the other side of the country. Army tanks on the streets below didn't make sense. Patrick had assured my parents Cape Town itself was "as white as Minnesota"—a hubbub of ex-pats and State Department diplomats like himself. It wasn't personal safety that worried me. It was harder to dismiss the occasional waves of anxiety about the newness of everything—marriage, Foreign Service, marriage and Foreign Service together, a new public relations job, making friends. As a diplomat's wife, I had no idea what was expected of me. Until I had a job, my plan was to watch the other wives, get the idea of how it all worked.

My father said growing up I had a talent for retreating to the background in new situations until I found my footing. I suppose he was right. Happy by nature, it was easy to fit in anywhere once I acclimated. The same would be true in Cape Town. It was just the transition that might prove tricky. Good thing I was a quick study. I leaned my head on Patrick's shoulder, shoving the worries aside.

At the airport in Cape Town our host family found us before we found them. I would have been happier picking up keys at the embassy rather than meeting the couple. But the State Department had more rules than the Catholic Church. Protocol for incoming officials required a formal reception. Like the neighborhood Welcome Wagon in Minnesota, I would think of these formal procedures as government versions of the good behavior I had grown up with in the Midwest.

"Don't let the ponytail fool you, she's old enough for legal debauchery," Patrick said to Henry and Jody with a wink, anticipating the inevitable question that always came with introductions. The ponytail did make me look ten years younger. My original plan was to meet the Hilliards with my hair down. That went kaput when the Cape Town wind made it impossible to see in front of myself through a maze of crazy blonde tangles.

My attire at work had always been a dark suit with my shoulder-length hair down. The comments came anyway. My boss joked to more than one naysayer, "Don't let the dimples and blonde hair fool you. Not only can she step up to the plate, she can hit it out of the ballpark." So I wasn't surprised when the Hilliards were taken aback. It didn't help that I was nine years younger than Patrick, not that he looked his age either. Together, we were an ad for the All American couple—him with his athletic build and Homecoming King good looks, me the prototype of Norwegian ancestry that runs deep in our country's Heartland.

Henry laughed at the debauchery comment. The two men walked ahead of me and Jody to their black BMW in the loading zone. I noticed the diplomatic plates right away. Puffed with pride, for a nanosecond I was a celebrity stepping into a sleek sedan after the Oscars. I had to admit, it *was* nice being met by another American couple.

Excitement about the residence fluttered through me. Proximity to the beach would make up for the flat itself. I had prepared myself for institutional drab. Decorating had always been fun. If I could transform a room of IKEA furniture into a warm nest, used government-issue pieces wouldn't be too much of a challenge. Jet lagged, disoriented, I half-listened as Henry went on about the current racial tension.

"Truth is, the place is a powder keg. These stop-start negotiations have everybody on edge with de Klerk's hair-trigger police backing crazy Buthelezi and his Zulus. Who knows if this election will even—"

"C'mon, Henry. You don't want to scare Mary before she's had a chance to fall in love with the place." Patrick yanked my ponytail with a wink. "It's nothing to worry about, just De Klerk flexing enough muscle to keep a lid on things."

His words drifted through my head but I wasn't listening. The drive took us along the edge of Khayelitsha Township, like Boipatong, another one of the designated areas for blacks under the apartheid regime. I had never seen real squalor in the small town where I grew up, much less in the corporate bubble of high-end hospitality. From my window I watched as row upon row of rundown matchbox bungalows gave way to a slum— lean-to's, shacks that looked like a good wind would level them. How did they survive the fierce Cape winds?

Skin-and-bone dogs rummaged through trash in the streets. Kids huddled on one corner, played in the dirt. Laundry hung on lines between dirty posts. The stench of smoke from fire barrels used for heating came through the car windows. Instinctively, I drew back.

We rounded a bend in the road. Monolithic Table Mountain came into view, straight ahead in all its breathtaking glory. It seemed to pop out of nowhere, a behemoth presence, so sheer the cliffs, so level its top that it didn't look real, this rock table in the sky. The landscape had changed within half a mile. Graceful European homes set deep on their lots gave an air of understated elegance. Manicured lawns bordered by flowerbeds painted a picture of idyllic living, shady streets made for leisurely morning walks and neighborly chats. I let out a breath.

Patrick pinched me. "Didn't I tell you it was beautiful, Mar?"

Without taking my eyes off the scenery, I answered with an elbow to his ribs. A sign read *Kaapstad*, Afrikaans for Cape Town. Henry offered the backstory. Dutch settlers, Boers, had landed in Cape Town in the 1650s on their search for a shortcut to the West Indies. As settlers moved inland, whole nations of African tribes moved south. Eventually the settlers and natives clashed, each claiming the land. Boer settlers have considered this home ever since.

Calvinist to the core, Afrikaners had it on direct authority from God that it was the mission of this tiny band of Europeans to convert the country to Christianity. I flashed on the Pilgrims landing at Plymouth Rock. Like Afrikaners, they made a deal with God that if He saved them, they would devote their lives to the cause. That part hadn't worked any better with American Indians than it had with blacks in South Africa. Natives went underground to practice their traditional religions. But unlike Europeans wiping out American Indians, the white minority in South Africa had to find another way to control the black majority. Gunpowder gave them their answer. Three hundred years later, Dutch Afrikaners still ran the country.

Henry drove us into the business district, streets lined with grand buildings befitting a seat of government evoking three centuries of white rule. When Afrikaners and their English-speaking brethren (Brits, French), couldn't agree on one capital city, they came up with three—Cape Town, the Mother City in the west as the legislative seat; the judicial seat would be Bloemfontein in the middle of the country; Pretoria would stand as the administrative center. U.S. ambassadors assigned to South Africa split their time between Pretoria and Cape Town with a six-month rotation.

No woman would have come up with such an arrangement, given the logistics of setting up house in two places, moving every six months. Patrick told me Cape Town was a beautiful city compared with the more industrial Pretoria. I couldn't believe our good fortune in landing the post. Henry pointed out the U.S. Embassy where Patrick would spend most days. An American flag billowed in the wind, a condition I would learn was a constant. That explained railings along the sidewalks.

We turned west toward Sea Point, a narrow stretch of land between Table Mountain and the Atlantic Ocean. Salt air told me when we reached the coast. Henry leaned toward the back seat. "Mary, this neighborhood has always been elite, 'Whites Only'."

"But it's not segregated now, right?"

Jody leaned over the seat. "It doesn't take long here to get spoiled, Mary. A few months and you'll never want to leave. The blacks you'll see around here are either domestic workers or gardeners who come in from the townships with permission."

Victoria and Albert Road paralleled a wide promenade along the ocean. The scene mimicked photos Patrick had shown me of San Diego where he grew up. It may have been thirty minutes from the black township, but Sea Point might as well have been a different planet. Locals in shorts and flip-flops walked their dogs, jogged, rode bikes. Sailboats in the distance completed the laid back ambiance. This was definitely more the "vacation destination" image Patrick had painted. With a stifled grin, I pushed my knee against his. He pushed back. *See? I told you*, that push said. The government flat might not be anything to write home about but the setting was straight out of *Sunset* magazine.

A paraglider appeared in the sky over Table Mountain. "That's Lion's Head Peak." Patrick said it was known by the Dutch as *Leeuwen Kop* (Lion's Head); Signal Hill was known as *Leeuwen Staart* (Lion's Tail). Together the shape resembled a crouching lion.

"It's like he's watching over us."

Henry pulled up in front of a nondescript highrise building. The guys retrieved our suitcases from the trunk while Jody spoke to the security guard at the door. She introduced us to Mr. Khumalo, a big black man who greeted us with downcast eyes, the deferential manner a vestige of servitude in the dying days of apartheid. Jody led us to the elevator, then punched the sixth-floor button. I braced myself. Henry and Jody stayed back as Patrick and I stepped inside.

My mouth dropped open. We looked at each other in awe, then back at the flat. Light flooded the room from floor-to-ceiling windows. It bounced off the walls and high ceilings as if through a prism, sunlight refracted into a dazzling spectrum of color. Glass doors opened to a wide, wrap-around deck which made the flat feel even bigger. Patrick and I walked toward the window in careful steps as if approaching the edge of a cliff. The whole world was outside that window. Waves pounded the jagged rocks below, spray and foam drenching the sand. As far as the eye could see was nothing but ocean and sky.

An involuntary burst of glee escaped my lips. Patrick threw his arm around my shoulder. Jody and Henry giggled, clearly pleased they'd kept mum.

Our tight-lipped hosts led us on a tour, both grinning at our obvious surprise. The living room was an Ethan Allen showroom. My best friend Veronica had worked at one in Minneapolis. At lunch we would meet there to ogle the classic dark wood furniture, multiple pay levels above what we could afford in our twenties. Now the showroom was mine, at least for two years.

Ethan Allen continued in the dining room. A mahogany table for eight looked elegant with its matching glass-door

China hutch. Pale curtains fluttered in the open windows. We followed Jody into the kitchen. She gave us pointers on the range, the coffeemaker, showed us the laundry area. The pantry was stocked with paper products. A round table filled the breakfast nook surrounded by glass on three sides, the ocean view a panorama. On the table sat a basket of fruit, snacks, coffee and wine from Henry and Jody. With that to get us started, they left us on our own.

Patrick and I giggled as we tiptoed through the flat again, not quite convinced it was ours. The three bedrooms had the same Ethan Allen furniture. The third one would be our home office that could double as a guest room. The master would be at the opposite end of the hall with the ocean view. The middle bedroom had no windows—the designated "safe room" outfitted for lockdown with a buzzer that connected directly to the embassy. My stomach turned. A nice palm in front of the door would help me ignore it.

Patrick's hand in mine, I led him back to the living room, then through the slider to the deck. Cool sea air hit us in the face. Container ships in the distance slid in stealth—metal hulks in the Monet seascape. Whitecaps whipped into foam peaks that disappeared with each swell. The whole place was alive.

In our first quiet moment, jet lag slammed us. The master bedroom had blackout curtains that would have helped quell the chaos of our circadian rhythms. Instead, we turned the sofa around to face the sea. Too tired to talk, we drank wine from our welcome basket and listened to the hush of waves at low tide. In utter contentment we let exhaustion take its toll.

Two

White Beaches

September 1992

A storm that night left the sky a deep indigo blue, the day already hot in the African sun. Patrick didn't report to the embassy until Monday. The weekend was ours. He was anxious to show me his favorite spots around the Cape Peninsula. A three-hour drive would bring us to the southern tip of Africa where the Indian and Atlantic Oceans converged at the Cape of Good Hope, geography I had read about in grammar school, now in my backyard.

Azisa, the building maid, was on her way down the hall when we left the flat. We introduced ourselves. Most Americans in the diplomatic community had live-in help. No wonder it was such a desirable post—plenty of sunshine, good food, a favorable exchange rate, big game reserves three hours away, the Atlantic coast at your doorstep, domestic help. Diplomatic families ending their embassy post would refer maids and nannies to the incoming tenants as a way to keep the help employed.

For security reasons Patrick had nixed the idea of live-in domestic help. Home would be the one place he could let down his guard in his intelligence-sensitive world. Azisa would be our part-time maid. It was only the two of us with no kids. Besides, I liked to cook. As backup, Azisa could do whatever cleaning I didn't. It was a perfect arrangement.

High voltage lights activated when we stepped into the underground parking garage, the place bright as daylight. Patrick checked the government late model sedan, a black Toyota, for signs of tampering. Scanning for an explosive device was protocol for Americans in a high-threat post. The State Department had a set list of rules for just about everything.

First on our list of stops was a grocery store, then a bank. The Pick & Pay market we had seen on our drive into Sea Point was a few blocks from the flat. There's nothing like an unfamiliar market to make you feel disoriented.

Patrick and I walked down each aisle, examining the inventory, mentally aligning items with their U.S. counterparts. We made our way to the produce section with its colorful bins of citrus—plums, pears, litchi. With our limited rand, the South African currency equivalent to a U.S. quarter at the time, we bought fruit, drinks, and biscuits to go with our gift basket meats and cheeses.

A tourist on holiday would never have guessed the state of political tension, much less violence, anywhere near Cape Town.

The place was a storybook scene. The Victoria and Alfred Waterfront gave way to a curved ribbon of highway hugging the rugged cliffs as we passed one stunning beach after another. Named after the queen and her second son—who made a big splash with locals when he visited Cape Town as a 16-year-old Royal Navy Midshipman in 1860—Victoria Road was a direct path from Sea Point to Bantry Bay, then on to Clifton Beaches, eventually winding its way to the Cape of Good Hope. These names were foreign to me, dots on a map. Patrick could have been a local the way he pointed out this beach, that village, favorite spots during his nine-month post before we met.

The breathtaking drive passed quaint towns, ancient fishing villages, and rocky points jutting out of endless white-sand beaches. Wrecked ships littered the landscape, testament to centuries of sailing the treacherous seas that left twenty-five hundred vessels grounded. Those were the ones that didn't sink. The Cape of Good Hope with its gale-force winds was infamously known as the "graveyard of ships." I would have to get used to the constant wind. Back home I hated it. Here it tempered the heat. Body lotion would become my new best friend in an effort to keep my skin from leathering like a lizard. My hair was another story.

Patrick pulled over. He took my hand as we climbed over boulders the size of VW Bugs until we reached the sand. "How's that for a view?" He turned me around. Table Mountain loomed in the background, a massive formation towering over the city, the Cape Basin a verdant Shangri-la at its feet. Billowing white clouds hung over the mountaintop like a tablecloth ready to drop into place.

What a gorgeous sight. If only Mom could see it. A sucker-punch to the gut reminded me she was a hemisphere away.

All of a sudden Patrick flung me back in a dramatic dip, then pulled me into a long kiss. "Who says I'm not romantic?"

Feeling safe and small in his arms, I looked up at my handsome husband. "It's not 'romantic' that I question. It's 'spontaneous'."

"You don't think that Robert Redfordesque move was spontaneous?"

"Maybe. Let's see if you can up that." I flicked off my sandals on the way to the surf. Hikers on Table Mountain could have heard the scream that followed. Melted ice would have been warmer than the Atlantic Ocean. Patrick bent over in laughter. He had warned me—warm air, cold water. But I had to venture into the sea, immerse my whole body, feel it, embrace it. I high-stepped it back to the sand. He threw his arms around me, rubbing my shoulders as he held me close, his body heat warm against me.

"You're spontaneous enough for both of us, Mar. Tell you what…I'll be spontaneous when it doesn't involve misery." Misery—he couldn't have been more wrong. I was the luckiest woman in the world.

Not in a million years could I have seen what lay ahead.

The next day we unpacked our things, which wasn't much in the four suitcases. The rest was en route by airfreight and container ship—personal belongings like framed photos, CDs, books, pieces of accent furniture, our Honda Civic. The flat had everything else, including three televisions. Not one had a cable box. A big rugby match between South Africa's *Springboks* and New Zealand's *All Blacks* would be on the next day, the contest the Holy Grail of sport in South Africa that fueled ongoing debate over which team was better, as unanswerable a question as the American counterpart over best all-time quarterback—Joe Montana or Tom Brady.

Patrick was a real jock. In school he played football, basketball, swam, played lacrosse. He skied, biked, hiked, sailed, and fished. In college he had worked for a local construction company; in law school it was salmon fishing in Alaska. Mastering a physical challenge was part of who he was, what he loved to do. It was also part of his job. He may have been a diplomat in a three-piece suit, but Patrick's security responsibilities required both stamina and weaponry skills. Physical training was ongoing, with basketball his sport of choice on a mission. All the same, he saw it as his diplomatic duty to follow South Africa's national sport. We headed into town for a cable box in time for the rugby match.

Fruit stands lined the sidewalk in front of the electronics store. A black man selling fruit watched as the sedan slid into place. I closed the cap on my hand lotion, careful not to let my wedding ring slide off my thigh.

"Mary, am I close enough to the curb? This thing's a tank compared to the Honda."

I swung the door open. It lodged between two fruit crates. "Can you pull up a little?" My hand on the door, I watched in slow motion as my wedding ring rolled off my thigh into the gutter. I jumped out. Patrick cut the ignition.

"My ring fell in the gutter," I shouted to the vendor. He said nothing, his face a blank. Dropping to one knee, I searched along the curb. Patrick came around the car. The vendor sprang up. A commotion followed. The thief took off down the sidewalk, knocking into people and crates until he disappeared.

Patrick began questioning bystanders. He did a double take when I bolted past him after the thief. At the corner I searched in every direction. Nothing. He was gone. I returned to Patrick. Of course none of the bystanders had seen anything. Patrick started toward me. Distraught, I got back in the car, slamming the door. He stood for a moment—shoulders slumped—then went inside the electronics store.

Nine weeks, that's how long I had worn the wedding ring, my most prized possession. Patrick had put so much into it. We had taken a trip to the Diamond District in New York City to educate ourselves. Patrick made note of designs I liked. But he didn't buy a ring. Two weeks later he planned a surprise weekend. The Blue Ridge Mountains in Virginia were seventy-five miles from our condo. After a satisfying day-hike in Shenandoah National Park, we changed for dinner. Patrick had made a reservation at Blue Meadows Lodge an hour before sunset.

It was a beautiful warm evening. The world aglow in orange light, he pulled out a pear-shaped diamond with a gold band. It was the single most romantic moment of my twenty-nine years. Now the ring was gone on our second day. I guess Cape Town wasn't "as white as Minnesota." I kicked myself for letting the ring roll off my thigh. It was the darn wind. Every time we got in the car I had the hand lotion out.

Back at the flat Patrick fussed with the cable box with no mention of the theft. He seemed unconcerned about it. Worse, his ability to switch gears seamlessly irritated me. I took matters into my own hands. When Patrick heard I had called the local radio station with the offer of a reward, he threw his arms in the air. They slapped down at his sides in resignation at what would happen next.

The calls started. One tip led us to a dark dead-end road in a rough area. After that we ignored the calls. The phone must have rung two dozen times that evening until we took it off the hook at bedtime. The next day we returned to the fruit stand, this time with the reward. I looked around for the vendor-thief. As we got out of the car, movement caught my eye—the thief. He was half a block away, no doubt tipped off by our government plates.

"That's him!"

Patrick sprinted toward the guy, approaching from one side. I caught up on the other. We had him cornered. Patrick leaned close, his voice calm. "I have three hundred rand in my pocket. Hand over the ring and it's yours."

Nothing. The man's face was a blank. It was all I could do not to slap him. Patrick must have read my thoughts. He grabbed him by the shirt collar. With the other hand he flashed his Special Agent badge. Wrenching his arm fee, the man motioned Patrick to let go. He did with a step back. Without making eye contact with either of us the vendor pulled a wad of tissue from his pocket. He handed it to me. Sure enough, my ring was in the dirty tissue. The man turned to Patrick with his hand open.

"Wait! How do we know he hasn't swapped out the stones? I want a jeweler to see it."

"You gonna make me babysit until she finds one herself, or tell me where?"

I ran the three-block distance. The jeweler listened as I summarized the theft in breathless spurts. A pen-shaped device would turn green if the stones were real. I waited. The light turned green. In a sardonic tone the jeweler told me it would have been hard to pawn the ring, a unique design that would have let the buyer know it was stolen. That was little comfort. But the ring was back on my finger.

I retraced my steps. "You're lucky he doesn't call the authorities on you," I said through clenched teeth. Patrick handed over the promised reward. The thief took off. Aware of bystanders watching the transaction, Patrick and I jumped in the car and sped away.

At the flat I concocted hors d'oeuvres of fruit and cheese from our snack supply. Patrick popped open a local Cabernet. On the deck we toasted our good fortune.

"Ya know, Mary, we're lucky this turned out the way it did. Spontaneity isn't always the best plan."

"That's an oxymoron."

"What if that man had been armed? Think how my report to the State Department would look—'Top Security Attaché's wife sustains life-threatening injuries in pursuit of thief.'"

"Or—'Top Security Attaché's Wife Loses Diamond Ring to Lowlife Thief.'"

"And 'Lives to See Another Day'."

"Hon, I couldn't help myself."

Patrick glanced at the headline of the morning *Argus* on the patio table.

MASSACRE IN CISKEI 29 SHOT DEAD

Twenty-eight ANC supporters, including Secretary-General Cyril Ramaphosa and one soldier, had been attacked by what were believed to be government-backed forces supporting Buthelezi's Inkatha Freedom Party. From all accounts the march had been peaceful until Ciskei troops fired on the crowd. It was Boipatong all over again.

"Hon, my ring was simple theft."

"Nothing here is simple. You do not want to be a blue-eyed blonde in pursuit of a black man. Even in Cape Town. And I don't want to be one either. You put us both in danger."

How could he see my bravery as poor impulse control? I fought the urge to argue. "You're right. I hadn't thought of it that way. It's just that I never let my brothers get away with anything. I couldn't believe that man would steal my ring."

"You can't just follow your impulse, Mary. This really could've ended very differently. The embassy might've had to get involved."

I looked at him askance. "Are you worried about me or your job?"

His mouth twisted in a sarcastic grin.

"If it's any consolation, I wouldn't have given chase had you not been there."

"I'm glad to hear that." He gave me a perfunctory kiss, his irritation subdued but not gone. He was right. It was also easier for him to bring up protocol—a report to the State Department—than to express his real concern. My husband was adept at talking about security issues. Feelings were another matter.

It was early in our marriage, but like all couples, we had already developed our own system of coded communication. Patrick's feelings were presented as concern over a breach of protocol because that's how he thought. That's how he was trained. Well trained. The man I married was compassionate to the core. But in his line of work, expressing emotion could be dangerous. I had learned to look for the feelings beneath his words. This time it was easy. Sometimes it was like decoding an acronym.

Patrick had known Cape Town wasn't as safe as he had made it sound to my parents. He could have warned me to be careful. But he couldn't bring himself to do that, reveal any hint of a flaw in the place he loved so much, wanted me to love. What my husband didn't know was that I could love imperfection. Growing up with seven siblings had taught me that flaws were a fact of life. In my family we had to forgive, move on or live in a constant state of tension. And so we learned to love one another, flaws and all.

But Patrick was a perfectionist. He had to be with a job where the margin for error was miniscule. His mother had been a teacher who pushed him hard. She understood that his innate intelligence could take him far in life. Now he pushed himself. Flaws were considered weaknesses, maybe not in others, but that was the bar he set for himself. Patrick always strove to improve his already polished skills, learn more, and do better. When it came to security, flaws could be fatal. Had something happened to me that day, he never would have forgiven himself.

In that moment I understood that nothing could have prepared me for South Africa. I would have to recalibrate my worldview, take danger into account for the first time in my life. It wasn't clear how I would keep awareness from morphing into fear. Nor was it clear how this new outlook would change me.

But I knew it would.

The *Springboks* lost to New Zealand, forty-one to thirteen. Patrick said there were simply too many errors from the Boks—their halfbacks were terrible, their defensive structures even worse, scrums and lineouts a shambles. He said it was no surprise given the eleven-year dry spell. The U.N. General Assembly had imposed an international boycott against South Africa as pressure to end apartheid. Economic sanctions may have hurt the financial system but the rugby boycott struck at the very soul of white Afrikaners with their Calvinist belief in racial superiority. That explained why black South Africans cheered for New Zealand during the game. Rugby as the national sport was synonymous with apartheid.

The morning sun caressed my bare arms as I sat overlooking the rocky coastline. Container ships slid by in the distance. Before long, one would dock along the Victoria and Alfred Waterfront with our belongings. In spite of Ethan Allen I missed my things, missed familiarity.

The *Argus* that morning had an op-ed piece about the Ciskei Massacre. Mandela had withdrawn from negotiations in response to the second bloodbath in three months, vocal in his accusation that President de Klerk's National Party had backed Buthelezi's Inkatha Freedom Party to fight Mandela and the ANC. The president repeated the same denial he had issued about Boipatong as he scrambled to bring Mandela back to the negotiating table.

Boipatong had left forty-nine dead. Ciskei, twenty-nine. The Rodney King riots, fifty-three. It seemed we hadn't come very far in our own race wars. For the first time I began to wonder if maybe Henry had been right the day he drove us to Sea Point when he said if the negotiation process didn't get back on track soon, the election might not happen. Every time negotiations stalled, more violence erupted.

Death was one thing, violence another. I had grown up around death. As coroner of our town, Dad treated the deceased with the respect and dignity of a family member. Those who died were our neighbors, townsfolk like us. It defied belief, the idea of dead bodies lying in the street waiting to be tossed into a truck for removal. Those were the images on TV, whether bloodshed in the townships or outside the stadium in Ciskei. I reminded myself that Cape Town was ex-pats and government people. And the occasional thief.

Patrick left early for work in the government car. Our Honda was still somewhere on a ship in the Atlantic. Walking suited me, especially along the promenade on a beautiful morning that refused to be ignored. Cape Town did indeed seem like another world, Sea Point a bubble within that world, far from turmoil in the outskirts. Decked in shorts, tank top and flip-flops, I left Azisa to her mopping. Bidding Mr. Khumalo good day at the door, I headed out for the twenty-minute walk to Clifton Beaches.

At ten in the morning it was already seventy-five degrees. Heaven. The waterfront promenade was alive with locals, tourists, black nannies pushing white babies in prams. Pride swept through me at my status as a local as long as I didn't look at the big picture. I spent most of my first eighteen years in Moorhead where my father knew by name the friends and neighbors whose funerals he arranged. My mother managed our household of eight children where I was seventh in the line-up.

In America, unlike South Africa, no one fought over ownership of the land, at least not once we pretty much decimated the American Indian. In the Midwest more than a century earlier, people were given acreage in exchange for moving to the area and farming the land. The Northern Pacific Railway brought settlers to the northwest part of Minnesota to take advantage of the Homestead Act of 1851. Goods were hauled by ox cart from St. Cloud onto steamboats for the journey north to Manitoba, Canada and beyond. As a little girl, I imagined one day the river would carry me to the big city. My dad used to joke that as a transcontinental city, I need look no further than our own backyard. By 1881 Moorhead had a reputation as "Sin City" with more than a hundred bars at a time when neighboring Fargo, North Dakota didn't allow the sale of alcohol. The real "Sin City" in Nevada would later usurp our town's reputation, forever stripping it of its claim to fame. No one, and I mean no one, would mistake Moorhead for Las Vegas.

My plan growing up had always been to leave Moorhead. But once out of school, I wasn't sure what was expected of me. College, of course—the American Dream went hand-in-hand with higher education. That's what we were taught. It's what we believed. My sisters talked about college, marriage, kids. I'm not sure about my brothers. Beyond college, I didn't know what I wanted to do with my life.

The one certainty was that it would be something different from the one my mother had lived, maybe even different from the ones my sisters would lead, for a while anyway. Marriage and children would come someday. In the meantime, I intended to experience the world, at least all of it that I could find in Minneapolis. No one in my family, including me, could have imagined I would be the wife of a diplomat, strolling along the Atlantic seaboard half a world away in South Africa, happy as you please in shorts and a tank top.

By the holiday atmosphere on the promenade, you would never know anyone worked. A life of leisure did not appeal to me, maybe because I had never known one. Mom was the hardest working woman in my world with eight little ones and a home to run. Most of us kids were pretty easy. The single oblong balloon among us took as much of her energy as the seven round ones put together. But she managed to handle it all, a master of organization and negotiation. Over the course of my childhood I had learned those skills to a tee. They had gotten me where I was with my career in a man's corporate world. I had had to push hard.

In the beginning, most people at work misread my agreeable temperament as weakness. "You catch more flies with honey than vinegar," my mom used to say. Growing up in a passel of siblings hones one's ability to get along. Or maybe it came naturally. Either way, I loved people. So assertiveness with a smile not only came easily, it brought opportunities to showcase my skills. From there, it was one rung at a time up the ladder. The satisfaction of a job well done fueled me. Work became my life—that, and my girlfriends. Wine dates were a highlight of my week.

How I loved my single life. As Mary Byron I had become my own version of Mary Richards, with several Rhodas. Girlfriends were a mainstay, my siblings in the city. When we married, Patrick hadn't balked at my keeping my surname, a lyrical short one shared with the famous eighteenth century English poet, Lord Byron. Byron and McGhee had a nice ring, Patrick said. The State Department did not agree, insisting it was inappropriate for a couple in Foreign Service. Maybe it would confuse the host government or be seen as too liberal in another country. Maybe it just made State Department forms harder to fill out. The reasoning wasn't clear to me. But in South Africa I would be known as Mrs. McGhee. It was only for two years. I could do that. As a self-supporting woman who had done fine on her own for a decade, my identity at twenty-nine was hardly shaky.

Patrick had been behind my career from the start, a given in today's culture, but not so much in the 1980s. The late hours at work when my hotel had a big event weren't an issue. He would cook for himself. On the rare occasion both of us were home, we would cook together. I was free to be Mary Byron with a life that existed before Patrick, one of the things I loved about him. Equality was the bedrock of our marriage. Byron and McGhee made a good team. That made it easier to put my career on short-term hold to support this crucial juncture of his.

A successful first, full post would open doors for Patrick, especially this assignment with its danger and weighted historical significance. Besides, my career wasn't on ice. A job in Cape Town would add to my professional pedigree. In the end, the two-year sidetrack would work in my favor. It would help me adjust to life in a foreign country too, with me immersed in my career, Patrick in his, just as we had lived in D.C.

Leaving the promenade, I retraced the steps Patrick and I had taken our first weekend and found my way to the third of Clifton Beaches, a broad swath of unencumbered sand. A wooden stairway led to the shore. Flip-flops in hand, I jogged to the water. In a frenzied African Toyi-Toyi dance, I alternated jumping on one foot then the other in the numbing cold, shocked again at the disparity between the warm air and the icy Atlantic. A sign caught my eye.

I frolicked through the foam until I reached it. Welded to a rusty metal pipe deep in the sand it read: *Slegs Blankes* and under it, "Whites Only." It didn't make sense. Why would the sign still be up almost two years after apartheid laws had been repealed? I looked around at the sunbathers. All white. Two black men in blue worker's uniforms stabbed at trash with their spears, others dumped rubbish from trash cans into a bin, a few swept the stairs, and still others watered palm trees shading beach-goers. It was a time-travel scene back to the civil rights era in the sixties.

A gorgeous Rhodesian ridgeback alongside a white-haired gentleman interrupted my dream as they walked in my direction. "Goeiedag," the man said, along with a string of words I
couldn't decipher.

"Goeiedag." The grin that followed was no doubt elicited by my butchered Afrikaans.

"Are you enjoying your holiday?" He signaled the ridgeback to sit.

I smiled. "This beach, those mountains…it's just spectacular."

"They call those the Twelve Apost—"
The ridgeback jumped to his feet, hackles raised, growling at something behind us. We turned around. A black worker lunged toward us with his spear in mid-air. The dog yanked against his leash, teeth bared. The worker dropped the spear. He fell backward in the sand. The Afrikaner commanded his dog into a down-stay. The ridgeback obeyed, upper lip stuck at the top of one razor canine in a low growl.

"Bongani, you know Duke won't hurt you."

"Yes, sir." The black man kept his eyes downcast in the same servile manner as Mr. Khumalo. "Goeiedag, Lady."

I returned the greeting in Afrikaans, then plucked the candy wrapper from my leg where it had lodged after its narrow escape from the spear. With a step forward, I put it in his bag.

"I'm enjoying your beautiful country. Thank you for keeping it clean."

The old Afrikaner did a double take. "If you don't let yourself get too caught up in some of our wretched ways, you won't feel as guilty. Try it."

Unsure how to respond, I glanced again at the black man. The Afrikaner and I bade goodbye and continued on our way in opposite directions. The worker returned to his chore. My pale arms were already pink. Five tubes of Coppertone were en route, which did me no good. Children played at the water's edge with their buckets and shovels under the watchful eyes of black nannies. I wondered if the young women brought their own children to the beach. No. "Whites Only." I walked by them, avoiding eye contact, wishing I were any skin color other than white, even the bright red I would be by the time I got back to the flat.

A honk drew my attention. A township van—a kombi—was parked at the roadside, doors open to pick up workers. Bongani was the last to get in. He noticed me. I started to wave, but thought better of it.

No one would be removing the "Whites Only" sign at Clifton Beach anytime soon.

Three
Uninvited Guests

October 1992

Patrick spent his early weeks at the embassy dealing with escalating violence in the townships, working to prevent another crisis like the Ciskei Massacre while planning security measures to minimize the impact of that violence on our officers and American residents. After a long interruption in negotiations—almost four months following the June massacre in Boipatong—Mandela and President de Klerk agreed to resume talks. In an effort to stem the violence, both men signed a "Record of Understanding" which established an independent body to oversee the white state-police operations.

Most important was that Mandela and President de Klerk had also agreed that no acts of violence, whatever their origin, would stop the peace process. Negotiations would move forward. Foreign Prime Minister Botha asked the United Nations to send a special envoy to play a peacekeeping role. The whole world watched to see if South Africa would end in democracy or mayhem. Chief Buthelezi was still a wild card, as Ambassador Lyman referred to him, the ANC's strongest opponent. Mandela was going to need help bringing him around. I didn't know it then, but that assist would come from U.S. Ambassador Lyman.

Keeping the ambassador and the Foreign Service community safe required a continual updating of the situation on the ground. At the embassy Patrick got the lay of the land—info about his coworkers—who was an ally, who was not, among both American and Afrikaner officials. My husband was adept not only at reading people but at drawing them to him. Warm by nature, wary by occupation, Patrick kept his guard up without losing the ability to engage with those he worked for and worked with, as well as those under him. Trustworthy and friendly make a winning combination in any field.

As a civilian State Department security agent, Patrick was responsible for all matters affecting the safety of the embassy in Cape Town—he hired and managed local security forces, kept his ears to the ground, was liaison to the government (President de Klerk's National Party), and hired security to report to him on safety issues inside Mandela's ANC and Buthelezi's Inkatha Freedom Party that might impact the embassy. To secure officers and staff, Patrick ran all emergency drills and lockdowns. In South Africa, Patrick's job began to make sense. He was part intelligence agent, gathering word from his operatives on the street and within political parties; part operations manager, overseeing marines and implementing security drills at the embassy; part diplomat, as liaison working with the foreign government; and part protective security for the ambassador and his family. The job description was vague, written in language that could cover everything, easily adapted by the mission. No one could say "That's not in my job description" because it probably was somewhere between the lines.

His job might have made more sense to *me*, but I still could not explain it to my mom or siblings, beyond the basics —we were there to help bring the major parties together toward a democratic election. Maybe it was the breadth of his job that was what Patrick loved about it—the problem-solving, each day something new. It's no wonder the courtroom paled in comparison. Litigation based on precedent, the past as guide, couldn't hold a candle to Foreign Service, which had no such template. At least it couldn't for Patrick.

At first I was envious of his job, or any job for that matter, but especially one doing meaningful work. Diplomatic spouses required clearance, formal permission to seek employment. My "Request to Work" application was pending. But the wheels of government move slow. I had to be patient. To kill time the most obvious draw for my attention was our flat. Beautiful as it was, I welcomed the opportunity to make it more like home than an embassy-leased residence, Ethan Allen notwithstanding. Our smaller belongings had arrived by airfreight. It was like Christmas seeing things I hadn't seen since before we left D.C.—photos, dishes, and clothes. The bigger items, along with our car, were still en route by ship.

Once I finished adding personal touches to the flat it was time to update my resume in preparation for the approved work request. In the dining room I organized my files into neat stacks. Drawn by the always-stunning view of the Atlantic out the window, my resume took a lower priority. It was too beautiful a day to be inside. A good dinner for Patrick—chicken curry, a favorite—would be a nice surprise to go with our new homey touches. Once I started my job there would be fewer opportunities for cooking fun weeknight dinners. My staples were simple, fast. But with time on my hands I could fiddle with fussier meals.

It turned out that exploring on foot not only was good exercise but another way to acclimate to the neighborhood. Mr. Khumalo bowed his head, avoiding my eyes with his usual "Good day, Lady." It was hard to ignore the political reality beyond our living room with a guard stationed at the building entrance. But I tried.

The local market was a straight shoot four blocks down Sea Point Road. The weather was perfect. Sun sparkled on the water, the sidewalk, the cars, everything in this paradise bathed in dazzling light. At the end of the second block, I hesitated with vague unease. I turned around. Nothing.

Shoulders rigid, I raised and lowered them a few times to shake out the tension. Patrick's work may require he move through the world with eyes in the back of his head, but I had no intention of spending two years with my nerves on edge. Odd about the phone, though. The last few days I hadn't been able to get a dial tone right away and could hear what was going on in the lobby, as if someone had forgotten to hang up. Putting the receiver on and off the hook a few times did the trick. It crossed my mind that if I could hear them, they could hear me. I hadn't mentioned the crossed wires to Patrick.

Other than this new snag, the only calls I got anyway were from Mr. Khumalo to notify me of visitors, which in the first few weeks consisted of embassy staff coming to repair or deliver things. Until I could land a job, that was the extent of my social life, that and my chats with Azisa. No wonder I was paranoid. Too much time alone can do funny things to your head. The devil's workshop, as the nuns used to say. A woman headed toward me from the opposite direction. We exchanged smiles. I relaxed.

In the fourth block the uneasy feeling returned, this time a ball of lead in my stomach. I ducked into the market and waited for my eyes to adjust. The unsettled feeling remained. Change of plan—I would gather the essentials on my list. The rest could wait. I found the chicken and spices, the two-percent milk and that would be it. Brands were unfamiliar, prices in rand hard to compute in my distracted state. A man further down the refrigerator section stared at me. I turned to him. He looked away. I resumed my search. He resumed his stare.

The creepy feeling took hold. The two-percent could wait. With the closest carton of milk in hand I sped through the empty cashier line. In no time I was outside with my bag. Footsteps behind me got louder. If someone was following me, they sure weren't very good at it. More annoyed than frightened, I picked up my pace.

At our building a look of surprise came over Mr. Khumalo. He unlocked the main door. A nod was all I could manage on my way to the lift. On the sixth floor the stink of cigarette smoke filled the hall. I didn't move. There were two flats on our floor. Mrs. Osborne did not smoke. It wasn't until I reached for my keys that I remembered the General Service Operator—GSO in that acronym-based government lingo—was coming from the embassy to replace the lights high on our bedroom wall. They hadn't worked since our arrival.

The door to our flat was ajar. "Hello? Mr. Sorensen?" Silence. I leaned the grocery bag against the wall then called out again, louder. No response. Inside the flat, smoke mingled with the stench of body odor and alcohol. I tiptoed through the living room, calling his name. In the dining room I stopped cold. My tidy stacks of paper that had filled the table thirty minutes earlier lay scattered on the floor, strewn across chairs, as if blown by the wind. One stood upright against the curtain ready to read. No windows were open, the hallway enclosed.

The front door slammed. I whirled around, trying to steady my nerves. No one was there. Yanking the door open, I searched the hall. It was empty. In a mad dash toward the lift, one toe of my flip-flop caught, throwing me off balance long enough to pause. *What if he'd been armed, Mary?* A shudder ran through me. Patrick was right. The safe room—from there I would buzz the embassy. No. If it *was* Mr. Sorensen, I would never live it down, tagged as the newbie who hit the alarm before the first month was out.

I locked the door behind me. It took a moment for the switchboard to get through to Patrick's office. "Mar, what's up?"

"Someone's broken in."

For a moment he was silent. When he spoke his voice had no sign of urgency. "Leave the flat. Meet me at the end of the block in five. Take the stairs."

Grocery bag still in the hallway, I ran to the stairs and leapt down two at a time until I reached the rear exit. My heart pounded, knees wobbled. Why hadn't Patrick sounded alarmed? Or worried? His black sedan was nowhere in sight in either direction. Of course he hadn't sounded alarmed. He wouldn't. His job had no room for emotional reaction. Even if his wife were in danger. Especially if his wife were in danger.

Ten minutes later the car rounded the corner. Patrick pushed open the passenger door. I jumped in. My fingers fumbled with the seatbelt. "Someone—"

Patrick put a finger to his lips. A mile down the road he stopped at a secluded spot. "Let's walk."

It was late morning, the air muggy under heavy cloud cover. My flip-flops slid under the gravel, one strap loose from my mad dash out of the flat. Even wearing his suit and wingtip shoes, Patrick was down the stairs ahead of me. I trotted on the sand to catch up. "Patrick, stop. What's going on?"

He led me by the arm to a shaded area between boulders. I searched his face for some indication. "You're scaring me."

He leaned against a boulder with a long sigh, but didn't meet my eyes. "We're being watched."

My mouth fell open. "What?"

"The government is having us trailed."

"What government?"

"The National Party, De Klerk's goons." Patrick looked at me for the first time since I had gotten in the car.

"Why? What do they want?"

"You're not in any danger. They're just messing with our heads to get us to leave. I'm not the most popular guy around here. They see us as interference with my reports back to the State Department about guerilla warfare in the streets while de Klerk and Mandela go on with this tug-o-war."

I didn't hear what he said after *They're messing with our heads*. No wonder Patrick didn't sound alarmed on the phone—he had known all along. I looked at him for several seconds as the pieces fell into place.

"So now you know." Regret tinged his words.

"Then there really *was* someone following me to the market. There really *was* someone in our flat."

He grimaced.

"And you knew this was going on." My voice was an octave lower.

"No. I mean...I suspected but wasn't a hundred percent sure."

"You suspected but weren't a hundred per—why in God's name would you not tell me, sure or not?"

"I knew you'd freak out. And there was a chance they wouldn't do it."

My voice stayed low in restraint. "I'm not freaking out because I *knew* what was going on, but because I *didn't*."

With one wing-tip shoe he poked at the sand. "Mar, I'm used to giving information on a need-to-know basis. There's no point getting people stirred up until I have all the facts."

My glare could've sparked fire on the boulder. "I'm not 'people.' I'm your wife. Here I thought I was going crazy thinking someone had followed me, that someone had broken into the flat."

"I didn't want to worry you unnecessarily." He gave me a sheepish glance. "I see now I was wrong."

"You can't protect me all the time. Once I'm working I'll be out there in the world."

He scrunched his neck with closed eyes, his go-to response whenever things got tense between us. My go-to response was to make things worse. I moved a few feet away, forefinger back and forth over my top lip like the bow of a violin. Then I turned around. Neither of us made eye contact. "I'll need to get your suit pants cleaned." Wet sand from an earlier cloudburst stuck like glitter around his cuffs.

"Don't do that, hon. I'm not treating you like The Little Woman. I had my reasons."

"Patrick, you're the only person I have in this whole hemisphere. Literally. You need to trust me, share information that affects me. I'd say being stalked qualifies."

Silence.

"You said part of what you loved about me was my strength and independence. Then you go and act like Tarzan. Why do you want to teach me to shoot if you don't want me to know I might have to? Why couldn't you tell me we were being watched? I don't get why you can't just talk to me about the situation."

"I thought the need for weaponry lessons was obvious. You don't see elephants anywhere, do you? Anything could happen if they can't get this election off the ground."

"There's no need for sarcasm. And yes, thank you for that intelligence. I think I had that one."

He stepped toward me. "See? You're insulted if I tell you something you already know and angry if I don't tell you everything I know. I didn't tell you about the surveillance because I didn't think the government would jump on us so quickly. My job is to keep people from overreacting. It's hard to turn that on and off. I've never had a wife with me on the job. We're not exactly typical newlyweds in some Virginia suburb."

"No, we're not. And that's the point. Tell me what I need to know. I'll try not to get hysterical."

Patrick scoffed. "Now who's being sarcastic?" He looked beyond me at the ocean as if he couldn't bear to watch my face at the words he was about to say. "Okay. Here's what you need to know—assume you're being watched—and trailed—at all times. Be careful what you say in public. Don't trust anyone, and I mean anyone, even other embassy families. It's fine to make friends, but you should be very careful with what you confide."

Stunned, I stared at him.

He turned his palms upward. "It's protocol, hon."

"How can I go two years without making friends? That's not something *I* can turn on and off."

"You have me. That'll have to do."

How could I tell him girlfriends were different, that he didn't want to hear about my loneliness or my irritation at his poker nights when the job already has so much of him.

"Okay, we're being trailed. Is that all?"

"No." He shifted his weight. "You have to assume our phone is bugged...and that listening devices have been installed throughout the flat. They must've mentioned this as a possibility at your security briefing in D.C."

"Was Mr. Sorensen's coming in to replace the bedroom lights just a ruse to—? Oh my God! Patrick, are you telling me people have been listening to us? We've made love about a hundred times!"

He smirked. "I wish."

"Are civil liberties nonexistent here? The government can listen to the most intimate aspects of our lives?"

Silence.

"So, other than the entire South African government listening to everything we say and do, needing to watch my back at all times, never trusting anyone—which leaves out making real friends— and talking to my parents over a bugged phone, is there anything else?"

Our eyes locked in a standoff. "I'm sorry, Mary. I wanted you to fall in love with this place, love it as much as I do. If I'd told you some of this routine stuff before we left home, it would've colored everything."

"Routine?"

Regret registered on his face as soon as the words were out. "Government surveillance is just another occupational hazard in Foreign Service, more so in an intelligence-gathering job."

"Patrick, we have to trust each other. I'm not expecting you to spill classified information, but I can't be shut out of your entire world, which right now is work."

"Okay, you made your point. But hon…it's not easy drawing the line between divulging things in one part of my life and not another when I'm in both places every day. It's safer to stick with a need-to-know basis." He caught himself. "Except now I won't."

I stared at him, wondering if I knew this man at all.

"I have to get back to the embassy."

Neither of us spoke in the now known-to-be-bugged car. What a fool I'd been. We had relinquished privacy the minute we stepped off the plane in Johannesburg. My mind reeled at the thought of our sex life caught on surveillance. My face flushed.

We had crossed a threshold into some other realm. Private conversations in our own home would no longer be spontaneous, including playful banter. I would now have to pick and choose those things worthy of a meeting on the deck where crashing surf would afford us privacy. Phone calls to my parents would no longer include a true account of my life here. Language would be vetted, devoid of details. The same would be true of friends. I would trust no one. I wasn't completely sure I trusted my husband.

Table Mountain came into view. Had I been standing on top overlooking Cape Town with not a soul in sight, I could not have been as lonely as in that moment on the Victoria and Albert Roadway driving back to the fishbowl I had hoped to call home.

Patrick was gone when I woke up in the morning. On my bedside table was his usual note, "A& F," the reference to Luther Vandross's *Always and Forever*. A dishtowel covered something next to the coffee pot too. I lifted the towel. Mr. Potato Head stared back at me with one eye. A note was under him. "Try removing body parts when I act like a jerk." It wasn't the first time Patrick had brought home some funny thing or other that an officer at the end of his post had left for the guys. Mr. Potato Head with a note wasn't exactly an apology, but at least it meant Patrick understood he had hurt me. That was something.

Despite the good intentions of the signed agreement between Mandela and President de Klerk, the violence did not stop. Defunct apartheid laws continued to be enforced. It was one thing for black and white leaders to work together for a new South Africa. But Afrikaners long ago had deemed their position superior by law. That didn't make change easy. Racial segregation had been the practice dating back to the white settlers' permanent landing in 1652, long before apartheid had been formally instituted as state policy in 1948.

The townships were racially discriminatory in that "black" African; "colored" (mixed-race); and "Indian" people were ordered by the Group Areas Act of 1950 to live separately, the literal meaning of the word apartheid. Colored South Africans, as progeny of the original Afrikaner settlers, enjoyed a somewhat higher status than blacks as the progeny of the original Afrikaner settler. When it became clear the Dutch would stay in Cape Town and claim it as a layover to the West Indies, girls from orphanages back in Holland were sent to join the sailors. Until they arrived, the Dutch commingled with native *San nomads*, giving birth to what later became the "colored" race.

Determining one's race was a mixed bag of criteria that employed several techniques used in the classification of non-whites. Skin color was one, along with other physical characteristics such as a nose width (they actually measured) and curliness of hair. The Pencil Test consisted of sticking a pencil into the hair. If the curl was tight enough to hold the pencil, the person was deemed black. If the pencil fell out, other characteristics were used to make the determination. Even within black townships, ethnic groups were often segregated into separate areas for Zulus, Xhosas, Sothosand others.

The white race was easier to categorize with two classifications—Afrikaners, descendants of the original Dutch settlers, and "other whites"—English-speakers of British descent. Afrikaners considered these "other whites" imposters, foreigners who had stayed on after the Boer Wars in which they fought the Dutch but never severed ties to their European native country as Afrikaners had centuries earlier. Not only were these other English-speakers considered to be inferior, they were not trusted by the Afrikaner National Party. Afrikaners seemed to trust other Afrikaners, period. Those Calvinist roots ran deep.

Under apartheid laws, race determined freedom of movement. When the old Afrikaner on Clifton Beaches referred to "our wretched ways," one of them included a law requiring non-whites to carry a passbook at all times—identifying them by race—as a way to control where they could and could not go, where they could and could not work. It was designed to keep all non-whites out of cities except for specific permitted work. Police routinely stopped people and asked for their passbooks. The system was so strict that our neighbors said their gardener even had to have a permission slip to cross the street to talk to another neighbor since his document only allowed him to work at their house.

Those guilty of not having their passbooks could be arrested on the spot and thrown in jail. As a young anti-apartheid activist in Johannesburg, Nelson Mandela had been the first black man to burn his passbook, one of a long list of anti-government gestures that eventually earned him life in prison for treason. For blacks in the passbook system, harassment, fines, and arrests were a constant threat.

But townships had an unemployment rate of ninety percent with no local jobs and little transportation. Blacks struggling to support their families were compelled to violate the pass laws and travel far to find work in the cities as garbage men, drivers, and maids.

Domestic workers could live in a family's home if they were sponsored. Some workers stayed all week in the white homes, cooking, cleaning, living in the servant's quarters, which most homes had. Babies back in the townships were cared for by elders, grannies. Men whose wives stayed in town with families had mistresses. HIV and TB were rampant. In rural areas where agriculture and wineries flourished, blacks found jobs on the farms where they traded labor for wine. So not only were they separated from their families in the townships, they were becoming alcoholics.

It was a bitterly cold day in February of 1990. I was in my office at the hotel in D.C. when the phone rang. Grateful for the break from my ad campaign, I answered on the second ring.

"Mandela is free!" Patrick was so loud I had to hold the receiver away from my ear. Mandela's message had resonated with him during his nine-month post in Cape Town before we met. He had been with Ambassador Edward Perkins, the first black ambassador to South Africa. It was a dicey assignment. At that time the Reagan administration had chosen a policy of "constructive engagement" in South Africa to keep American business interests intact. The president was reluctant to impose outright sanctions against a government in which the white minority, only thirteen percent of the population, owned ninety percent of the land. The United States in the early nineties was still South Africa's second largest trading partner.

But things changed as South Africa reached the brink of civil war. Archbishop Desmond Tutu and black South African leaders called on our government to pressure American businesses not to trade with their country as a way to put the squeeze on then-South African President Botha's white National Party to end apartheid and release Nelson Mandela from prison.

Over President Reagan's veto in 1986 Congress passed the Comprehensive Anti-Apartheid Act, establishing economic sanctions which prohibited future investments, bank loans and trade. More than two hundred of the U.S. businesses in South Africa sold their operations. Those that didn't tried to minimize the impact of apartheid.

Needless to say, the white minority government was not happy with the U.S. It was into this prickly environment that Patrick would accompany Ambassador Edward Perkins on his diplomatic mission in 1987 to end apartheid. Patrick's assignment was supposed to be short term—thirty days to replace another agent. Thirty days turned into a nine-month mission to keep the ambassador and the embassy safe. It had been no easy task. Many politicians in the U.S. saw Ambassador Perkins as a black face chosen to mask President Reagan's earlier refusal to get tough with South Africa when he put U.S. economic interest over human rights.

To make matters worse, our country had done an about-face not just with sanctions but with jumping on board the freedom train. Slow to support Mandela, it wasn't until the struggle for a united democratic South Africa resonated with the American public that President Reagan changed U.S. policy. In his memoir former, Ambassador Perkins said the president's decision to send him as an anti-apartheid agent of change in 1987 on the heels of sanctions a year earlier made it hard to convince leaders on both sides, black and white, not only that we meant business about ending legalized racism but that a black man had been chosen to represent the United States to a white minority government that clearly had no respect for anyone of color.

On assignment, Ambassador Perkins was in danger for his life, distrusted by blacks as a puppet of Reagan's pro-Afrikaner government, disliked by whites who were feeling the sting of economic sanctions. The civil rights activist Reverend Jesse Jackson told Ambassador Perkins that our racist president was using a black man to refurbish his own image as non-racist. The reverend went on to warn Perkins that he would likely be killed by either blacks or whites, distrusted by both. Patrick's job as a Special Agent in Diplomatic Security included taking the ambassador into black townships where men stared him down and white cities where women in the street hissed at him.

Patrick's time there deeply affected him, witnessing firsthand the racial hatred, the effects of oppression, economic deprivation. So on that cold day in February of '90, he couldn't wait to tell me that Nelson Mandela was now a free man. In the months that followed his release, leaders the world over showered praise on Mandela for his continued pursuit of a democratic South Africa during his incarceration. President George H.W. Bush invited Mandela to the White House. How strange it must have been for him to go from a prisoner of almost three decades to a hero lauded by our nation. A few days before his arrival in the capital, Nelson Mandela had been cheered by three-quarters of a million New Yorkers in a tickertape parade.

Patrick was assigned the detail for Mandela's visit to D.C., a huge honor. The public speech would be at the Convention Center. The whole town was revved up. That appearance was all I could think about—that and how to honor the man most Americans saw as akin to single handedly taking down the Nazi regime. In a stash of mementos Patrick kept from his foreign travels, I found a colorful piece of batik. It would make a perfect scarf, my personal tribute to Mandela.

The night of the speech people waited more than six hours for him after a day packed with talks to various groups about the crimes of apartheid and his plan for moving toward democracy. The hours of anticipation fed the frenzy. At ten o'clock that night the Convention Center erupted into thunderous applause as Mandela finally took the stage, fist clenched over his head in triumph. Chills ran down my spine.

Mandela soaked it all in. After several minutes the applause wound down. But before he could speak, somewhere in the upper stands a voice began to sing. More people joined in. Then more. Soon the crowd was singing in one voice to *Nkosi Sikeleli Afrika*—"Lord Bless Africa"—a song known around the world.

Patrick had brought home the Miriam Makeba album. I joined the crowd in song. On the floor and in the stands hundreds in the American audience danced the tribal Toyi-Toyi while thousands sang.

Mandela didn't try to stop it. With his trademark grin of joy he marveled at the tribute of respect. When he did finally quiet the crowd his first words sent it roaring again, "When we finally leave your shores, we shall do so fortified by the magnitude of your love, the greatness of your heart."

Then and there it registered that I was in the presence of a remarkable man. After decades in prison the brutality he and other ANC leaders suffered, the toll on Winnie and their children, it was unimaginable to me that Mandela could radiate such optimism without a shred of bitterness. At seventy-one years old he had no time to look back. He didn't want us to either. It was all about the future. Multiple times during the speech he was drowned out by the thunder of applause and foot-stomping from the masses. The energy was electric, contagious. None of us tried to hide tears. A surge of emotion pulsed through me, the power of group reaction in such a deeply affecting moment. Nelson Mandela changed me. Whatever else I may have wanted in life, a new driving force took shape—the need to witness the birth of a new South Africa.

How could I have known Patrick and I would do far more than witness it? We would be part of it.

Four

Town and Country

October 1992

Ambassador Lyman pushed Patrick to take a weekend day off, a mental break from the unrelenting pressure that comes with keeping a whole community safe during political upheaval, to say nothing of protecting the ambassador himself and his family. In short, Patrick was ordered to get a life, the luxury of a day off. That would end soon enough.

Social life as a couple had not been part of our life in D.C.

Most of Patrick's friends were single. He didn't know my girlfriends well because I was out with them when he traveled. At home we wanted it to be just the two of us to make up for lost time. How unlikely it was that in this foreign land we would have more of a social life than in the States. Patrick had made friends during his earlier post. I was finally going to meet the Donovans, these dear locals who meant so much to my husband.

The sun was high over Lion's Head Peak as we left the city on our way to Durbanville, a rural suburb on the northern outskirts of Cape Town. The route took us through miles of farmland, the irrigated land a patchwork of green and brown. I took pictures along the way to share with Mom and Dad in hopes the bucolic country landscape would counteract images of violence they saw on the news. Farmland turned to wine country, gentle hills undulating with rows of grapes. Patrick turned onto Franschhoek Road as if he had been there last week. We stopped in the driveway of a large Dutch-style house similar to those in Cape Town, flower beds bordering a well-manicured lawn.

Two massive German Shepherds trailed behind Richard and Michele as they trotted down the steps to greet us. Patrick was met with a good-ole-boy slap on the back from Richard as if there had been no five-year gap since his last visit.

"Hey, man, we didn't know if you were bringing your bloody American entourage or not. Figured we might need protection."

Michele hugged me. "Welcome, Mary. Richard's a real joker. I'm not sure he even remembers the dogs' attack command." She took my hand in hers like an old college roommate. Immediately I liked both of them. The dogs stayed close during our tour of the property, which started with the garden. Michele was clearly proud of her green thumb. Raised beds were thick with flowers, as well as a lush variety of vegetables and herbs, a patchwork of colors and textures.

The front door slammed. Two teenagers bounded out of the house.

"Hey…Simon…Teresa!" Patrick waved them over. "Come meet Mary."

The kids were Mini-Me's of Michele and Richard, blonde blue-eyed beauties typical of Nordic heritage. Patrick shot them all kinds of questions to catch up. Rehashing the story of his "magic tooth" brought boisterous laughter. On his earlier visit Patrick would wow the kids flipping his fake tooth out like a hidden quarter that suddenly appears, much to the kids' astonishment and delight.

The tooth itself wasn't so funny—disguised cyanide in the form of a capsule in case things ever went bad on foreign soil. It sometimes hit me that my husband harbored government secrets so weighty that he was provided a means to off himself rather than divulge them. First wife really meant first. That's quite an ultimatum. Mystery was built into his job. The hard part was to not ask what he couldn't tell me.

Verbal affection flowed easily between the Donovan's and Patrick. I hadn't seen him as relaxed and happy in public since we arrived in South Africa. The dogs trailed alongside Michele as we walked. Something told me all four Donovans had those attack commands on the tips of their tongue. An animal person one hundred percent, I didn't initiate contact. If they were working dogs, they would decide when the time was right to check me out. Or Michele would.

Michele commanded the massive duo into a sit position. "And now officially meet Julie & Kelly."

Their eyes stayed locked on her, ready for their next command.

The German Shepherds I had ever seen were TV police dogs, canines not to be messed with under the complete control of their handler, like Julie and Kelly. Yet it was clear they could hardly restrain themselves from a greeting once the release command was given.

It was, and they did, with thorough sniffs.

A puppy appeared out of nowhere, all wiggly and licky. Michele gave a command in Afrikaans. The puppy sat. "This is Toby. Simon found him after school in the gym parking lot."

Young Simon Donovan reminded me of Patrick. Saving a homeless animal was exactly what my husband would have done too. His stepfather had been a rancher in Montana, a real cowboy. Whit taught Patrick about horses, how to care for wildlife, respect nature, the land. The older man also loved stories about the American frontier in Zane Grey novels. And he was a fan of Western movies. A copy of Clint Eastwood's *Fistful of Dollars* was in our collection at the flat. Westerns often included dogs, so maybe there would be one in our future.

Michele and I worked our way to the house in nonstop conversation. How wonderful to be with friends in a normal environment, a safe environment. Michele led me to a poolside covered patio in the expansive backyard. Conversation moved from teas—*rooibos*, or red tea, a favorite for both of us—to nutrition and yoga, travel and children. Yes, we planned on them someday. Richard grilled fish on the *braai*, our version of a barbeque, as he and Patrick caught up. Today we would have special catch—abalone and crayfish, delicacies on the South African coast.

The afternoon feast was served by Agrinette, the maid, or the PC name, "domestic worker." Banter between her and Michele seemed natural, as if she were part of the family, a sort of Alice from *The Brady Bunch*. "Goeiedag," I greeted her in Afrikaans, thrilled she actually understood me. Like most South Africans, she spoke at least three languages—Afrikaans, required by the minority government, and English, which she spoke with the Donovans, though both Michele and Richard managed some Xhosa and did speak Afrikaans.

Conversation over lunch flowed with the help of the Durbanville Hills Chenin Blanc Richard had chosen. At first I was a bit reserved. The four of us covered local traditions, housing, travel and movies, compared South African and American words—*flat* vs. *apartment*, *robot* vs. *traffic light*, *lekker* vs. *great*. I asked them as many questions about South Africa as they asked me about America. We all clicked. My reserve fell away as I became comfortable. Once in a while Patrick would check on me with a wink.

Richard regaled us with stories of Patrick's earlier visit, the life he had before me. Of course the topic of the elections came up, Michele's and Richard's perspectives as locals on Mandela, De Klerk, the latest violence—where to go, where not to go. In a shift to lighter topics before the meal ended, I mentioned the blustery wind that had nearly blown us over that morning. Richard explained that that was the work of the "Cape Doctor," a reference to the southeasterly winds that often ramped up to ninety-nine miles per hour, literally blowing large trucks off the road. He also explained the cloud-cover "tablecloth" that hovered over Table Mountain in certain conditions.

Michele and Richard's lifestyle was the complete opposite of ours. Michele was a busy mom with two kids—carpooling, birthday parties—the whole thing. Richard owned and managed his own security alarm company. With so much in common, we lived very differently—a family-oriented rural existence versus our career-oriented one in the hubbub of D.C. The big city still held allure for me, the vibrant feel being surrounded by theater, shops, restaurants, politics, and in D.C., annual visits each spring from every middle school student in the country. I loved it.

It wasn't out of the question that Patrick and I would one day live a quieter life. I tried to imagine him with kids and dogs and a regular job. He loved the outdoors—mountain sports, water sports, hiking, fishing. He may even have preferred country life. But school and work schedules were two major obstacles to travel. My next thought wasn't so comforting.

Adventure was hard-wired into Patrick. Kids and dogs would tie us down. And travel alone would never be enough. As much as he loved nature, my husband would need an element of risk—at the very least, the possibility of attack by wildlife. Where that left the prospect of children I wasn't sure. But we had time to figure it out.

The loud clap of Patrick's hands snapped me back to the present. Michele set a lovely crystal platter on the table, the tiramisu a work of art with its delicate layers of sweetness. "I can't believe you remembered my fave, Michele." Patrick grinned in appreciation. If I hadn't already liked Michele, that gesture of affection would've sold me. For a single guy far from home, little things make a big difference. In the first months of our marriage I had mastered very few dessert recipes, my mom's lemon meringue and Grandma McGhee's mud pie the exceptions. With all my down time, I could give the tiramisu a try.

I could see our friendship with this couple would be a lifelong one.

It had gotten dusky. Embassy security strongly recommended no one drive at night in this high-alert environment. Reluctantly we said goodbye, and the four of us agreed to another get-together. Richard had a favorite Greek restaurant near our flat—Mykonos. At last we had a social life to look forward to—occasional dinners out with Richard and Michelle.

On the drive home I was full of good food and the warm, satisfying feel of friendship. It had been so relaxing, just one couple visiting another. No government goons. No hidden eyes. How badly we had needed this dose of normal life. For one afternoon we had been a million miles away from the ubiquitous turmoil that had become a way of life. One nagging thought popped to mind after the visit. Patrick, Richard and Michele were well-versed in South African history. My knowledge was limited to all things apartheid. I hit the Cape Town Public Library for a crash course.

The timeline read like an EKG of clashes that ranged from

skirmishes to war, starting with the first Zulu and Xhosa tribes in the 1400s; the arrival of Dutch settlers, Boers, in the 1650s; and the British who followed two hundred years later with plans to expand their empire.

Diamonds and gold, that's what changed the course of history. Discovery of these precious resources sparked a battle between the Dutch and Brits at the turn of the twentieth century—the Boer Wars. The end result was a mass uprooting of rural populations of blacks as well as rural white Afrikaners who fled in droves to the mines to work as cheap labor. Indigenous black people were lured or often compelled to move from rural areas by a variety of means common in colonialism—dispossession of good farmland, expropriation of livestock, hut "taxes."

This influx of workers resulted in "the poor white problem." Housing shortages, sanitation crises, public health epidemics like influenza fed into racial and moral panics about the proximity of black workers who lived in the same urban neighborhoods as whites. Townships—separate neighborhoods for blacks—sprouted up across Johannesburg and other urban centers as firms sought an unending supply of black workers during the high-growth era of the 1930s.

These early townships gave rise to the infamous hostel systems that housed up to sixteen workers per sleeping room for eleven months of the year with a one-month break to visit families in the homelands. Mid-century when other countries in Africa were fighting for independence from colonial rule, Dutch Afrikaners worried blacks might rebel against the white minority. That's when they came up with apartheid.

Township residence was assigned by the government based on tribal affiliation rather than marriage or family unit. Each of six tribes had its own distinct language. No way could they ever unite. Families were broken up, husbands and wives separated based on tribal ancestry. Afrikaners had effectively colonized their own country with a system of governance guaranteed to keep them in economic power.

It was romance, or in this case lack of it, that changed the tide of history. A prince in his native Xhosa homeland in the bush, Nelson Mandela had been educated at the best schools as the one who carried the future of his family tribe. (He was given the name Nelson by a white teacher who found his Xhosa name—Rolihlahla—hard to pronounce.) When he came of age, an arranged marriage sent the young prince fleeing to the city. In 1952 Nelson Mandela was a young lawyer in Johannesburg working with black victims of segregation.

The future leader was in position.

Walter Sisulu, an anti-apartheid activist, met Mandela when the African National Congress formed in 1912 with a platform of change through nonviolence inspired by Mahatma Gandhi during his years in South Africa. Walter Sisulu saw in the young lawyer a man who could be groomed to lead the party.

During apartheid the ANC had been banned as illegal, its leaders exiled, including its then-President, Oliver Tambo. But Tambo never stopped working to end apartheid practices. In London he garnered the attention of world leaders in his anti-apartheid speeches, writings, meetings with government officials and anti-apartheid supporters. Historians say he was probably more effective exiled in London than he might have been in his own country.

In prison, Mandela, with help from Winnie, had stayed in contact with Oliver Tambo. That communication allowed the two leaders to continue their work. Winnie and Archbishop Desmond Tutu led the public charge to release Mandela. In the meantime prison was Mandela's office. He had never left the job. And he had never lost hope. That was the Mandela I heard at the Convention Center in D.C.

This backstory brought me up to date after our visit to the Donovans.

By 1992, when we were there, all that stood in the way of a united democratic South Africa was for President de Klerk and Mr. Mandela to agree on terms. But that was far from easy. The latest bump was President de Klerk's push for a two-phase transition to multi-party rule with an appointed transitional government. The ANC, Mandela, wanted a single stage transition to majority rule determined by a non-racial election—one person, one vote.

Other sticking points included minority rights, property rights, indemnity from prosecution for politically motivated crimes. Agreement on those issues would turn negotiations into a slow moving train over the next two years and generate violence that threatened to throw the country into civil war.

As the weeks went on, I watched my back, assumed everyone listened in on my phone calls. I even kept a whistle close by so I could blast the eavesdropper's eardrums, a futile gesture reminding them that I was onto their antics. My scheme didn't change anything but gave me a fleeting sense of control. My husband would not have approved of these tactics, nor would he have approved of my walking a few extra blocks to lead the goons off course when doing errands on foot.

Following our argument on the beach, Patrick kept his word and let me know what he could about the political situation without divulging anything that wouldn't be public knowledge in a few days. But it was one small way to be part of his secret world. One evening on the beach he told me negotiations had stalled again. Mandela stood by his demand that majority vote would determine the configuration of Parliament. De Klerk stood firm for a policy that would keep whites in economic power. Why wouldn't he? White Afrikaners enjoyed one of the highest standards of living in the world. Black townships had the highest murder rate, along with high infant mortality, despite world class medical facilities. Twenty-five years earlier, Dr. Christian Barnard, a South African cardiac surgeon and descendent of Dutch missionaries, had performed the first human-to-human heart transplant. At the same time, access to health care for blacks remained elusive.

In negotiations President de Klerk put his foot down—there would be no deal with Mandela if he couldn't guarantee white economic control. Apartheid would end but the president demanded there be no seizure of Afrikaner property or industry. Whites feared blacks would do to them what they had done to blacks. Mandela compromised. Afrikaners would maintain their lifestyle.

In fact, the *Argus* reported that a tidal wave of foreign funding amounting to R17.5 billion was poised to pour into the Joburg stock exchange after the elections as British investors and bankers scrambled for a piece of the action. The elections were seen by many international fund managers as a watershed event signaling a degree of political stability that would make it easier for them to invest in South Africa. Morgan Stanley and Prudential were on board to open offices in Joburg.

But President de Klerk needn't have worried. Mandela wasn't interested in confiscation or punishment. Equality, a voice for all—that was the first step to better lives for black South Africans. The people would decide who controlled government in a one person-one vote election. While these compromises were pounded out at the negotiation table, suspicion grew in the townships about what Mandela was agreeing to. Rumor and misinformation spread like a contagious disease, with the same result—more death.

As the sun set one evening on the beach, Patrick told me there had been three deadly incidents over the weekend—Friday night, eight blacks died in an attack at a rail station northeast of Johannesburg; a rural white family of four was killed in an apparent robbery south of Johannesburg; and six blacks died in a hand grenade explosion in Sebokeng Township.

The guilt-shame came in waves of emotion as I noted each location, all in or near Joburg. My parents would learn of these incidents on the news. They kept a map of South Africa on the fridge with Cape Town circled in red, another around Johannesburg showing the expanse in between. Thanks in part to the University of Cape Town, our neck of the woods was white and liberal, more open to change. My parents knew that. A pang of homesickness stung me, thinking about them.

On these walks with Patrick, I was careful not to react, especially with fear. Private conversations about the political unrest on the beach below our flat were what passed for emotional intimacy anymore. Government goons listening to us in the flat gave me and Patrick a bond of sorts, the illusion of closeness in conspiring to outwit them. But I was lonely. Some days my contact was limited to the domestic workers in our building. Most of the time it was small talk with Azisa. The maid lived in Langa Township and rode the kombi into Cape Town with her daughter, Noli, (Xhosa for "tenderness"), who worked in a home nearby. Even my innocuous conversations with her would be cut short if the building manager was around.

One day while reading a letter from Mom and Dad, I called Azisa over to the kitchen table to show her photos they had sent. A puzzled look came over her face as she studied the snow-covered landscape. "How do kids with no shoes go outside?"

"Everyone wears boots. It's a huge hassle to get bundled up. My mom used to make sure us kids had all gone to the bathroom before she zipped the last jacket, or she would be doing it all over again in five minutes."

"No South African could live in such a country."

"Why ever not?"

"We could not afford boots." She looked me dead in the eye as she handed back the photo. "Thank you for showing me the picture, Lady." And with that she went back to her work. No, of course they couldn't afford boots. Not here. But if they were in the United States they would at least be able to work, go to school, compete, get jobs wherever the jobs were located. That would be South Africa's future too if we could get to an election. Azisa never spoke about hope for the future, but she must have had some. Perhaps its fragility prevented her from voicing it, as if the words might jinx it.

The prickly guilt-shame ran through me at the great good fortune of being born white and free, a concept so basic to my understanding of the world that it was difficult to grasp the reality of oppression. No shoes. How had I not seen poverty as part of oppression? It was still hard from inside my white bubble, the layers of restriction unthinkable for a girl who grew up being told she could be anything. What did black mothers tell their kids when they talked about their dreams? One time my sister Marcy told me I was too old to be like Dorothy Hamill with her Olympic Gold medal. I was fifteen. It crushed me. What if she had told me that dream could never come true because of the color of my skin?

As time went on, I tried to look at the white world, at least inside our flat, through Azisa's eyes. Over time, she became more relaxed, seemed to enjoy our talks as much as I did. She had become less reticent as we chatted, though I could not convince her to call me "Mary" instead of "Lady" even in the flat. She would tell me about her family in the township. I would continue to show her photos from home. In that small way we began to forge some semblance of friendship. She seemed fascinated by Minnesota snow, which to her looked very strange—foreign, beautiful, cold. Even limited conversations with Azisa brightened my day.

Loneliness wasn't unexpected. It was early in the assignment. I had anticipated a period of adjustment. But I didn't know how to direct my energy without the structure of a job and found myself watching the clock for Patrick to come home. No one had told me about this part of marriage, the waiting. It hadn't occurred to me that getting a permit to work would take so long, or that I would feel so dependent without a job. I had been in charge of my life since leaving home for college a decade earlier. Now I was in charge of dinner.

And so I waited for what had become the best part of my day—the end of it.

Five
I Become My Mother

November 1992

The smell of curry met Patrick as he walked in from work, exhausted as usual. First he would lock up his sensitive documents, swap his suit for jeans and finally drop on the sofa. Then it was my turn to tell him about my day, hear about his, though I'm sure he shared little of what actually went on at the embassy. That was okay. I just wanted to talk.

Dinner was a high point of my day, with Patrick the beneficiary of my culinary accomplishments. After converting measurements to metric, I mastered a few recipes from *The Joy of Cooking*. Planning meals, shopping for ingredients, cooking the meal gave me some degree of focus while I waited for the ambassador to grant my work approval request. I had sent several resumes out to high-end hotels. It couldn't hurt to set up a few interviews. As an added skill to wow potential employers, I had practiced their language with my Afrikaans tapes. It was not an easy language for me—West Germanic descended from the Dutch, spoken only in South Africa and Namibia.

In spite of the curry aroma, Patrick didn't follow his usual routine. Instead he handed me an official looking letter written on embassy stationery. The ambassador had given it to Patrick in person. So why the long face? I got my answer. The ambassador had denied my "Request to Seek Employment." Patrick had been as surprised when he got it as I was now. The reason for denial had something to do with forfeiting my diplomatic immunity if employed in a foreign country.

"What does that even mean—'diplomatic immunity'?"

"It means that if you'd stabbed the thief who ran off with your ring you'd be prosecuted for assault with a deadly weapon and the U.S. Government wouldn't be able to intervene."

My jaw dropped.

"I'm kidding. The point is our embassy doesn't want you to work."

"But the literature said spousal employment was negotiable."

"Yeah, well Boipatong and Ciskei nixed that. We're on high alert until this election."

"You mean I'm stuck here for two years without a job, without friends, trusting no one, being watched? Patrick, this is ridiculous. There must be an awful lot of unhappy spouses in Foreign Service, that's all I can say."

He rubbed my shoulders. "This is my fault, hon. I should've told you more about what it would be like for you as a diplomatic spouse. It never occurred to me you might not be able to work."

I wrenched away from him. "It's no one's fault. I just have to figure out what I'm going to do for two years." On my way out of the room I tossed the letter on the entry table.

It was a miserable weekend, testing the limits of my frustration. I fell into a pool of self-pity. What was I doing here? I had given up everything to follow this man to the other side of the earth only to be shuffled into passive domesticity—scrutinized, told what I could and couldn't do, robbed of privacy and denied purposeful work. I wasn't allowed to speak my mind, socialize freely with whom I wanted, or even walk to the grocery store without being followed. Our flat was bugged, our phone tapped. De Klerk's minions were probably reading the letters I'd been writing to my mom and sisters.

I did my best not to take it out on Patrick, but my mood hung over us all weekend. How I longed for a girlfriend to confide in. No, there would be no confiding. It was up to me to come up with a plan.

Monday morning I stayed in pajamas long after my second cup of coffee. I looked around the flat as if for the first time, beyond Ethan Allen. It was a masculine space, the dark furniture and minimalist decor suitable for government families coming and going. Transient. Impermanent. People like us. The apartment in Minneapolis I had shared with my friend Debbie had been such a warm, welcoming place—fabric upholstery instead of leather, color instead of muted earth tones, floral wallpaper instead of paint.

I would never feel at home here. We were intruders, uninvited guests. Mom and Dad had been so worried about my going to South Africa. Luckily, my brother Kevin had paved the way as a Foreign Service officer with a post in Yemen. That helped. But they had to like Patrick, trust him. When I took him home the first time, it was hard to imagine what they would talk about. Neither of my parents had been interested in politics as far as I could tell. If they had rousing discussions about world events I wasn't aware of it.

Then it came to me—fishing. Dad and my brothers were avid fishermen. Commercial salmon fishing every summer in Alaska to pay for law school at USD had turned Patrick into a serious man of the sea. My husband was as comfortable on a boat as he was in an ambassador's living room. By the end of our five-day visit, Mom and Dad's worries about my going to the other side of the world were lost somewhere between Patrick's cleaning fish and clearing the dinner table.

Mom hadn't said it in so many words but her feelings were clear. She liked him. Dad, too. As we stood by the car to say goodbye Mom took me by the shoulders and looked at me, hard, as if she might never see me again. Whatever dreams she might've had before marriage and children, she had given up for the eight of us. In her eyes she told me to go—go live a life full of wonder and exploration, a life where each day would bring new adventure, the opposite of the one she had lived.

In that moment I believe Mom validated my decision to nurture my marriage, postpone a family, relish every new experience we might find in ourselves as a married couple. There's no way to be sure what was in her mind. I just know that when we said goodbye that afternoon, her blessings went with me.

Friends had been envious of our travel to an exotic locale. South Africa sounded so romantic. And the lifestyle in Cape Town fed into it—dignitaries living in mansions with drivers, nannies, cooks, housekeepers. It's a powerful fantasy as long as you ignore the oppression that drives an imperialist economy. Guilt plagued me when I described such a life to my friends, a girlish pretend world wrought from too many fairy tales.

But I also talked about the mission—our being there to make sure the election took place, followed by a peaceful transition of power with black majority rule. It was a noble cause. We would witness history, be part of it. That topped the exotic foreign locale on the other side of the world.

Landing the Cape Town post was a stroke of good fortune. It could have been any other of the two hundred and sixty-five American embassies with a comparable assignment around the world. A foreign agent could find himself in Paris immersed in culture on the Left Bank or in Asia fighting human trafficking. Patrick's first post in Cape Town had been nine months instead of the full two years, but he was no longer eligible to throw his hat in the ring for a longer assignment. Reassignment of Foreign Service officers every two years kept them from getting too comfy in one place. Patrick's upcoming assignment would be like a first post. We had some say in where we would go, but the State Department would make the final decision.

In D.C. we waited for news. Life would change for us wherever we were sent. Patrick had come home one night with a list of vacant embassy posts. World map spread across the dining table, I smoothed out the folds, quivering with excitement. "Djibouti, Eritrea, Kyrgyz Republic. Wait. What happened to Paris, Dublin, Wellington?" One look at the list and I grasped the full impact of giving up control. Foreign was one thing. Far-flung countries I'd never heard of, quite another.

Patrick leaned over the map. "I don't care where we go. We'll be together."

Well, I did care, though I didn't say so. No one, including me, would envy my going to Outer Mongolia. Surely, with six choices there had to be some reasonable chance of a good post. Highlighter in hand, we marked desirable locations on the map for further research.

The next day I left work early and headed to the U.S. State Department Foreign Service Library with our list. The library wasn't open to the public. As Patrick's significant other I had long ago been vetted so I could attend diplomatic events. The library would have everything I needed to know about our future home. Today, it's hard to imagine doing research without the internet. In 1992, research meant footwork, a brick and mortar library. A card catalogue.

Patrick and I had set our criteria for a desirable post—climate, culture, living conditions, accommodations, security, danger or hardship pay, health issues, air quality, language training required, items allowed to ship, children's education, embassy jobs available for spouses. I would take notes on each post that met our criteria so we could know exactly what we were getting ourselves into when we filled out the State Department list of possible choices.

The Foreign Service Library itself was daunting. After clearing security I confronted the massive collection of books, pamphlets, maps, all related to the business of diplomacy—espionage, treaties, trade relations, and on and on. A wall shelf held reports on most of the embassies, including the one in Cape Town. What a beautiful city. But that was out. I focused on the others. This was my process for weeks.

Every night Patrick and I would go over my notes. One evening after dinner we spread the map out on the dining table as usual with my notes for that day. All through dinner Patrick had been in a teasing mood, which I found mildly irritating as time closed in on the date to submit our list. He leaned over Eastern Europe, I took the Western part.

"They know we're used to harsh winters. Maybe it'll be one of these new embassies in the former Soviet republics."

My head came up so fast it bumped his chin.

"Ow!" A sly smile took shape.

"You're not serious."

"There is one other possibility…did I mention Cape Town?" In mock protection, he lifted one arm to his face.

"Cape Town!"

"Don't get too excited. I did a little more investigating. It's a long shot. I doubt they would let me go back for a full tour."

He turned around and poured us each a glass of wine from the bottle on the dinner table. "But I have a feeling there might be a chance. Slim to none, but a chance." We clicked glasses in a cross-fingers toast.

Patrick took our list of six choices with him to the State Department. Cape Town was at the top.

Talk of my taking weaponry lessons fell by the wayside after the argument on the beach when Patrick finally told me about our being under surveillance. Two months later the topic of guns came up again, triggered by more violence. It happened at the King William's Town Golf Club in the Eastern Cape. Five black men armed with rifles and grenades burst into a crowded dining room, killing four whites there with their wine-tasting club. Fifteen white diners and two black waitresses were injured, some seriously, by gunfire, shrapnel and flying glass.

"Does the ambassador think Buthelezi is behind it?"

"Princeton agrees with Mandela that De Klerk is arming and training Buthelezi's forces to fight the ANC. He can deny all he wants, but black resistance fighters don't go from knives and clubs to high-caliber guns and grenades without somebody funding them."

Patrick suspected the violence would get worse the closer we got to an election. One week after the King William's Town killing, he and I drove to the shooting range on the industrial edge of town, the same place Patrick and the marines had their scheduled practices. After completing the paperwork, I proceeded with a private arms lesson with the master marksman instructor on the kinds of handguns I would learn to use, different ammunitions, how to load, check, clean each weapon. My jitters dissipated as I handled each piece.

Guns weren't completely new to me. I had been around them all my life. My dad hunted in the fall deer season, as did my brothers and most of the men in our part of the world. Once I held my father's rifle. I had had no desire to shoot it then. And I had no desire to shoot one now. News of violence made it into the *Argus* every day, and that was just the publicly reported incidents. But it was our flat being broken into that had shaken me to the core. Patrick's long hours left me feeling vulnerable. Weaponry lessons made sense, but they were also proof that Patrick was concerned for my safety, even at home in Sea Point.

The instructor remained in the observation area while I followed Patrick to the open range. The weight of the Colt 45 shocked me. In movies the good guy whips out his weapon deftly. In my hand, it was a cast iron skillet and about as heavy. Patrick helped secure my safety glasses, positioned me in the proper stance, then stepped aside. I faced the life-sized target, a weighted paper shaped like a man hanging from a wire. Intimidation swept over me, whether from both men watching or the lifelike replica, I wasn't sure. My mouth went dry, palms turned clammy.

Gun tight in my hands, I pulled the trigger. It was all I could do to hold onto the thing. Patrick caught me by the shoulder as I stumbled backward. "Got quite a kickback, huh?"

"Oh God, did I hit anything?"

"Almost." Patrick restrained a smile. Again he helped me into position, the squeeze of my shoulders a coded hug unreadable from the instructor's vantage point. This time I was prepared for the shot. It hit the target. The next was easier, as was the next and the next. Each bullet hit somewhere on the paper man. As my nerves settled, the gun was less like a skillet and more like a saucepan. The last few shots hit dead center, right in the heart. A buzz of adrenaline raced through me, my body buoyant.

The instructor bounded from the observation area. He yanked the bullet-ridden paper off the wire clips. Rolling it into a tube, he handed it to me. "Nice job."

The Spelling Bee in grammar school had always been a thrill to win, the reward of a new rosary every month. That was nothing compared to this prize, the punctured paper target. I took the souvenir, a big grin plastered on my face. Patrick's too. I had proved a worthy student in front of the instructor.

The glow lasted as we started home. My dad would be so proud. No. Dad wouldn't be proud. He would be worried. This wasn't a deer hunt. And it wasn't target practice. I had somehow disassociated the skill of shooting from the act of killing. It was hard to imagine a situation in which I might need to defend myself. But Patrick must have known there would come such a time when I would need the gun. And shoot to kill.

Bottle of wine in one hand, glasses in the other, Patrick joined me on the deck to watch the sunset. Swapping his suit for jeans, he looked relaxed. I turned my book over on the table.

"You must've had a good day."

"Good day isn't a category. But I do have good news." He leaned down and kissed me, then poured the wine, a local Sauvignon Blanc. Settling into a chair, he propped his sandaled feet on the deck rail.

"You're going to drop a shoe over the rail one of these days. What news?"

"Ambassador Lyman and his wife Helen are here from Pretoria…which means we'll be having lots of diplomatic events."

"Is 'diplomatic event' military code for 'party'? And will I get to meet Nelson Mandela?"

"Better. You'll get to meet Helen Lyman." With an outstretched leg I caught the tip of his sandal and sent it over the rail. "Cute. Very cute. Did you notice the tide? One of us is going swimming."

"I'm sure Helen Lyman is very nice. But I'd rather meet Mandela."

"You will. But right now Helen is more important. She'll show you the ropes, help you get to know the other wives. Are you gonna get my sandal before the tide does?"

"Why not be spontaneous and come in with me."

"There you go with your 'be spontaneous' campaign. And Mary, just as a heads-up—you need to dial it back. Spontaneity is not the way to blend in."

"I'm not a diplomatic spouse right now. I'm a lover with a hot babe."

Patrick tossed a throw pillow at me. Ten minutes later we were on the beach.

Yale. Harvard. Stanford. Born in San Francisco to a grocer father and housewife mother whose sons' names reflected the dream of immigrant parents determined their children go to college, Ambassador Princeton Lyman had been interested in world events his entire life. As a boy, Princeton helped out at the family grocery store after school, hard work and education core values growing up. He recalls that his father read all four San Francisco daily newspapers. In the store, the radio stayed on all day for the news, international events of particular interest for a city on the Pacific Rim in the post-WWII period.

By the time he graduated high school, Princeton Lyman was convinced his career would be in foreign affairs. As Ambassador Lyman in 1992, he had thirty years of diplomatic service by the time he arrived in South Africa.

President de Klerk and Nelson Mandela had declined U.S. offers of direct help from savvy negotiators. But they were not opposed to facilitators in the negotiation process. Before Ambassador Lyman had even presented his credentials—along with a letter from President George Walker Bush in which he encouraged De Klerk and Mandela to bring the parties together—the ambassador was told by the government that his assistance was welcome. The process was at an impasse, the two men unable to reach a solution on how to proceed with a restructured government based on a nonracial election.

Though the U.S. would not have a place at the negotiating table, Ambassador Lyman would immerse himself as a facilitator behind the scenes. Little did I know at the time what a crucial role he would play in bringing together the major parties, a monumental challenge, given their diverse agendas.

Patrick may have been eager for me to meet Helen, but it was my husband's boss who intrigued me.

Six

The Diplomat's Wife

November 1992

It came by courier. The heavy linen envelope was embossed with the U.S. Embassy insignia, our address handwritten in cursive with blue ink. I grabbed a frosted glass of lemonade and settled on the deck lounge. Pounding surf obliterated everything but the sound of my heartbeat, which had kicked up several notches since I picked up the envelope.

Swiping my hand dry from the frosted glass, I slid a fingernail under the flap to open the letter. It was a formal invitation. Ambassador Lyman and his wife Helen were hosting an official welcome dinner for me and Patrick at their home. A thrill fluttered through me, followed by the sinking realization that I had nothing appropriate to wear. Time was something I had plenty of, with no job, so it wouldn't be hard to go downtown to shop for the perfect dress—something in deep blue to complement my eyes. Gold earrings and an understated necklace would finish it off, for a simple but elegant look. *Blend in, Mary.*

While this dinner was protocol for welcoming an embassy official, I suspected it was also an opportunity to suss out the new guy, and the new guy's wife. My outfit had to be right. The advantage of not being star-struck helped with nerves. In my job as director of public relations I had dealt with all kinds of high profile guests. In D.C., Patrick and I had attended foreign embassy functions at the White House. But this would be my first diplomatic event at an American post as Mrs. McGhee. I wanted Patrick to be proud.

It was a balmy evening, the night of the dinner, warm weather a sign that we were moving into the summer season, our winter in the States. The ever-present wind had tamped down to a pleasant breeze. I hadn't tried anything fancy with my hair. Long and loose would be easier to run a brush through before we rang the doorbell.

The ambassador's home was in Bishopscourt, twenty minutes inland, Cape Town's wealthiest neighborhood, a favorite enclave of high level diplomats. The drive alone was worth the invitation. We wound our way along leafy streets as we gained in elevation until we reached the top. Ambassador Lyman's was the end house, a sprawling pitched-roof home on park-like grounds. At the wrought iron gate, three guards stood at a hut. One approached and greeted Patrick.

"Lone Ranger and Tonto are expecting us." Patrick handed the guard his I.D. The man nodded, then looked over at me. After inspecting my identification he did the customary check under the car with a mirrored-end rod to check for an explosive device. Cleared, we drove on. "Princeton and Helen," Patrick said with a smile in response to my confused look at the Lone Ranger and Tonto reference.

The property looked to be completely fenced, topped with razor wire and security lights, cameras. A long driveway hidden from the street by mature landscaping brought us to a second gate. Again we stopped for clearance. Finally Patrick pulled the government sedan into one of the spaces marked "guest." A wide stone path led us across the yard—lush grass lined with marsh roses, birds of paradise, bright geraniums in every color, all of it manicured to perfection. That first day in Cape Town, we had passed Khayelitsha Township on the other side of the mountain. I hadn't noticed a single flower.

A quick run of a hairbrush through my hair, and I rang the bell, eager to thwart Patrick's "legal debauchery" comment, not that he would say that in this company. Patrick was nothing if not professional. An African house lady opened the door. We stepped into the foyer. Before she could speak, a blur of blue silk appeared from behind, shuffling the maid aside.

"Thank you, Takisha. Patrick, welcome." The gracious woman shook his hand, then took mine in both of hers. "Mrs. McGhee...Mary, hello. I'm Helen Lyman."

"Hello, Mrs. Lyman. I'm so pleased to meet you. Thank you for having us."

"Please, call me Helen." She looked to be about my mother's age with the air of sophistication that comes from a lifetime of world travel. The daughter of Jewish immigrants who had escaped just before the worst of the Nazi atrocities, Helen had been a career diplomat's spouse for three decades. Princeton told her when they were dating in high school that he had decided on a career in Foreign Service. Helen almost broke up with him. She told him she could barely face the prospect of traveling the world, moving from place to place every two years, much less with children.

Helen and Princeton were a real team, like us. She had supported the two of them with her degree in social work while Princeton finished graduate school. They had had their share of separations with his tours abroad as he worked his way up the State Department career ladder, but her life wasn't without excitement. She and their three school-aged daughters had joined him in South Korea and in Ethiopia for his work with humanitarian aid in the 1980s, where she taught at the American school.

I tried to imagine her life as a diplomatic spouse with three little kids, making it all work in posts across the globe. It wouldn't take long for me to figure out Helen Lyman was special. The ropes were the least of what I could learn from her. In less than three minutes, I liked Helen Lyman. It was clear she was comfortable with who she was, happy in her life as a diplomatic spouse. That was no small thing for someone as lost as I was that fall of '92.

The petite brunette led us into a drawing room, the rustling of her voluminous skirt announcing our arrival to three other couples mingling over drinks. Patrick squeezed my hand. The ambassador nodded to him from across the room. He came toward us. The man had to be mid-fifties but his trim body and friendly demeanor gave him a youthful quality. Patrick kept my hand in his while introducing us to the others, all high-ranking Americans in positions of authority at the embassy, along with their wives. At least a decade stood between me and everyone else.

The drawing room was beautiful with classic European furniture in dark woods. Ornately framed African artwork hung next to paintings depicting American genre scenes, all carefully curated by a committee focused solely on the embassy collection to reflect the perfect mix of national pride while paying homage to the culture of South Africa.

Glass doors opened to the patio. The garden was an oasis with a stunning array of protea, the national flower. How my mother would have loved it. I wasn't sure the exotic flowering plant would grow in Minnesota, yet if anyone could make it happen it would be Mom. A balmy breeze fluttered the sheer curtains, as if to say "just one more beautiful evening in Cape Town."

Armed with drinks—a local Boschendal Chardonnay for me, a Castle beer for Patrick—we split up and found our way into conversation. The housemaid in her crisp uniform glided toward me with a silver platter of hors d'oeuvres as I walked toward the wives. As a PR director, I had become a master at balancing wine and a small plate in one hand, leaving the other free to shake hands. Sampling a chicken skewer with Cape Malay curry, I leaned across an invisible crevasse to guard against spilling. The staged moment of preoccupation gave me a chance to catch up with the women's conversation—gossip about their domestic help—while comparing my outfit with theirs to make sure I had made the right call.

The dining room was a picture of elegance, the table set with fine china, sterling cutlery, birds of paradise in tall vases on the side tables, low flower centerpieces on the main one. Seating would be according to protocol, which meant I would not be next to my husband. Perhaps because we were newcomers, our host set protocol aside. The ambassador pulled out the chair next to Patrick's for me, then took his place at the head of the table. Across from us a picture window framed a view of the mountains, breathtaking against the gold hue of a setting sun.

Wine poured freely as the hum of chatter pierced by an occasional high laugh filled the room. Geography led the conversation—where we were from in the States and, from there, common interests, which led to golf. No one said anything about political strife, violence in the townships, or
the latest killings.

"Them are fightin' words, my friend. I'll take you on. Patrick, you choose the course…we'll make it a foursome."

Patrick scoffed. "Stellenbosch is out of my league. But I'll take you on in basketball."

"You gentlemen aren't the only athletes in the room." Helen glanced at the other wives. "Mary, do you play tennis?"

"I do."

"Be forewarned, Helen, Mary played in college. And she has a mean competitive streak." It was actually Patrick who had the mean competitive streak. But I was onto him with his deftly-placed bait.

"Then I'll have a challenge. You must come over and play. Tashika will fix us a nice lunch afterward and we can get to know each other better."

Patrick nudged my knee under the table.

"I'd like that. Thank you." Conversation resumed with more talk of sports, which the men played, what sport at what level. My mind drifted. Fork in mid-air, I wondered if this same innocuous banter had filled dining rooms in Cape Town for three hundred years of white rule. The topic turned to the depreciating rand. Current events were my cue. I waited for a break.

"Mr. Ambassador, this morning I read an op-ed piece in the *Argus* about how the ANC might react to this latest spate of murders in the townships. What do you think Mandela will do?"

An awkward silence fell over the room like cloud cover over Table Mountain. The econ officer's wife whispered something to her husband.

"More lobster, Mary? Tashika, bring Mrs. McGhee—"

"It's all right, Helen." The ambassador took a sip of wine as everyone turned to him. Patrick tensed up next to me. "This last crisis has the ANC threatening to break off negotiations with President de Klerk altogether if the violence doesn't stop."

"Can we do anything? I mean, the emba—?" Patrick cleared his throat, cutting me off.

The ambassador glanced at him, then back to me. "You mean *can I* do anything," he said with a teasing smile. Heat rushed to my face. "Mandela knows retaliation would threaten any hope for an election." The ambassador looked at the other guests to draw them in. "And yes, I *can* do something. Just this morning I presented both Mandela and President de Klerk with a letter from President Bush. He's offered to send Henry Kissinger to help move forward with an interim constitution."

"I'm sure if anyone can help negotiate, it's Mr. Kissinger."

Patrick's shoulders slumped. The ambassador continued.

"I agree, Mary. But it turns out Mr. Mandela doesn't want an interim constitution. He wants a complete overhaul—a new constitution. You'll read about it in the *Argus* next week, but it turns out both men feel this is South Africa's problem, up to them to resolve."

"Oh. But surely you—"

"My goodness, Princeton, our guests will end up with acid reflux if we try to solve all our diplomatic challenges over one dinner." Helen topped off her husband's wine, her hand lightly on his with a quick look, some silent communication transpiring between them. "Mary, I understand from Patrick that you were in public relations back in the States."

The ambassador turned to me. "Public relations, that rings a bell. Wait…didn't you apply for diplomatic clearance to work?"

"Yes, I did." My voice faltered, noting Patrick's downcast eyes.

The ambassador chuckled. "Well, I can see tennis is not going to be enough to keep you out of trouble. Since you're interested in the mission, and with your background working with people, you might fit right in as a community liaison."

A collective gasp preceded the sound of wine glasses filling.

"Why don't you drop by the embassy Monday. I'll have Beverly see what we can do."

Helen pushed her chair back. When she stood to address the guests, a tone of insistence came through beneath her saccharine voice.

"Gentlemen, I'm sure you would enjoy a brandy in the drawing room. Princeton has a new telescope I'm sure he would love to show off. Ladies, if you'll join me on the terrace, I'll have Tashika bring us some sherry."

The evening wound down as we chatted on the patio. Just as arriving early or late to a diplomatic event is a major faux pas, so is failure to depart at the appropriate hour. The group dispersed with gracious chitchat as we took our turns thanking the ambassador and Helen for a lovely evening.

Patrick was silent in the car.

"I didn't mean for the job thing to come up, hon."

He scoffed. "Is it really so hard to blend in?"

"I did blend in. The other wives are great, especially Helen. You heard her invite me over for tennis and you heard me accept."

Silence.

"It's just that it seemed crazy not to talk about the violence, how it might affect the election. Isn't that a topic of shared concern? I apologize if I embarrassed you."

"Maybe you shouldn't have had that second glass of wine."

"Patrick," I chuckled, "you're kidding…I was not out of line."

"No. Worse…you stood out from the other wives. There's a time and a place, Mary. You embarrassed Helen by asking Princeton to talk about high level intelligence."

"You mean I embarrassed *you*. And he said it would be in the paper next week. I wouldn't call that high level intelligence."

Patrick slammed his palm against the steering wheel. "That's not the point. Hon, can't you support me here? It's two years, that's it. All I'm asking is that you blend in."

I stared straight ahead with a mumble. "Spend my days playing tennis and shopping."

"Like that's a big sacrifice."

Heat rose to my face. "I don't see how my getting a job at the embassy can be interpreted as not supporting your career. If anything, I'd think you'd be pleased. You knew I wanted to work. You were all for it. I didn't go to college to play tennis and shop."

"No. And you made sure everyone knew it. 'Look how educated I am. Look what an important job I had in the States. You women may be Stepford Wives but I'm part of the mission.'"

"Hon, that's not fair. I can blend in with or without a job. I'm just not big on pretending."

His tone was cold. "No, you're big on travel and adventure. Well, now you're here and it's not so adventurous." He scoffed out loud in disgust. "You mock the protocol. You think blending in turns you into 'The Little Woman' and God forbid you should be like your mother."

"My mother has nothing to do with this."

"You knew there would be some of that, Mary. If the idea of blending in was so offensive maybe you should've thought twice about what you were getting into."

My mouth dropped. Headlights from an oncoming car flashed light across his face, jaw set in restraint. "Patrick, you're twisting everything. Whatever you're imagining is in your head. As far as I know, I'm not guilty of any violation of protocol."

"No? Really? In case you hadn't noticed, this was a welcome dinner, a social event in the ambassador's home specifically held to introduce us, not for you to confront him about what the U.S. is or isn't doing. Really, Mary, if being like other wives is too much of a stretch, maybe you should go home."

"Go home! What are you talking about?"

"You could probably get your old job back."

"Patrick, you're not being fair. I was not out of line."

The conversation was over. He kept his eyes locked on the road.

Sea Point had rolled up its sidewalks for the night. Storm clouds blocked the moon. In dark silence we drove to the flat. How could we have seen the evening so differently? Was Patrick right? Had I been inappropriate, misunderstood some prohibition about bringing up the one thing that was really important? It wasn't about the embassy job. Patrick was disappointed when my work request was denied. And it wasn't about the other wives. They liked me. Helen liked me. I have good sensors about people. My career in public relations depends on it. That's not what upset him. But what?

We pulled into the parking garage. Neither of us said a word in the elevator or inside the flat. I grabbed my toothbrush on the way to the guest room. Careful to avoid eye contact, I mumbled goodnight as we passed in the hall. When the door was shut and the TV on, I dropped on the bed, burying my face in the pillow to muffle my noisy sobs of anguish. Did he actually mean what he said? Think he'd be better off without me? Had I been out of line bringing up the whole reason for the mission? There's no way I could have taken such a big misstep to justify Patrick's reaction. I was missing something.

Then it dawned on me, the unspoken rule. Cape Town was a world still immersed in the genteel way of life that had reigned for three hundred years, a planet in its own orbit far removed from the raw struggle for survival on the other side of the mountain. Rule number one—don't point out the discrepancy. Especially at a dinner party.

By living like Afrikaners—their homes, their neighborhoods, their lives, all of it safe, untouched by violence—we could distance from a reality no one wanted to confront. But how could we sit around a dinner table enjoying good food and wine without any mention of why we were here in the first place? That seemed crazy. It made us no better than every generation before us who looked at that same view over dinner and talked about golf. If pretending was protocol, then yes, I had breached it.

Of course, that was it. What a dummy I had been to miss the real message that day on the beach when Patrick came clean about the surveillance. Not only was authentic friendship off the table, personal sharing taboo, but so was talk of the real world where, for all intents and purposes, apartheid continued.

It was about putting on blinders to keep from acknowledging to ourselves or anyone else our complicity, "our wretched ways." The white Afrikaner on the beach wasn't referring to Dutch rulers. He meant us, all white people.

Blending in had nothing to do with what I wore or who I made friends with, or even about drawing attention by having a job. What Patrick really meant was that I should live inside the bubble and pretend our hands were clean, that everything would be fine because the U.S. would save South Africa from oppression at the hands of another.

If not having girlfriends was going to be tough, it was nothing compared with this. I had never turned away from truth. And reacting to that truth had always been a part of who I was, my heart an open book. Tears came easily over hurt animals, abuse of any kind. Now I was supposed to ignore murder outside our doors because it was inappropriate dinner conversation? Not suffer over kids who had no shoes, no roof? If collective pretending was the way to protect against reality and the broken heart it would surely bring, it was too late. I was already halfway there.

This epiphany brought new waves of homesickness. As a Girl Scout at summer camp, I had missed my mom and dad so much I marked off the days until they would come rescue me. No one would be coming to South Africa to rescue me. I yanked the covers over my head and cried myself to sleep.

Sun threw shards of light across the room. It was quiet. I tiptoed down the hall to our bedroom. The door was open. Patrick was gone. Wow. He couldn't wait to leave for work. Fine. Let him stay mad. He was the one who couldn't handle things. Don't talk. Don't feel. Don't confide. *You have me, Mary, that'll have to do.* But he didn't want to talk, much less listen. Did he think our marriage would thrive on neglect when I couldn't confide my feelings for fear the weight of dependency would hobble him?

I was on my own. At last it was clear.

On the way to the kitchen, I stopped. Patrick was on the couch dead asleep, legs sticking out from a blanket too short to cover him. My hurt had already given way to anger. Feeling righteous, I continued to the kitchen. The hiss and drip of coffee brewing sounded abrasive as I stared out the window, the glorious Atlantic an incongruous sheet of glass in the morning light.

I startled. Patrick hugged me from behind. "Hon, I'm sorry." His voice was low, soft. I turned around. Tears filled his eyes. He started to speak, then pulled me close again. "I didn't mean what I said. You have to know that."

His remorse caught me off guard. I had to accept his apology but wasn't ready. He couldn't undo such harsh words so easily. I hugged him back, tight. "It's okay, hon. We can talk later."

He took me by the shoulders, our faces close. "Tonight."

Then he was off to work. My head hurt, my stomach churned. A terrible nights' sleep hadn't helped. Going back to bed was pointless. The coffee tasted bitter, my stomach a pool of acid. I sat on the sofa, staring at the ocean, eyes unfocused. *You should leave, Mary, go home…go home.* A stack of Patrick's shirts stared at me from the ironing basket. I started on the mindless task. The radio kept me company, just as it had my mom when she ironed.

If only I could really talk to her. But that was pointless. What would I tell her? That all my education and hard work had been for naught; that I wasn't working, not in public relations, not in Foreign Service, not in anything? That my husband no longer wanted me by his side? That I had become a whiny, clingy wife who couldn't cope with the demands of diplomatic life? That the next two years would consist of ironing shirts, cooking dinner, grocery shopping while the world as we know it came to an end?

I might as well have been in Minnesota with a house full of kids.

By noon I forced myself to eat a piece of toast. The promenade, my happy place, would lift my spirits with people and sea air. Fifteen minutes of zombie-walking convinced me the effort was hopeless. My mind stayed stuck. *You should go home…go home…go home.* The worst thing was that part of me believed that if he had said those words, he must have believed them in some dark corner of his mind. An elderly couple walked toward me, hand-in-hand. A new wave of anguish surged through me. They had maneuvered decades of marriage and still showed the affection of lovers. Three months into ours, Patrick and I were strangers. I ran the rest of the way to the flat, holding back tears until Mr. Khumalo greeted me and the elevator door closed.

In the flat I stared at the ocean over a cup of tea. How had things gotten so bad so quickly? I had to face the truth that my vision of what life would be in South Africa was one hundred and eighty degrees from reality. Something had to change. And I had to change it. Never one to shrink from a challenge, this time would be no exception. Surely Patrick didn't think I would really pack up and go home. He had to know me better than that. But one thing was clear—it was up to me to figure out my life as a diplomatic spouse, an unemployed diplomatic spouse. And it was up to me to get us back on track. We had to talk.

Our conversation would go better with his stomach full. That night I made a pot roast with veggies, a favorite of Patrick's. Dinnertime passed. No Patrick. He hadn't mentioned a late meeting and he hadn't called. Each hour of waiting brought more emotion until I had a mix of anger, disappointment, hurt, funneling through me. The phone rang. A last minute meeting was running long. He would be late. The apology was sincere. It was just as well. Depleted emotionally and physically, it wasn't a good time for a charged conversation. By the time he found his warm plate in the oven I would be fast asleep.

It was to be the first of many non-conversations about issues that would get swept under the carpet, superseded by his demands at the embassy. Emotions would stay tangled, unspoken. There was no way to ignore the growing malaise between us.

Seven
Woman of Desire

November 1992

Patrick left early for another seven am meeting, his days ever longer to accommodate a busy schedule. In the kitchen next to the coffee pot, Mr. Potato Head stood armless with one eye missing. I smirked. If only it were that easy, apology via clever talisman. That wasn't enough if we couldn't talk things through once in a while. Patrick had cut deep. I couldn't close the gaping wound by myself, in spite of the message from Mr. Potato Head that he owned part of the problem.

My meeting at the embassy turned out to be fruitless. The officer in the Community Liaison position had postponed her decision to leave the job. It might become available in the not-too-distant future. But I was too disheartened for any glass-half-full perspective. It was back to waiting. True to her word, Helen Lyman invited me over the next week to play tennis. I was so happy to spend time with her. During our two-out-of-three match, we would stop to let the parade of funny looking guinea fowl cross the court and disappear into the bushes. The yard was a veritable paradise.

After Helen won the third set in a tiebreak, she led me to the veranda where Tashika served us iced tea. It was easy to like Helen. She initiated conversation about her life as a new diplomatic spouse, regaling me with funny stories about life with Princeton and their three daughters in South Korea and Ethiopia in an open, unguarded manner. I relaxed with her. Still, I was careful to keep comments about my own life general, free of detail. *Don't trust anyone, Mary, not even other embassy families.*

Helen must have sensed my loneliness. Stories about her life were a gesture of comfort, opening up about her own struggles as a new diplomatic spouse inviting me to do the same. I couldn't imagine how she did it, given the stress of relocation—moving every few years, setting up house, getting the girls into school, trying to provide some semblance of normal childhood, making friends that she would leave when the post ended. Had she been as lonely as I was now?

Helen talked in code, but the subtext was clear—Mary, I understand how hard this is, your first post, a difficult and dangerous post at that. You won't be lonely for long. You'll find your way and come to enjoy the privilege of living in a new culture. I know you're not comfortable opening up yet, but know that I'm here for you.

I was envious of her, wanted to be past the hard part of this first post. She also told me it would be a mistake to anticipate future posts based on this one, that they were all different. "Future" posts. The word struck me. I was quite sure I would never get used to this one, much less contemplate the ones ahead. But Helen's company offered the companionship of girl talk. That was enough. Though she was old enough to be my mother, I decided that morning that Helen Lyman would be my mentor. But she already knew that.

The emotional assist of companionship gave me a boost. If I couldn't get a job, volunteer work would do. The *Argus* had published a short piece about an American film shooting in town with Robert Mitchum and Bo Derek. The article even included information about where the stars were staying.

The Ritz was two blocks from our flat. My gut urge was to meet with hotel management to volunteer my services organizing the visit of their high-profile visitors, a project right in my wheelhouse. That would be impossible, of course. The Ritz would have competent public relations staff. Besides, the ambassador would see it as thumbing my nose at protocol. Instead, I would play it low key with a letter for Ms. Derek–an introduction and offer of assistance, one young woman to another in a foreign country. A few rand would convince the reception clerk to slip it under her door.

With renewed purpose, I headed out, zigzagging my way around three blocks to mess with my shadow's head. I was no doubt in better shape than the dolt trailing me. Let him earn his rat's pay. The long walk did me good, cleared my head. With my energy, my smarts, I would find my footing. Then I would figure out how Patrick and I could recapture our newlywed feel. Work would revive me. And I would be around Americans.

As I walked through the lobby, the same feeling came over me that always did stepping into a luxury hotel—the thrill of glamour, the air of possibility, myriad people with important lives coming and going through the revolving door. At the registration desk I waited while the man in front of me queried the clerk about a suitable off-site restaurant for a large crew. A movie crew. Before she could answer I stepped to his side.

"Are you here with the Robert Mitchum film?" I used my confident PR manner. "Hi. My name is Mary McGhee. My husband is in diplomatic service here. I would be happy to show your crew around town and recommend restaurants, sights, must-see attractions." Not that I had been to many myself. But I knew my job. The rest I could figure out. He looked me over in the quick-glance way men do.

"Are you available to work on the movie?"

It was too much to hope that it would be this easy. I tempered my enthusiasm so it wouldn't sound like the desperation it was. "As a matter of fact I am."

He extended his hand. "I'm Bob Bradshaw, the producer. Pleased to meet you, Mrs. McGhee. Come with me, there's someone I'd like you to meet." With a parting glance at the clerk, I followed him up the lift to the penthouse. The luxury flat was complete with a Juliette deck and views of magnificent Table Mountain on one side, the Atlantic Ocean on the other.

Bob introduced me to the star. Robert Mitchum looked relaxed on the sofa with a drink in hand. Older than I had remembered him on screen, he still had a commanding presence with that trademark low sexy voice.

"Mrs. McGhee, what's your interest in this movie?" I explained my background in public relations, including event planning, then volunteered my services for the project. He mimicked the same head-to-toe assessment as the other Bob. "No way. You're way too pretty to be behind the scenes. We'll put you in the movie."

"No, no. I'm flattered but I'm really at my best behind—"

"Do you know how many people would kill for this opportunity?" His eyes twinkled.

Of course I did. The audition was later that afternoon in a conference room buzzing with at least fifty locals—blacks, coloreds, Indians. I was the sole blonde. Taking a seat along the wall, I waited. An hour later a young man led me to the front where I sat across the table from another young man and repeated what I had told Bob & Bob. The casting agent liked my dimples. It turned out the script called for a woman journalist, a bit part with no lines.

He hired me on the spot with instructions to show up on the set the next morning with seven bright-colored outfits.

At home I pulled out every possible piece of clothing until the bed was covered in overlapping pink and orange outfits, the dominant color in my honeymoon wardrobe. The afternoon melted down with multiple clothing changes in alternate combinations. The front door opened. I ran to meet Patrick. "You won't believe what happened today. I'm going to be very busy for the next few weeks."

"Doing what? Hold on while I change." Comfortable in jeans, I led him out to the deck and told him the whole story of how I had landed a role in *Woman of Desire*.

"You won't be doing any sex scenes with Mitchum, will you?"

The throw pillow hit him in the face. He grabbed it with a chuckle. We had one of those evenings fueled by the energy of everything falling into place. Patrick told me not to worry about the ambassador, that mine was a short-term gig with no compensation. Later, in the kitchen drying dishes, he put his hands under my arms and lifted me up, then lowered me into a kiss. "There's something I'd like to report to my *Woman of Desire* journalist." I giggled under his kiss. Walking backwards, he guided us into the bedroom with a swift kick to close the door in classic Twentieth Century Fox style.

An entire downtown block had been cordoned off for the massive tent that served as base. An assistant checked me in, then I met the cast and crew. Everyone seemed friendly. The air was filled with anticipation, the good kind of uncertainty that comes with lots of moving parts all eager to coalesce.

Peter, an older actor from Cape Town who was also an extra, offered to coach me in my small role. What a relief. His scoop about the movie was that it was a mystery/thriller with erotic overtones. Bo Derek was a huge draw for everyone, still a perfect "10." Her mother had joined her for the trip. My event planner know-how would kick in later when I helped her plan Bo's thirty-sixth birthday celebration on the set.

The movie filmed from sundown to sunrise after government buildings closed for business. For the next two weeks Patrick and I would be ships passing in the night. Every morning after filming ended I would crawl into bed with him. It was a lovely way to end my day and start his. Sleep during the day proved difficult, the bright African sun relentless. I got by with less than normal energy, boosted by my involvement with the movie.

At last I was at home in Cape Town with friends, coworkers, a place to be and time to be there, for two weeks anyway.

A huge wrap party marked the end of on-site filming. It would be the perfect occasion for me to introduce Patrick. If he would go. His much-needed sleep disrupted by my nocturnal schedule, he had been unusually tired the last two weeks. The stress at work didn't help. All he wanted was to come home, eat dinner and go to bed. I had to change his mind for the party. The night after filming ended I made a special meal to tell him about it.

"Nah, not interested. Really, Mar, you should go."

I couldn't tell whether he was serious. We ate in silence for a moment.

"Okay. I will." Surprised, he stared at me. "Patrick, I want to go. It's been great being busy, being around people again."

He nodded, then went back to eating. And that was the end of that. Calling his bluff had been momentarily satisfying, a way to discharge a small dose of residual anger from his admonition that I should go home.

But if he wasn't coming with me to the party, that brought up another issue. I would have to drive the Honda—a manual—shifting gears on a long mountain road from Sea Point to Llandudno. On my first few outings I had nearly blown out the clutch on the hillside. Peter, my acting coach and fellow local, was the answer to my dilemma. A locally well-known pianist, Peter was gregarious, easy to befriend. We had bonded during a long bar scene where we suspected that, given the trouble Mitchum had with his lines, he was actually drunk. The scene had required multiple takes.

The morning of the party, I asked Patrick again if he was sure he didn't want to go. He was getting dressed for work. "I'm sure."

"Okay. So I'm going with another member of the cast—a guy— since I'm not all that comfortable with the stick shift."

Patrick stopped shuffling his foot into the sock. "What guy?"

"Peter. The actor from the bar scene we worked on for hours? I told you about him."

Patrick didn't say anything. That evening he zipped my dress just as the phone rang. Mr. Khumalo announced our visitor. "So you'll have a glass of wine with Peter, yes?"

"Now I'm playing the father, meeting your date?"

My kiss brushed his lips. "You didn't want to come. Don't make this a slight on you."

"Ten minutes, that's it."

The jealous streak was a side I had seen years ago when he first met my friend David in Minneapolis. The day of the vice-premier of China's arrival at the hotel, Patrick had popped into my office to ask for my help in restricting guest access to the west lobby the next afternoon. On my way to meet with the head of maintenance, Patrick and I met at the elevator. He was on his way to the lounge for a drink. When the elevator door opened, he blocked it with his whole body as if protecting me from assault. We were alone.

Suddenly nervous, heat flushed my face. "So, how long have you been a security guard?"

Patrick suppressed grin. "Special Agent." He looked at my red face. "That's okay. It's a complicated role." He spoke with not an ounce of condescension. Emboldened, I offered to show him and the other agents around town. It was, after all, part of my job to work with visiting groups. The hit was thinly disguised but something told me he would accept.

The next evening, my roommate Debbie and I met him and another special agent in the lobby. My guess had been correct that a man like Patrick would be on time. As the four of us stepped outside the hotel, he moved toward the street to hail a cab. I was one step ahead of him. The one at the curb was for us, I said. The look of surprise on his face morphed into a smile. Once again I was embarrassed. Once again, he responded with warmth.

Looking like a much more relaxed man than the one I had met curbside the previous day, Patrick had changed from his three-piece suit into khaki pants and a dark, long sleeved shirt. I had changed from my black suit and white blouse into gray pants and a black sweater, the dark background a perfect contrast to the blonde hair that fell past my shoulders in soft waves. Debbie had suggested I try a rich red lipgloss. With that added touch, I was a different woman.

The other agent took the front seat. Deb and I got in back. Patrick had to stoop low to climb in next to me. His aftershave was subtle, masculine musky. Scrunched between him and Debbie, I nestled behind his shoulder to give him more room. Even without the suit, the shades, the authority, Patrick was a presence. The cab driver eyed him in the rear view mirror with a questioning look. I leaned forward and told him the name of the restaurant, grateful to establish some semblance of my own authority in a second small gesture.

Patrick was strong. I could not be passive in the company of such men. They misread me. Girlfriends teased me about the need to assert myself in the kind, sweet way of those who are stronger than they look. In my job I had learned to take charge without hesitation, stave off any sense of doubt over whether I could handle the task, whatever it was. That demonstration of confidence had brought business opportunities that gave me a chance to earn my stripes, eventually landing me in my job as director of public relations. I wanted Patrick to witness my capable, independent self.

At the restaurant I approached the bar to order a glass of wine. Patrick stepped forward. "What's your pleasure?" Accustomed to ordering my own drink, I was taken aback, feeling feminine in a way I had not for a long time, the way women do when they're not in charge of everything. He ordered the drinks. We found Debbie and the other agent in a booth. I slid in first. Patrick squeezed in beside me for the second time in half an hour. Again, my face flushed.

A friend waved from another table. The black man approached us, an impressive figure in the trendy 1980s high-waist jeans and herringbone sports jacket. Patrick straightened his shoulders and did a double take, first at me, then at the man, who stuck out his hand. "Hi, I'm David. I work with Mary. Didn't I see you at the hotel with the Chinese delegation?"

That initial jealous reaction told me Patrick was interested. David in Minneapolis had been no more threat than Peter in Cape Town. No one was. Still, maybe taunting Patrick a bit over not coming to the wrap party was my way of showing him—and myself—that I wasn't wholly dependent on him for companionship.

For the first time in weeks I had something of my own bordering on independence. That was hard to come by. Breaking free of diplomatic restrictions was a momentary coup. But once again, I found myself reacting like a child to Patrick's protective overtones. I had wanted him to be jealous, at least a little, as payment for not coming to the party. But the rebellion only drove us further into our designated roles of Reason versus Feeling.

"You might actually enjoy Peter. He's a well-known jazz musician locally, and an actor with the local troupe." Patrick knows how much I love jazz. And he's not a fan of celebrity. I wasn't helping the situation but I didn't care. The doorbell rang. It was Peter.

"Mary, you look lovely." What is it about that thick British accent that makes everything sound more elegant, more sincere? Peter leaned forward and kissed me on the cheek. I motioned him in. Patrick got up from the chair, a look of confusion on his face. He reached out his hand.

"Nice to meet you, Peter. Mary has told me about you." Patrick threw me a sidelong glance with a twinkle in his eyes. "Come in, come in."

Peter, a bear of a man close to my father's age with gray-white hair, lumbered into the room. With a suppressed groan, he lowered himself into a chair. "The old hip. Man, I don't know how Mitchum does it, after all the bones he's broken in Westerns. I would've paid out of pocket for a stunt man."

"Mary tells me you're a musician. I hate to typecast, but my guess is this is more up your alley than Chardonnay." Peter took the glass of scotch. Patrick poured another for himself and a glass of wine for me.

Half an hour later, it was Peter, not Patrick, who nudged us off to the party.

"You'll be missed," I said to Patrick with a kiss. On his pillow he would find my note: *"A + F"* (Always and Forever). Next to it would be Mr. Potato Head, sans left ear.

At last I had something exciting to write about to Mom and my sister Marcy. I told them all about the movie—Mitchum, how he told me he had broken over a hundred bones in his moviemaking career; how much he missed chili, to which I offered him my famous homemade version; how I had invited the entire cast to the flat for drinks. And of course, I described the wrap party. Then it was over. Time on the set had reminded me how peopled my world had been at home. One actor, another local, sensed my loneliness. He invited me for tennis, after which we had coffee. Conversation centered mostly on movies, his past acting gigs. He asked me about the embassy, which was common. People were curious. My answers were general.

One day when Keith and I stopped for a cold drink, the questions became more pointed as he asked about Patrick's job, security issues, my life here and at home.

That was a red flag. My gut tightened in confirmation to be wary.

These kinds of pseudo-friendships had become a frequent occurrence as people sought visas to leave the country. "White flight" was the term used to describe the exodus of Afrikaners, Brits, American expats who fled with their wealth, fearful of either an impending civil war or confiscation of property by blacks after the election.

As violence escalated and spilled from the townships, whites were attacked by militant radicals when they happened to be in the wrong place at the wrong time. People wanted out. But visas were tightly controlled. I wondered if my contact with Keith was more about his wanting my help than friendship. Did he think I could get him a visa? Was he reporting on me to the South African government? I severed our contact.

My life shrank back to its insular form. Nine weeks after our arrival in Cape Town I still hadn't found my footing.

Eight
Freed from Domesticity

November 1992

Two weeks after the ambassador's dinner, I got notice from the embassy's administrative officer that I was to schedule an interview for the now-open position of Community Liaison Officer. The ambassador had made it sound so casual, "*drop by the embassy, Mary...*" but clearly I wasn't a shoo-in.

"An interview sounds so formal. It's a little intimidating."

Patrick sat on the bed putting his shoes on for work. "Nah, just protocol. You'll do fine."

"It's not the Foreign Service Officer test you had to take, is it?" Patrick had described the written and oral exam in which two out of three applicants failed. He said it had been harder to pass than his state bar.

"Nope. They're just making sure they have the best and the brightest representing the U.S. on foreign soil. That would be you."

"You're biased."

"Yep." He kissed me on his way out the door. "A word of advice…don't wear your hair in a ponytail. They'll think you faked your I.D." Patrick suggested I arrive fifteen minutes early to allow time to go through the metal detector, a commonplace exercise in 2018 but, at that time, a practice reserved for government and other high security buildings.

Marine Post One checked my diplomatic passport, glancing twice at me, then my photo, to confirm I was Mrs. McGhee. He buzzed me through to the main embassy where Admin Officer Brown met me, a stern looking woman with hair pulled back tight, two decades my senior. She escorted me into a windowless boardroom where the two other officers made up the interview panel.

"Be seated, Mrs. McGhee."

So much for small talk to break the ice.

In spite of Patrick's assurances, my stomach was in knots. Corporate America loves an articulate, confident employee who excels at connecting with all kinds of people, part of the skill set displayed in a job interview. Here I would measure my words.

The three officers stared at their clipboards rather than at me. A moment later, they began the process, each in turn with a question.

Officer One: "Mrs. McGhee, can you explain the ways in which you meet the criteria for the job of Community Liaison Officer?"

My mouth went dry at her humorless manner. My two-page resume was on the table right in front of them. Had they even looked at it?

"I...I was very successful at my corporate job back home as a project manager with strong organizational skills—meeting goals, coming in under budget." All three looked up from their clipboards. "Of course...this is government work. I understand I wouldn't be managing a budget."

Strike one, Mary.

In the awkward silence, they took notes. I babbled on, trying to undo my shaky start. "As Public Relations Director, I also utilized my writing skills for press releases and—"

So much for measured words.

"That's fine, Mrs. McGhee. Can you tell the panel why you want this job?"

An involuntary giggle nearly escaped. *I'm bored to death, Ambassador Lyman denied my Request to Seek Employment, I'm lonely as hell, and I'll probably have more privacy here than at home in our bugged flat!* "I'm capable, comfortable with responsibility, energetic, focused. I think I can be a real asset to the embassy."

What I had intended to come across as possessing the initiative of a self-starter sounded cocky. *Strike two, Mary.*

Admin Brown cleared her throat and straightened her shoulders. "Mrs. McGhee, as you are aware, an embassy serves its country and foreign citizens in numerous capacities. What is your knowledge base for international affairs?"

International affairs? Are you kidding? Two months ago I knew zilch about South Africa! Strike three, Mary. No, wait! Just be honest.

"I know that this is a dangerous but momentous time in South Africa's history—that the focus of the embassy right now is to support the democratic process and ensure that the first nonracial election in three hundred years takes place with a peaceful transition to majority rule." I let out a sigh of relief.

This time, the silence was less awkward, but their faces remained blank. More scribbling.

Officer One again: "Mrs. McGhee, do you speak Afrikaans or Xhosa?"

Strike four. I explained about my study of both languages on tape before arriving, but how I had failed to master either. A slight smile emerged from Officer Two, a look of superiority mixed with derision. An upcoming class in Xhosa would offer whatever candidate they selected an opportunity to learn the language spoken in most of the townships.
Whatever candidate they selected.

Officer Three: "How would you describe your social, interpersonal and communication skills, especially the ability to work with people from other cultures?"

"As PR director for a luxury hotel, I met numerous dignitaries from around the world—the vice-premier of China; King Olav of Norway; Presidents Bush and Gorbachev; King Gustaf and Princess Silvia of Sweden..."

Silence. Stares.

Good one, Mary. How many dignitaries live in poverty-ridden townships? Fix it!
"So I'm quite used to showing the deference and respect due those from different cultural backgrounds and economic levels." I shifted in the chair.

Admin Brown: "Our regional security officer runs unscheduled lockdown drills. If you were in the lobby with members of a visiting congressional delegation and a real lockdown were announced, how would you handle it?"
Finally, an easy question. "At my hotel, we had more than one fire drill while I was with some celebrity or notable leader." My shoulders relaxed. "At the embassy, if a lockdown occurred, I would calmly escort our congressional guests to a safe area and stay with them for the duration, explaining the efficacy of embassy protocol in dealing with emergency situations."

Silence. Scribbles.

The questions continued, easier ones. Describe my knowledge of the Cape Area. (My husband had been here before and was showing me around the city, the wine country, the peninsula). Finally they put down their pens. Admin Brown thanked me for my candor, then escorted me out of the conference room to a bench where I was instructed to wait.

Eyes closed, I leaned my head back. Hiking the Blue Ridge Mountains had been less exhausting than that grill. And this was a spouse interview. I had totally blown it—no knowledge of international affairs, no Xhosa or Afrikaans, total disaster naming high-level dignitaries as my exposure to other cultures. What seemed like fifteen minutes was less than five. Admin Brown motioned me back to the room.

Blank looks on the interviewer's faces said it all. I sat on the edge of the chair.

Admin Brown took her place at the table, then reached across it to shake my hand. "Congratulations, Mrs. McGhee. Welcome aboard. You start tomorrow."

Hello, Cloud Nine. An hour after walking through the door I was an employee of the United States Embassy, a turn of events beyond my wildest dreams. To think I would have been happy with a job in PR. I was part of the mission, maybe just a cog in the wheel, but that wheel was about to roll into history.

Later that evening on the deck, I told Patrick all about the interview while we celebrated with a bottle of Reserve Cabernet. The moon hung low, luminous to match my mood. Patrick joked that I had been relieved of my tennis-playing days in the nick of time, his tone free of sarcasm, light with relief that at long last it had all worked out with a job.

The next morning I sprang out of bed. My outfit lay over the chair—a dark blue suit with white silk blouse for my first official day at the embassy. The look was conservative, the dark blue a good contrast for my hair, the white silk the best complement for it. Dark blue pumps and small gold earrings finished it off.

Instead of kissing Patrick goodbye, we left together. At a stoplight a swarm of kids surrounded the car. I tensed. One of the little boys approached Patrick—why is your wheel on that side? Rather than brushing him off Patrick reached behind the passenger seat and pulled out a canvas bag filled with candy, granola bars. One at a time he handed them out. Mothers watched from the shade of a tree across the street. Had this been his routine every morning?

My shoulders relaxed when the light turned green. I hadn't been aware of my nerves. News on TV had no shortage of images—burning barricades, black youths throwing stones, overturning cars. It hadn't escaped my notice that I had reacted like the white minority I had come here to oust. Guilt. Shame.

At the heart of the city center, Patrick pulled into his parking spot at the embassy. Puffed with pride, I followed him through the same process as the previous day, this time without the pre-interview nerves—first the metal detector, then Marine Post One, who nodded as Patrick flashed his badge with a quick look at my diplomatic passport in lieu of the I.D. badge that would come later as my embassy credential.

Inside the building we walked down the main hallway past huge framed portraits of President George H.W. Bush and Secretary of State James Baker. These official photos hung in every embassy around the world. Chills went down my spine. It was all so grand, so historic. Our first stop was the RSO office, Patrick's office. I was his first appointment of the day. Fingerprints came first, followed by a photo I.D. Next was the paperwork, the official application with questions for the background check, three references to vouch for my character.

Three levels of security clearance—Top Secret, Secret, and Confidential—dictated the limits of one's access to classified national security information. Form questions included my allegiance to the United States; foreign influence; sexual behavior; personal conduct; financial considerations; alcohol consumption; drug involvement; emotional, mental, and personality disorders; criminal conduct; security violations; outside activities; and misuse of information technology systems. The State Department would know more about me than my own mother.

The clearance process is a long one, three to six months. Certain areas of the embassy would be off limits until I got my Secret clearance. Paperwork took up most of the morning. Next, Patrick introduced me to the staff and officers. Some of the faces were familiar from the ambassador's dinner. Most were a blur by the time I met the next person. One stood out—the consul general's administrative assistant, Beverly, who took my hand in both of hers. She radiated assurance, warmth. My affinity was immediate. Beverly hadn't been at the ambassador's dinner but she looked familiar. I was sure we had met.

Patrick kept us moving until we stopped at the office of my interviewer extraordinaire, Admin Officer Brown, to whom I would report. The woman smiled, knocking ten years from her face. Patrick squeezed my hand and left.

My new boss showed me to my office across the hall from hers. In addition to my role as community liaison officer, I would also work on the USAID Self-Help programs. My first task was to review and evaluate applications from locals for start-up projects in the townships and green light—in movie-speak—those that looked promising for funding from USAID. After the election there would be business opportunities for blacks in their own neighborhoods, a much-needed boost for the ninety percent unemployment rate in the townships.

My first task was to order the pile of submissions by date, some months old. I scrutinized those that had been accepted and noted the criteria, then turned to those projects that had been turned away to find out why. The list of reasons was heartbreaking, many having to do with basic logistics. Transportation into the embassy to fill out an application proved difficult for most from the townships. Kombis—the informal transportation used by blacks to get into the city—were inconsistent, unreliable. People had few cars. Petrol was expensive for those who did. My mind flashed to my own ride in a kombi.

During our early days I had had the urge to explore beyond Sea Point, go into town without a driver. Kombi vans were a common sight in our neighborhood as they dropped domestic workers off in Sea Point. One day I waved one down to take me into the city. The van was packed. I paid my rand and took a seat next to a black woman who turned her face to the window as I approached. Every eye was on me, the single white person. Oh, no! Did they assume I was an Afrikaner? *No, No, I'm not*, I wanted to yell. *I'm American, here to oust your oppressors.* Yet I sensed fear. I was in their space. And they had no idea who I was.

In his capacity as regional security officer, my husband rebuked me for my spontaneous adventure. "The kombi is dangerous. It's no place for a white woman." Defensive, I started to respond, but stopped. Patrick was simply doing his job as protector-in chief, paternalistic by definition. Rather than fall into my scripted role of rebellion against authority, I remembered that it was up to me to keep the piece, remind him we were lovers. And I did.

Other than the unpleasantness of Patrick's admonition, my ride in the kombi gave me insight into the first barrier faced by those who had to come to the embassy to complete the application. No faxing. Even if the technology existed, the poor townships would hardly have access. Mail by post presented another hurdle—getting to a post office to buy a stamp. The most determined applicants made it happen.

My priority became expediting those applications waiting for approval. Then I would tackle the "cold file." Once completed, my job was to submit applications that proved viable to a review board for approval. The last step of the process involved my going into the township to visit the site—in an embassy car accompanied by a driver familiar with the slums.

At the embassy it was clear everyone had very high regard for Ambassador Lyman, especially the way he was handling the prickly business of diplomacy with the three major players—Mandela, de Klerk, and Buthelezi. It turns out Princeton Lyman was no stranger to political turmoil. In the early 1960s, armed with a Ph.D. in political science, he headed to Washington to pursue a career in Foreign Service. President Kennedy had just been elected. In 1961 he created the USAID program in response to the growth of independence in Africa— nations who had fought for decolonization by European powers. By the 1980s Princeton Lyman was Deputy Assistant Secretary of State for African Affairs and had created development programs all over the continent. In 1992 President George Herbert Walker Bush made him ambassador to South Africa. The Cold War was over. Conservatives in Congress no longer considered Mandela's ANC a communist front, or his rival, Chief Buthelezi, a champion of capitalism. Mandela had been released from prison by then, negotiations with de Klerk begun. It looked like clear sailing for Ambassador Lyman.

By the time he arrived in the summer of 1992, the same time as Patrick and I, negotiations had collapsed and the country was in complete turmoil following the massacre at Boipatong. The ambassador was not in an easy position to offer help. South Africa still had a grudge about how slow the U.S. had been to support Mandela, and de Klerk still resented the Reagan-era sanctions that continued to grip the economy.

The USAID program was part of the ambassador's effort to bring the parties together, work with leaders in black organizations. These were the people who would have key roles in the government after the 1994 election. If we could get to the election. His first hurdle was to gain the trust of President de Klerk, Nelson Mandela, and Chief Buthelezi. It had not been easy for him and his staff to earn credibility with Zulus. But they had done just that in clandestine nighttime meetings with political contacts afraid for their lives. Patrick was involved on those occasions when the ambassador met with leaders of opposing groups, though he never gave me any details.

I didn't know all this background about the ambassador when I worked at the embassy. What I saw was a nice man with a nice wife who lived in a nice home and gave nice parties for political dignitaries. It would be years before I understood the immense talent and experience Ambassador Lyman brought to the table. His efforts were key in averting Buthelezi from going off the deep end and taking the country into civil war.

Dear Marcy,

I miss you! By the time you get this letter I will be going into my fourth week at the U.S. Embassy! Yes! The embassy! It turns out I couldn't work in PR (long story) and just when I felt like taking the next plane home, this job popped up. I went through the toughest interview ever, so I truly got it on my own, not because of Patrick. You have no idea how thrilled I am to be using my brain again. I have been freed from the Good Housekeeping life.

And that's not even the best thing about it—I am now part of the mission, the diplomatic effort to make sure this election happens. There's so much violence (please don't tell Mom and Dad. The news is bad enough). This job is without a doubt the most exciting thing I've ever done. Someday maybe I'll write a book...ha ha!

How is your new job? How is juggling the mom-work thing? If anyone can, my money's on you. How is little Gina? I am sure she is a brilliant first-grader and the cutest bug ever. One of these days I hope to give her a little cousin to play with. Patrick and I are talking about getting pregnant. Right now it's hard with his crazy busy job and everything that's going on here.

There isn't enough room on this Air Mail stationery to tell you how gorgeous this country is, and the beach is right outside our door. Sometimes it feels like a dream.

There is an embassy ball in a few weeks and I have to shop for a gown. You would love that, too… I know you love a good party. This is more like a fairytale ball. I'll send pics. And you be sure to send some of Gina. She'll be big by the time I see her.

Stay out of trouble and toast us next time you pop a cork.

All my love,

Mary

My stomach growled. It was barely noon. Still too excited to eat breakfast and wanting to make a good impression, I drove to the embassy early again with Patrick. All morning I had been immersed in reviewing projects for approval.

Beverly popped her head in the door. How did I feel about Cape Malay curry? She had a favorite lunchtime restaurant around the corner. It wasn't until we sat across the table that it hit me. No wonder she looked familiar. I had seen Beverly every morning on my run. She lived next door!

A diplomat in her third year at the Cape Town post, Beverly spoke about the country with the same love Patrick had back in D.C. Her description of the increasing unrest in town, in the country, reiterated Patrick's recaps during our secret walks since the break-in. Beverly's demeanor changed from gregarious to troubled, her melodic voice tightening as she explained that Americans had become personas non grata as the situation ramped up in the townships, black-on-black violence between competing factions at war over what spoils might be had under a new regime. Bev caught the look on my face. She changed her tone and made light of the situation, which only underscored the weight of her concern.

Like Patrick, Bev had a protective nature. Whether that was aimed at me specifically or was part of the job wasn't clear. What was clear was that the girlfriend I had yearned for sat across the table.

By the end of the first week I had settled in at the embassy. At home, Patrick listened as I recounted every detail of my day. We were a team again, Byron and McGhee, even if he couldn't talk about anything of substance. At least we talked. That's all I wanted.

The fall season brought one diplomatic event after another. As a community liaison officer, I managed to use my public relations background organizing community events for American families, most of which were held in the ambassador's or consul general's home. I was finally in my element. Protocol became my new best friend, one I would turn to often in the future.

Some of these diplomatic events were sophisticated affairs. Invitees included peace leaders, strategists, high-ranking diplomats like the Deputy Chief of Mission, the consul general and Foreign Service officers involved in building morale and goodwill among all during these touchy times.

For a typical event in which the embassy represented the U.S., dress was usually "business smart"—suits and ties for men, suit skirts or knee length cocktail dresses for women. Guests would arrive at the ambassador's home in chauffeur-driven vehicles. Depending on the event, press would attend along with a photographer or two.

The Annual Marine Birthday Ball at the Alphen Hotel was a different matter altogether. Formal wear was in order, men in tuxedos, women in floor-length gowns and up-dos. I had a few dresses to choose from, tags still on. One thing spouses understood about life with a diplomat—there would be plenty of opportunity for formal wear. Those who didn't ship dresses from home ordered them later from the States. We may have been living in the midst of political mayhem, but the latest fashions would still be very much on display at the Marine's Annual Birthday Ball.

The officer in charge asked me to help him, starting with choice of venue. We checked out hotel ballrooms across the city. From invitation lists to flag placement in the room, to arranging formal introductions, to table assignments—event planning was a detailed process. Custom dictated protocol for American diplomats, local officials, dignitaries, the occasional American actors filming in town. I so loved being involved, coordinating the plans, orchestrating the night, participating in such a venerable event.

Arrival of guests set the tone for the evening. It was magnificent. Marines in full dress blues made a tunnel with their ceremonial swords as we entered, Ambassador and Mrs. Lyman first, followed by other dignitaries, guests and staff. Cocktails preceded a five-course meal paired with lovely Cape wines. Formal speeches and dancing followed.

That was the highlight for me. I loved to dance, everything from 80's disco to country swing. An accomplished dancer, Patrick was quite patient with my fumbling at his fast swing moves. All eyes were on us when we took to the dance floor. That evening we didn't sit out one single number. Our last dance a slow one, Patrick held me close as we whispered to each other. When the song ended, we kissed. It was a perfect moment, a perfect evening.

The Marine Gunny Sergeant drew his ceremonial sword. It was time to cut the cake. In high pageantry he did the deed, steel blade slicing through alternating layers of chocolate cake, raspberry filling, cream cheese, peaked frosting. Steeped in tradition, the ceremony was so elegant. Wincing at the memory of how I mocked protocol in the beginning, I mentally dared anyone to not feel a surge of emotion, some sense of history if not pride at such a moment.

For all the hard parts of diplomatic life, this was the payoff.

Nine
Relief and Warlords

December 1992

Dumbstruck, I stared at Patrick. A stack of shirts lay on the bed. He packed the way he lived. Disciplined. Everything neat—ironed, starched, folded. He took his valise from the closet. His shaving kit went in first. As he avoided eye contact, his jaw was set in that way it got when he was stressed and tried not to let it slow him down.

Choosing my words carefully, I leaned in the doorjamb, struggling to keep my tone of anger and disbelief to a minimum. *I never told you because I knew you'd freak out.* "Hon, I don't understand how you can be going on a mission. You're already on a mission, a dangerous one. Why would they put you somewhere else?"

"It's sensitive. That's all I can tell you. It'll just be a couple of days." He opened a locked drawer and took out his weapon along with a few of the documents he kept secure. Things between us had been so much better with me working at the embassy. I wanted to support him, but this news had come out of nowhere.

I sat on the edge of the bed. "Patrick, we've been here three months, three months of political unrest. And now you're going somewhere even more volatile? What I am supposed to think?"

"Silence.

Silence was my husband's usual response when pushed. The non-answer irritated me, as if I were some outsider who couldn't be trusted. He kept packing.

"This is the hard part, Mar, when I can't tell you what you want to know."

"Don't be condescending." I grabbed a pillow and tugged at the manufacturer's tag.

He stopped fussing with the valise. "Hon, I can't tell you. And you know that, so I'm not sure why you're choosing this moment to nag me."

"Nag you? You walk in the door and tell me you're leaving for a few days and can't tell me where or why or how long. And I'm supposed to say, 'Okay, bye.'?"

"Yes."

I gritted my teeth, mouth closed. "Will you be able to call?"

"No."

Anger turned to frustration as I fought tears. Patrick could see I was distressed but made no effort to comfort me. Distress was really protest packaged better. I had no control. No say in the matter. The State Department could just whisk my husband away. It may not have been his choice but at least he had information.

Life in the dark was the part of diplomatic service I hated, would never get used to. Like everyone else who was not at the top, I was on the outside. Most of the time I lived with it—understood that Patrick couldn't tell me what went on at work. That seeped into our private life. No wonder emotional intimacy was difficult. Decisions came from on high, not from within or between. His going on a mission-within-a-mission had never occurred to me. He was needed here, at the embassy.

At home in the States it would have been no big deal for him to leave without notice. As the one person in this hemisphere I could trust, it was major. Cape Town had become increasingly dangerous, angry demonstrations reported in the paper every day, violence in the townships erupting like some horrific whack-a-mole game—fighting suppressed in one place only to pop up in another. Anything could happen. Sending the head of diplomatic security on assignment somewhere else must mean one thing—it would be more dangerous there than it was right here.

The first day we walked into our flat I decided to ignore the safe room. Sea Point was safe. If anything did happen, Patrick would be home from the embassy in a flash, like he had when I mistook government goons for an intruder breaking in. The safe room seemed like wasted space. Until now. With Patrick gone, that room would be my protection.

I studied my husband as he packed, willing him to wrap me in his arms and tell me he would return in two days. Instead, brow furrowed in concentration, he stayed focused on the task at hand as if I weren't in the room.

The man packing was no longer my beloved Patrick, but Diplomatic Security Special Agent in all his armor, internal fortitude in place of a flak jacket. It was the same look he had when I first laid eyes on him outside the hotel in Minneapolis. My breath caught watching him step out of the limo in those mirrored sunglasses, ready to do whatever he had to should a threat arise—cold, distant, in control. Gorgeous. Mysterious. A chill had gone down my spine, a tingle of magnetic attraction.

Now impenetrable wasn't so sexy. Arm's length was too much space between us when he was about to disappear to an unknown destination. But the space could not be breached. Patrick had been trained to suppress everything in him— especially emotions—to mobilize his senses into high gear. Survival mode.

A perfunctory kiss and he was gone. I leaned back on the bed, trying to grasp it. His leaving was a test, as if assignments back in the States had been dry runs for the real thing, now sprung on me without warning. The possibility that I might not be able to cope had never occurred to him. Strong independent Mary, Big City woman, the Mary Richards "me" back home. My husband would do what he needed to do on the job. He expected the same of me.

In the three months since our arrival we had trusted no one. Our reliance on one another as confidant had been a bond of sorts. *You have me, Mary, that'll have to do.* And now he was gone. And I was left on my own with the dreaded uncertainty of it all. Ordinary couples at least had the luxury of phone calls during a business trip. Mystery Mission would be my first without the support of friends, work, without communication of any kind.

Two weeks earlier I had accused Patrick of being a workaholic. The tape replayed in my head. "I feel like work is the most important thing in your life, like your need to climb the career ladder takes priority over everything."

The look on his face made me shudder.

"You think this is about my career? Mary, things are very touch-and-go here. If I screw up, someone—many someone's—could die. Yes, right now, my job is the most important thing in my life."

"More important than our marriage?" Immediately I regretted the question.

"If you want to make me choose between our marriage—which I take as stable, and the political mess out there, which could erupt into civil war with countless deaths—then yes."

How stupid of me, forcing him to say it out loud. But it wasn't just the job. Early on I accepted that there would always be a part of Patrick I didn't know, couldn't know. He would never let me all the way in, not really. But it was his ability to shut down feelings, function at survival level that frightened me.

Of course, the loneliness of one person didn't count for a hill of beans compared with the well-being of a whole country. Confrontation was just my awkward way of telling him how desperate I was that he see me, hear me, reassure me with affection. Confrontation always backfired.

I still hadn't learned to support Patrick the way he needed to be supported. And he still hadn't learned to recognize my needs. Unlike him, I wasn't a lone wolf. Take away my siblings, my girlfriends, coworkers, and I was lost, my innate strength honed by those around me. Maybe he saw that as weakness, needing other people. But that's who I was. Growing up in my world, when someone needed comfort, it was a hug or phone call away. Patrick needed only himself.

As happens in every marriage, the little hurts accumulate until you start shutting off part of your heart. Not locking it exactly, but waiting for that day somewhere down the road when something will happen to open it again. Hoping it *would* open again. I had been naive to think that mastering protocol would be the big challenge here. Emotionally I was on my own
On my own to copy, knowing Patrick was in some undisclosed dangerous place more dangerous than here, to cope with the reality that I could lose him.

A sickening twinge gripped my stomach. All I could do was wait. How I hated that word, its inherent passivity. But I would have to be strong—or fake being strong—be the wife Patrick believed me to be. The next few days would tell me whether or not I was that person.

A glass of Chardonnay would go nicely with my dinner salad. The living room TV was tuned to the evening news as usual, tonight welcome background noise. I half listened.

"...*U.N. efforts to provide humanitarian relief in Mogadishu continue to prove difficult with rebel factions controlling the airstrip...*"

On my way to the deck with dinner in hand, I turned it off. As if I didn't have enough to worry about in South Africa without adding Somalia's problems. Patrick could've gone to any number of unstable countries, but my guess was he was closer to home, maybe headed for Joburg where violence had erupted with increasing regularity the last few weeks. Images of bloodshed flickered in the breeze on the front page of the *Argus* sprawled across the lounge. I folded the paper and stuck it under a table leg, face down.

That night the bed was a sea of empty space. The wind howled, as it did most nights with storms off the Atlantic slamming into Cape Town. This wind was like no other. Handrails lined city sidewalks to keep Capetonians from flying into the air like Mary Poppins. Such a funny image. But the wind was no laughing matter. Tonight it sounded ominous. Branches from our potted trees scraped the glass like some creature clawing to get inside. A patio umbrella crashed against the deck rail. Sleep was impossible.

The clock said eleven-fifteen. A night owl, Bev would be up. I had come to appreciate her nurturing manner, taking me under her wing this past month. She clearly understood what it meant to be a newcomer, not only to South Africa but to the embassy. A phone call and five-minute walk later I was at her door for a glass of wine and the comfort of conversation.

The next morning I woke exhausted in my empty bed. Whatever coping I had would be shot if this was any measure of my quality of sleep the next few days. Half listening for the phone, I showered and dressed, then drove to the embassy with hopes of catching some hint of what was going on. That was unlikely, but work would be a diversion.

The pile of USAID applications stared at me. I stared back. Forcing myself to focus, I did manage to review a few, even make notes on those that looked promising. Two hours later, whatever concentration I had mustered left me. It was Friday, Girl's Night Out. Beverly had introduced me to a couple of other wives who missed their girlfriends back home. It was always a fun evening, the social highlight of my week. Bev checked in with me before leaving for the night. I begged off. Patrick might come home, or at least call. She gave me the name of the restaurant, just in case. A warm hug and she was gone.

Friday night was particularly lonely with my imagination conjuring all kinds of scary scenarios Patrick might be in. Saturday I woke exhausted. My whole body was on edge, spring loaded to answer the phone that refused to ring. He couldn't call, I knew that. It didn't matter. The phone was our single link. He could return to the embassy any moment.

The weekend dragged. I answered Mom's letter. The Mall of America had opened in Bloomington, Minnesota, with five hundred stores and an amusement park in the center. Another clipping had a photo of Bill and Hillary Clinton with the Gores after winning the election. Abbey Christiansen down the street had given birth to triplets. Our old milkman retired, but Mom didn't mind the new young one who liked to chat.

What an orderly world. I kept the clippings out to show Azisa, my one reliable daily contact. How I valued our talks. She was so curious about the U.S., a perceived fantasyland where everyone was rich and beautiful.

Of course the phone did not ring once all weekend. Monday, I made it through the day, then Tuesday, Wednesday.

No word. The days rolled by, one hardly different from the next. My concentration was shot. I moved through the day as if my ears were clogged with water, half hearing at warp speed the world around me. My appetite disappeared. Protein shakes became a mainstay.

At night I lay awake in the dark, listening to the wind, wondering where Patrick was, what kind of danger he was in. No news was good news, as if that were any comfort. Had he been hurt, I wouldn't know. Anything worse I would. That was my level of worry. At least he was alive—today.

A string of lousy nights undermined whatever coping I did have. Once home from the embassy, I would often break into tears out of sheer frustration coupled with my imagination working overtime from lack of sleep. The one thing I needed was the one thing I couldn't have—news that Patrick was safe. Knowledge is power—that was his mantra, my mantra. That meant I was the most powerless creature on the planet. Never in my life was I as un-tethered as in those awful days in December of 1992.

Christmas, my favorite holiday, was two weeks away. It barely registered. I felt no joy. The celebration of Christ's birth was not the date I awaited with the rest of the Christian world. Mine was the unknown date that Patrick would walk through the door. As Christmas Day drew closer, joy or no joy, I stuck to my usual traditions as a way to cope.

Warm weather didn't help the holiday mood. For the first time since leaving Minnesota, I yearned for the cold. There were no Christmas trees to buy. Dutch Calvinist Afrikaners didn't celebrate much of anything, much less Christmas. I dragged the sorry potted palm that sat in front of the safe room into the living room. That would have to do. Holiday CDs played in the background as I carefully placed ornaments on the delicate palm leaves.

Instead of evergreen, the aroma of Christmas cookies filled the air, Patrick's favorites—double chocolate chip, gingerbread men, wreath sugar cookies and coconut macaroons. Freezing might save them but it would also wreck them, so I left them out. The real reason was my Hallmark fantasy—I half-convinced myself Patrick would be home just because it was Christmas, just about as likely as snow falling on the deck. By now it was clear his mission was no minor detail. Whatever it was, wherever he was, it was best to brace myself for the long haul.

Friends invited me to Christmas lunch. I accepted. Wine flowed freely in holiday cheer, food and conversation bringing a welcome boost. That evening I called my parents. That was the best gift anyone could have given me, short of Patrick walking through the door. It was so good to hear their voices. I fought tears, my heart aching to tell them what was going on.

How had I ever taken my family, my parents for granted—Christmas with a real tree; Mom busy baking for the neighbors—our traditional gift—the kitchen sink lined with fruit cakes waiting to be wrapped and delivered. I could almost see her in there, radio on, singing to holiday music. The image brought memories of every Christmas of my childhood.

Another Friday brought another Girl's Night Out. Again I bowed out.

On the floor, sitting Indian-style, I wrapped a last minute gift. My mind was blank, save for an occasional wrong turn into my dark imagination. The holiday CD had ended. In the quiet I hadn't even noticed. A clicking sound at the door made me look up. I didn't move a muscle.

The door opened. Patrick.

I exhaled in a loud gasp. Thin, drawn, his complexion pale, he dropped his bag by the door, stumbling to the wing chair where he collapsed, head rolling to one side for support.

"Hon, my gosh! What's happened? You look awful." I crouched in front of him.

Grabbing me by the shoulders, he moved me out of the way. By the time I got to him in the bathroom, the poor guy had already unleashed the contents of his stomach. Leaning over the bowl for a good two minutes, he was unable to talk between throwing up and sputtering. I soaked a washcloth in cold water and ran it across his forehead. He was burning with fever.

It was all he could do to stay upright long enough for me to get his clothes off. In the shower he leaned against the fiberglass. Quickly I got the bed ready. Together we managed to get him close enough that he fell into it, arms akimbo, feet dangling to one side. I dragged his legs around to align him, then shimmied his shoulders onto the pillow. It was hard to keep the panic from my voice.

"Oh my God, hon, how long have you been like this?"

He opened his eyes—opaque, dull—then closed them without answering. He was fast asleep. I sat in the bedside chair. For the next forty-eight hours he woke to vomit, then would fall back to sleep. In fragmented patches between wake, sleep and vomiting, he told me where he'd been.

"Somalia? But why? I don't understand." The news I had turned off ten days earlier flashed to mind. Why hadn't I paid attention then to what Patrick told me now—the country had been in chaos for a year after rebels drove dictator Barre from Mogadishu with no central government to replace him. Warlords had been fighting for control. It was a complete breakdown of civil order.

"But why now if this has been going on for a year? And what did it have to do with the State Department in Cape Town?"

Patrick sipped water through a straw, hydrating one ounce at a time. Any more than that and his stomach would revolt.

"It's a mess." He dropped back on the pillow. "Nothing but fighting among warring factions—warlords and their minions. They blocked the U.N. choppers from delivering food. People were starving, Mary, hundreds of thousands of people. These gangs made off with everything—food and supplies—the minute a chopper landed. It was finally impossible for U.N. peacekeepers to stay. Americans and foreign diplomats were airlifted to Guam and Trenton."

"But…if they had to leave for their own safety, how could you be there?"

"We weren't at the embassy in Mogadishu. Gangs trashed it….armed looters stripped the place bare, taking everything—equipment, supplies, furniture." He closed his eyes, exhausted. I waited, trying to process what he had said. He opened his eyes again.

"But…how did we get involved in all this if there was no embassy, no diplomats to work with?"

"President Bush had to step in."

The maneuver was dubbed Operation Restore Hope. Patrick had accompanied Ambassador Robert Oakley from the U.N./U.S. mission as they met with rival warlords near Mogadishu. Ambassador Oakley had been trying to negotiate with warring factions, broker a ceasefire in some attempt to get peacekeepers back in the country. Without a U.N. presence to protect the people from rebels and the waters from pirates, it would be impossible for humanitarian relief efforts to get in there with food.

"Marines had been authorized to use all means necessary. By the time I got there, they had secured the beach and airfield so helicopters could land. They repaired the embassy enough to serve as a makeshift headquarters. President Bush is coming in a few weeks.

"My God, Patrick…you met with warlords? I mean…you were armed, right?"

He managed a wry grin before bolting to the bathroom. Along with the ambassador to Somalia, they traveled in a heavily armored jeep mounted with high-caliber machine guns. Patrick had both his pistol and an Uzi. *An Uzi!* A well-armed military escort plus two other diplomatic security agents accompanied him and the ambassador as they spoke with one warlord after another. When one meeting ended, they would slip away by helicopter to another camp outside Mogadishu for the next.

"The hard part about fending off attacks was trying to figure out who was who. I'm telling you, hon, it was almost impossible. They all wore civilian clothes, rebels and warlords —football jerseys, Nike tee shirts. The militia was all around but there was no way to know if they would be attacked, or who would attack them." His voice trailed off.

And that's how the story unfolded, in patches. Between wake and sleep I slipped out of bedroom to call the embassy doctor. An hour later he stopped by. Patrick woke long enough to answer a few questions. Possible diagnoses included some obscure African virus. Symptoms were hard to ferret out with dehydration and exhaustion complicating a diagnosis.

Grateful for a moment to myself during the exam, I went out on the deck for fresh air, nauseated after hearing about the mission, the danger he had been in. Yet I wanted to know. More important, Patrick wanted to tell me. He had been scared, waking up every morning not knowing if he would make it through another day. Every night he had written me a letter, in his head.

I recalled our first date, the look on Patrick's face when he told me he was committed to a life in Foreign Service. What such a life might entail, he never specified—things like swooping into a war-torn country to secure a landing strip for humanitarian aid to a starving population. I was so proud of him.

Bravery hadn't meant he was fearless, far from it. Fear opened his heart—let him face death with everything inside—no armor, the real Patrick. What I would have given to have those letters in writing. But I kept his words in my head, the truth he found beneath the terror—that in his darkest moment, it was me he wanted to talk to, me he needed.

What he hadn't said in the days that followed, what he hadn't needed to say, was what we both surmised about the mission—Somalia was a preview of South Africa's fate if President de Klerk and Nelson Mandela failed to negotiate a new constitution. Soon. Political turmoil could explode into full-blown war, resistance fighters and anti-apartheid holdouts doing the killing rather than famine.

It would be another decade before the release of *Black Hawk Down*, the true story of another ill-fated humanitarian effort in

Somalia. It was in October of 1993 when the infamous warlord Muhammed Farah Aideed's forces shot down two Black Hawk helicopters in a battle that resulted in the death of eighteen U.S. soldiers and hundreds of Somalis. In the movie, jersey-wearing warlords looked just like the ones Patrick had described.

Weakened from days of vomiting, Patrick slowly recovered from his illness. It hadn't been an African virus. The culprit turned out to be far more insidious. Based at the Exxon Corp compound, coming and going with two other diplomatic security special agents, he ate the same food as everyone else. The guy who cooked for the envoy also had lav duty.

I had never seen Patrick as sick as he was then, and never have since. His homecoming turned the tables on our roles, confirming what Patrick had seen in me all along—my own strength. He knew nothing of my sleepless nights, sudden bursts of tears, extra wine to calm my nerves. It was a charade, my imitation of strength a mask for desperation.

Yet I *had* coped, maybe not like a pro, but I had gotten through the ordeal, nursed Patrick back to health, kept everything together. For the first time, I understood protocol not as code for an elite group, but as a set of rules to guide behavior when order breaks down. I had stuck with my holiday traditions, showed up for work, met with Bev. That's what was expected. Somehow, just by following that path, I had indeed found some semblance of control.

It was short lived. Our Ethan Allen cocoon was about to suffer another blow.

By New Year's Eve, Patrick was still deathly ill. We had made a date to go out with the Donovans. That date had been one bright spot that kept me going while Patrick was gone. Patrick would most likely sleep all evening, Michele said, so why didn't I meet them at the Greek restaurant anyway. You couldn't pry me away from Patrick's side.

The bedroom was more comfortable but while he was sick, Patrick insisted we sleep in the safe room, door locked, alarm on. Weakened, dehydrated, he was vulnerable. That opened my eyes to his deep need to protect me, to feel safe himself. The term "post-traumatic stress" wasn't part of the popular lingo yet. I have no doubt that was part of his insistence about sleeping in the safe room, though, a measure of the impact fear for his life in Somalia had had.

New Year's Eve I was particularly glad to be holed up in the safe room. Fireworks were already exploding below us on the promenade by evening, a repeat of the previous month's Guy Fawkes Day celebrating King James's survival of a failed attack on his life orchestrated by the hapless Fawkes. Capetonians liked their fireworks displays, Guy Fawkes or New Year's Eve.

We slid *Father of the Bride* into the DVD player, the Steve Martin version, to drown out the noise. Two movies later, in spite of the racket outside, I had finally fallen asleep. It was just after midnight.

WOOOONKKK. WOOOONKKK.

The alarm! Both of us sat bolt upright, dazed. Patrick jumped out of bed and got to the alarm on the wall. "Get down!" He fumbled with the cover.

WOOOONKKK. WOOOONKKK.

The blasting noise overpowered the fireworks. My heart pounded so hard it was difficult to breathe. I did as Patrick said and crawled under the bed. The alarm cover was off. Blinking lights would indicate where the perpetrator was, who had broken into our flat. The alarm stopped. In spite of the fireworks and revelers outside, the room was calm again.

"Stay down, Mary."

I watched from beneath the bed as he opened the safe room door, baseball bat in hand, so weak he wobbled. Steadying himself against the wall, he gripped the bat over his shoulder, ready to swing. I waited. Nothing. A moment later he returned.

"It's okay. You'd better come see this."

Thinking Patrick wanted to show me damage to the front door lock, I trailed behind him into the living room. We stared at the lock, perfectly intact. No forced entry. That meant one thing—whoever had come in had used his key, clearly caught by surprise to find us home. I was horrified. Feeling violated sent a chill through me. Then my knees went weak.

Neither of us would get any sleep that night. We would stand guard. In the living room I propped pillows on the couch so Patrick could lie down. In our mutually buzzed state of hyper-alertness, our emotions flip-flopped between ventilating anger and expressing raw fear. Whoever had broken in was aware we had plans for the night and would be out celebrating past midnight. Had the government goons listened in on our call to the Donovans when we made plans for that evening? But what were they looking for? Our personal documents were locked in the usual drawer along with the gun now under his blanket on the couch.

Sometime after four in the morning the street noise died down. Jumping awake wide-eyed at the slightest sound, Patrick and I dozed on and off. The sun finally put an end to our efforts. Still rattled, now depleted, we wandered zombie-like through the flat. Picking over a light breakfast, we searched for something good to look forward to in 1993. I finally found something. Going home.

Ten

The Other Side of the Mountain

January 1993

The clock made a low hum seconds before the alarm went off. I caught it in time. Patrick didn't stir, his breathing slow, even. In the predawn light, his face was serene, free of furrows that crept in during the day as tension took hold. I hadn't slept well, in part from nerves, in part excitement that this day had finally come.

Slipping out of bed, I tiptoed into the dressing room. Everything in the closet looked wrong: too formal, too much color. Neutrals, that's what I needed, pulling out a pair of dark wash jeans and a navy V-neck sweater. No, jeans didn't seem right, not for this special day.

Mrs. Tambala had been waiting three weeks for my visit. So had I. Her project proposal and the difficulty we had had meeting at her home gave my visit urgency. This site evaluation had to be completed before we could move forward. As a manager in the USAID program creating projects for economic growth in poverty-ridden townships, this was a crucial part of the process, the final step before funds could be released. The jeans went back in the closet. A pair of charcoal slacks with a white silk blouse and the navy sweater would be more respectful.

The grass roots aspect of my job was one of the things that drew me, the chance to be with the very people we had come to help. Three weeks earlier Mrs. Tambala made the day-long journey to bring her application to the embassy. Transportation from the township of Khayelitsha was a kombi. Their stops were infrequent and unscheduled, which made it difficult to keep an appointment. Mrs. Tambala had walked at least a kilometer just to catch the ride. At the embassy she had gone through security, taken a seat, waited to plead her case.

As I approached her, she looked to be in her mid-thirties, not much older than me. She stood with a timid but warm smile that said I held her future in my hands. Her batik sari crossed one shoulder and draped to her calf. On her head was a tartan of alternating bands of bright cloth. She looked dignified in her ethnic garb.

Like most in her township, Mrs. Tambala spoke Xhosa. As I told the interview panel at the embassy, Patrick and I had studied Xhosa and Afrikaans using Berlitz tapes, with little success. Between my limited Xhosa and Mrs. Tambala's broken English, we made our way through the forms. Her sewing project was well developed, had the potential to create jobs for women in the township. It wasn't up to me to approve the project. What I could do was nominate it for consideration by a review committee of Foreign Service officials who administered the USAID program. I had no doubt that with a little financial support, Mrs. Tambala would make her project happen.

She could hardly control her enthusiasm, her spirit of positive energy. And I would be there to guide her through the process were it approved. I told her to check back in two weeks by phone. The excitement faded from her face. The township had no phone. Then she lit up again. A coin-operated public phone was two kilometers from her home. She would walk the distance, just as she had today to catch a ride on the kombi to Cape Town for this appointment. She promised to call in two weeks.

Two weeks came and went. No call from Mrs. Tambala. I fretted. Perhaps she had phoned when the line at work was busy, or I wasn't in the office. The public phone needed rand to make the call. She had saved coins to pay for the kombi ride to the embassy. Maybe the call and kombi fare combined were too much. I would have to adjust my thinking in this new environment, know that things we take for granted can be stumbling blocks here. All I could do was to wait for her call.

Two days later the phone rang. I was giddy at the sound of her voice. "Mrs. Tambala, are you safe?"

She spoke softly in broken English. Yes, she was fine. The public phone had been out of order. I strained to understand her mix of English and Xhosa. The language was hard to translate in my head, it's nuanced intonation and clicks difficult to interpret. In English, I spoke slowly and clearly, careful not to use contractions or slang. The committee had accepted her project. Now we needed to make a date for me to visit her home, evaluate her plan for how the project would work on site.

The phone beeped, hungry for more coins. Mrs. Tambala had none. We talked as fast as we could, given the language barrier, but managed to set an appointment before the line went dead.

When the rescheduled day came I missed our meeting. The night before my visit, violence erupted in Khayelitsha. The Regional Security Officer had restricted official U.S. travel to the township. My husband would make no exceptions, even for me. There was no way to reach Mrs. Tambala. Again, I waited for her to call me.

Two days later she phoned. We scheduled a new appointment. As the new date drew near torrential rains caused mass flooding in the township. It took Azisa an hour to get to our flat from her township, twice the usual time. Mud had leaked into her house and blocked the doors. Dirt roads, already rough, became impassable. I had to cancel my meeting with Mrs. Tambala, with no way to reach her.

Again, I waited. Again, she called. We set another date. And now that day was here. A hot shower was working its magic, erasing the effects of my restless night. A cold hand touched my shoulder. I jumped. Pat pulled me close with a kiss. Shampoo ran down my face onto his. "Why didn't you wake me up?" He nuzzled my neck with soft nibble-kisses.

"Oh, right, and tell Mrs. Tambala, 'No, it wasn't violence or torrential rain that kept me from our appointment. I was messing around with my husband in the shower. But let's reschedule again. I'm sure you didn't mind walking a mile to phone me.'"

"Do you know enough Xhosa to say all that?" He brushed the shampoo from my face. "You be careful today. Stay long enough to get what you need, then get out."

"Yes, Officer." I tweaked his nose.

A sideways smile relaxed his face. "Otherwise, I'll be forced to detain you," he said twirling a strand of shampooed hair, "and subject you to all kinds of things."

"You don't say. Like what?"

"A Special Agent could be pretty creative with a certain detainee."

"That doesn't give me much incentive to behave."

"Then how does a nice bottle of wine and a walk on the beach before dinner sound?"

"Not as interesting."

He slapped my tush and kissed me again. "I'm serious, Mar, stay close to Mr. Swandie."

I wrapped my hair in a towel. Two rows of dress pumps and heels stared at me from the closet. Neither made sense for trudging across what promised to be muddy ground. Digging behind them, I found the sneakers. African or American, women understood shoes. I would wear the sneakers and change into pumps. Mrs. Tambala would think me a practical, no-nonsense worker, more focused on our visit than fashion.

Now I was ready for the hard part: how to hide my hair. If you were to describe a Foreign Service worker who mimicked the look of the ruling Afrikaners, it would be me. Blacks in the township would have no way of knowing the blonde lady in the government mercedes was an anti-apartheid activist not an Afrikaner. My dad's Minnesota Twins baseball cap teetered on a high shelf. Perfect.

I stuffed my ponytail under the cap. "Dad, will I have a story to tell you." As an accessory it wasn't exactly haute couture, but it did the trick. Oversized sunglasses would cover most of my face. The outfit would show respect for Mrs. Tambala in her home, sunglasses and cap would help me blend in on the way in and out of the township.

The U.S. Embassy driver opened the door for me. Today Mr. Swandie would double as my bodyguard. He assured me we were taking the safest route, Settler's Highway. Khayelitsha was a mere thirty-five minutes away, but the township, like the others, was the embodiment of apartheid with overcrowded slums, the result of Afrikaners bringing cheap labor closer to the factories. I had seen the lean-tos of corrugated metal, tarp roofs, cardboard walls that first day as we drove from the airport to Sea Point, before it became clear the townships had limited running water, few sewers, no trash collection.

Khayelitsha was a dangerous place, violence never far from the surface. Brutal policing kept some kind of order, but fueled by inhumane living conditions, the police presence stoked increasing resentment. Tagged "black-on-black" violence, as if it were inherent, rather than fed by warring political parties, the fighting for scarce resources, Khayelitsha was known as the murder capital of South Africa. I reminded myself that Mr. Swandie had grown up there, spoke Xhosa. His manner may have been gentle, but he was a hulk, a man not to be messed with, a trait valued by the embassy for black drivers taking officials into dangerous territory.

The city gave way to the Cape Flats, a wide swath of prairie I might have seen in the Midwest with its tall grass wavering in the breeze. Thirty minutes later asphalt gave way to a rough frontage road. My stomach tightened. Images from news clips on TV ran through my head—cars being stopped and turned over, or carjacked; petrol bombs; necklacing—a particularly brutal form of murder in which a tire doused in petrol is placed around the victim's neck and set on fire, a public display of torture reserved for government informants. To this day the word "necklace" turns my stomach. There were no images of necklacing on TV, but gruesome reporting—with a reference to charred ground where a victim had burned to death was enough. I shoved the images away.

The frontage road turned into a dirt one, more a series of ruts than road in the wake of the punishing storm. Mr. Swandie drove slowly to avoid water splashing mud on the windshield. I bounced against the door as we maneuvered around big potholes and hit smaller ones. We passed a *shebeen*, a place where locals sold illegal liquor. A few men leaned against the wall taking a long look at the Mercedes. Up the road a queue had formed—men in coveralls, women, most likely maids, waiting for the kombi, which was approaching from the opposite direction. Mr. Swandie pulled the Mercedes over to let the kombi squeeze by.

Riders jostled to get inside the cramped vehicle. As it pulled away, those workers left in the road did a double take at our car. "Stay low, Mrs. McGhee." I sunk down in the seat. The car was as closed as a coffin. It would've been faster had I gotten out and walked. Two women in line at an outhouse stared. Another stopped to look as she hung wet clothes on a rope. Days of rain had left the air damp, even if sunlight could make it through the cramped, squalid housing. A little boy carrying a bucket of water stopped to look. He squatted on a soccer ball mired in mud for a ringside seat. The putrid smell of raw sewage added to smoke from early morning barrel fires nearly nauseated me.

The black polished sedan was a spectacle, unable to avoid attention amidst the shacks, its roof higher than most dwellings. Between people gawking and our slow pace, I was exposed, vulnerable in spite of Mr. Swandie. Lean-tos and huts lined both sides of the dirt road, the density adding to my sense of claustrophobia. Had vigilantes wanted to attack, we would be stuck. The road wasn't wide enough to turn the car around, even had we wanted to.

The Mercedes lumbered over deep ruts for another fifty yards. "Please, Lady, remind me the address." *Oh my God, is he lost?* The streets had no signage other than the occasional handwritten one on a slat of wood in the ground, and those were face down in the mud, except one that leaned against a trash can: *One Settler, One Bullet.* White Afrikaners stood warned. I was probably the only white woman within five kilometers of the township. And now we were lost. I repeated the address.

Mr. Swandie stopped the car alongside an older woman sweeping out her shack. He rolled down the window, addressing her in Xhosa. She stepped over to the sedan. Children came out of the shack. The woman caught sight of me. She shuffled the little ones behind her.

"It's okay," Mr. Swandie said, nodding toward the backseat. "Lady is American, here to help."

I lunged forward to the driver's side window. "Do you know Mrs. Tambala?" The woman frowned without answering. "She's going to start a sewing project. I am helping her."

The woman glared in silence.

"Mr. Swandie, tell her I'm here to help Mrs. Tambala."

Before he could say anything, the woman spoke. "I speak English. She is my cousin. Follow me."

I reached for the door handle. Mr. Swandie turned around. "No, Lady!"

"It's okay. I want to walk with her."

"No, Mrs. McGhee. We drive." The tone of his voice told me not to argue. He radioed our whereabouts to the embassy. At the pace of trudging oxen, we followed behind Mrs. Tambala's cousin, barefoot children in tow. Neighbors came out of their shacks watching intently, looks of confusion followed by suspicion.

Mr. Swandie came to a Jacuzzi-sized pothole. The car bounced, splashing dirty water on the kids. I gasped. They froze. One little boy jumped into the giant puddle. More water splashed. The other kids broke into laughter. They jumped into the pothole, too. I laughed. They ran to the next one with screams of delight.

Meager lean-tos gave way to more permanent homes—matchbox houses, "two rooms and a garage"—leased by the government. By this time there were a dozen little kids along with a couple of old women, the escort-cousin in the lead. Word of our impending arrival had reached Mrs. Tambala before we found her house.

Elegant in traditional dress, sans tartan, she waited at the gate to greet us. I gave in to the urge and ran to her, arms outstretched. She hugged me tight. It was such a relief to be out of the car, bystanders witnessing the embrace. We were welcome, had been expected. Once we recovered from our greeting, Mrs. Tambala and I looked at the muddy children, then at each other, and laughed.

Mr. Swandie waited in the car. Mrs. Tambala led me inside to inspect the layout for the project that had brought us together. "First things first," she said. Mrs. Tambala motioned me to a corner and pulled back a tarp that opened to the outside. There in a protected nook was a hole in the dirt. It took a moment to register. Yes, I understood and thanked her. Her face tensed when she said it was too dangerous for women to go to the big outhouse, even in daylight.

Sunlight streamed in with the tarp open. On one side of the room, a pot of water steamed over a hibachi-like stove. Women in colorful skirts and mismatched blouses sat on the floor. Two toddlers entertained themselves with wooden utensils. Mrs. Tambala offered me the one seat, a small wooden stool. In the middle of our group was a tiny basket with a newborn wrapped in swaddling. The cousin picked up the baby and held her out to me. My first instinct was to say no. I had never held an infant this small, a month old at most. I thought better of it. As I cradled the baby my whole body began to relax.

The baby squirmed, her face blotchy. One tiny fist emerged from the swaddling.

Mrs. Tambala set the teacups on a low table. "Do you have children, Mrs. McGhee?"

"No. Not yet."

"Someday."

I smiled. Patrick and I had agreed to postpone kids, the logistics of foreign travel in an unstable world hardly conducive to family life. We had not discussed when a good time would be, but it certainly wasn't now. I was content holding the sweet baby. Mrs. Tambala came close, her left hand on me, right hand on the baby.

"This is Mandisa...she is our future. It is she who brings us all together."

The room had fallen quiet, women and children listening, watching. I laid the baby back in her basket on the floor. The other women moved in close and formed a circle, incorporating me into the formation. A girl began to sing what must have been a traditional Xhosa song. The women joined in, the children too, their voices soft and clear, blending into one.

The next moment we were swaying, our movements synchronized in song, all of us looking at baby Mandisa. I didn't know the Xhosa song, but the melody was easy, like something I had sung as a schoolgirl at St. Francis. How odd to stand in this humble dwelling half a world away in a strange place with people who looked different from me, spoke different from me, lived different from me, feeling undeniably connected.

We resumed our places to enjoy the customary *rooibos* tea steaming in the pretty teacups. Mrs. Tambala kept the chipped one for herself, as any good hostess would. I admired the porcelain, thinking about my own collection as a girl, the outings with my mother to antique shops. A warm flush passed through me. I would write in my journal about this day, share it with Mom.

The cousin spoke better English than Mrs. Tambala. With her help, we carried on the discussion we had started weeks ago about the sewing project—how she planned to set up the room, the garments, how she would get them to market, and the number of jobs she would create. Mrs. Tambala could've been a businesswoman anywhere with her innovative ideas, which stood out, given the impoverished setting she had to work around.

The fact that she and her cousin spoke any English at all surprised me. The Bantu Education Act of 1953 linked education to taxes, which meant far less money spent on educating blacks than whites. It was meant to isolate Africans, keep them in their designated role as cheap labor in apartheid society. At school, children were taught in their tribal language, not English, a strategy to keep blacks from participation in the white, English-speaking government. High school students protesting the laws were gunned down in the Soweto Revolt of 1976. So Mrs. Tambala's learning English must have been very difficult in a township with few books in English or other educational resources.

The afternoon ticked by, the three of us talking at least two hours. The other women tended the children, prepared dinner. The little ones began fussing. They had been so good during our discussion. And I did not want to overstay my welcome.

One little boy pushed another into me. I braced to keep my balance on the stool, but teetered sideways to the floor. Mrs. Tambala jumped up, began scolding the children. I burst out laughing. Sensing approval, the little ones crawled up on me, giggling, vying for attention. I tickled one, then another, and another, filling the room with the squealing sounds of play.

In the tussle, my cap fell off. Blonde hair tumbled over my shoulders. The first boy stood up, mouth agape. He reached for my hair. I smiled. "It's okay." He hesitated, then touched the loose strands, a look of astonishment on his face. Was it possible he had never seen a white woman, much less touched one? The other little boys gathered around, little girls too, each waiting their turn to feel the strange flaxen hair.

Mrs. Tambala shook her head in apology, scolding the children. Our voices became overpowered by men yelling outside. I peeked through the tarp door. Mr. Swandie stood next to the car surrounded by angry young men. He caught my eye. "Lady, we go...NOW!"

Mrs. Tambala had seen what was going on. Our eyes locked for a moment, neither of us able to find words. Quickly she motioned me out the door. "Go. Go." I glanced at the children, at baby Mandisa, then ran outside to the car. My cap! I twirled around. Mrs. Tambala met me halfway with it.

Mr. Swandie had the back door of the car open. With his big brawny arms he lifted me off my feet, shoving me inside. "Stay on the floor, Lady!" Swinging his body to and fro he pressed the men back until he made it in and slammed the door. He started the engine. The car lurched forward with hard jolts. Men surrounded the Mercedes, rocking it side-to-side. Then they pounded the roof. The car lurched forward.

Curled on the floor, I pulled the Minnesota Twins cap tight. At least if I was going to die, my dad would be with me.

Angry voices behind the men yelled "Boer settler!" Mr. Swandie revved the engine to a threatening roar. The car pulled away. The pounding stopped. The bumpy road of ruts and potholes kept us at a crawl, but Mr. Swandie kept moving. A rock slammed the rear window, cracking the glass. Another followed, then another, hitting the roof, the hood. In slow motion we picked up speed. At the end of the road the car bumped over the asphalt ridge where the dirt ended. The road smoothed out. We had reached Settlers Way, the highway back to Cape Town. My breathing slowed as the gap widened between us and the mob.

I was still in a cocoon on the floor. "Mr. Swandie, is it okay to come up?" He didn't answer. My voice had come out muffled in my curled up position. Louder, I asked again.

"Yes, Mrs. McGhee." My legs wobbled as I slid onto the seat. Table Mountain lay straight ahead. He drove fast. Sweat poured down the back of his clean-shaven neck into the collar of his white dress shirt.

I leaned forward. "Are you okay, Mr. Swandie?"

"Yes, Lady." His voice was thick.

Neither of us spoke the rest of the way, each alone with our own thoughts. I stared out the window in a daze, trying to make sense of what just happened. What if we hadn't gotten away? A ball of lead pushed hard against my chest. The thought hadn't formed into words yet, but slowly it came into focus. I wanted to blurt out my gratitude to Mr. Swandie, commend him on his fast action. My voice stuck. No doubt he was thinking I was the crazy do-gooder white lady who almost got us killed.

"We'll be back in Cape Town soon, Lady. You're safe now."

He sounded as if he were assuring himself as much as me. As we got close to Sea Point, my heartbeat returned to normal sinus rhythm. The ball of lead in my chest refused to abate, leaving me vaguely nauseated. I just wanted to go home. Mr. Swandie stopped at the flat entrance. He came around to open my door. I got out. My legs nearly buckled.

"Mr. Swandie…I…I—"

"Yes, Lady." He bowed his head, then got in the car and drove away.

The sun was still high. Inside the flat I sat on the couch in a state of bewilderment. I had no idea of the time, nor how long I had been there when Patrick walked in and found me waiting for him.

Eleven
Lost and Found

February/March 1993

My visit to Mrs. Tambala came none too soon. Bloodshed in the townships made the news every night— black rivalry between Mandela's and Buthelezi followers—while De Klerk sat back and watched negotiations stumble to a halt. Stress on Patrick was relentless, demanding late hours at the office, last minute travel to hot spots, always planning the next security detail. At the embassy I rarely saw him unless it was for safety drills, which we had more often these days. Morale was low. The strain wore on everyone.

President De Klerk and Nelson Mandela finally came to an agreement that changed the direction of negotiations. De Klerk's National Party agreed that Mandela and the ANC would be the principal party in negotiations. Buthelezi would be secondary until he dropped his demand for a separate Zulu nation. And 1993 would be devoted to writing a new constitution.

How long that would take was the question on everyone's mind at the embassy. In the meantime, Patrick was on the front lines, holding back the tsunami of building rage. Travel by embassy officials to the townships was grounded. Instead of visits for the self-help projects, I continued to plan tours and events for the American community with the goal of building morale, one of my responsibilities as Community Liaison Officer. As publisher of our American community newsletter, *Cape Pointer*, I upped the request for input. That brought visitors.

My office was an open door, a place where people could hang out—get their mail, hear the latest on upcoming events or help with planning one — a baby shower, tennis tournament, wine tasting. Fiction and biography titles in the small library shelved in my office rotated more quickly. Staff would come in for a book but stay for a talk. Right away, I spotted when Bev needed a shoulder, or the visa officer to blow off steam about a colleague.

My work at the embassy had morphed into the closest thing to my job in public relations back home. Busy, productive, my world was peopled again. Charles Monroe—the one Political Officer—was a regular. Charles was also on the USAID committee, which meant we worked together on various community projects. The man was easy to talk to and liked to regale whoever would listen with stories of motorcycle trips across the U.S. And he played guitar. The guy was not your typical statesman.

Charles had his ear to the ground with duties that included attendance at functions (particularly rallies), befriending locals, reporting on political activities. That made him my source for the inside scoop outside the embassy. Where Patrick's information was sensitive, Charles's was not. "Unaccompanied"—that was his designated status. Reluctant to bring their children into South Africa's volatile environment, his wife had chosen to remain in the States. No one could blame her. Had I become pregnant, I might have gone home.

Restrictions on township visits made sense, but I was restless, yearned to be involved at the grassroots level. More than anything, I was curious about the rallies. Rabble-rousing events, these political gatherings were rarely dangerous.

One day I was wrapping up paperwork on my USAID self-help projects. It was unlikely I would be the one to see them through as things stood now with restrictions to the townships. Charles had project information that would be useful for my successor. I stood in the doorway of his office until he looked up.

"Tell me you figured out a way to airdrop me into Khayelitsha to finish my projects."

"Not likely," he said with a big toothy grin. "But hey, there's a rally tonight at the university. If you want a firsthand look, this would be a good one. Patrick's welcome, too."

That night over roast beef and Yorkshire pudding I brought it up.

"Mary, I spend every waking hour keeping the lid on things. Why would I want to go to a rally and watch everybody get worked into a lather of near-hysteria?"

"I know...but now that I'm not out in the field anymore, I'm curious. It's right here in Cape Town, at the university. The local police are on board. And I'd be safe. Charles knows his way around these things."

He responded with a sardonic sideways glance. "Charles. Right."

I leaned back in the chair, arms folded. "Is this going to be another Peter-and-the-wrap-party?"

"Let's just drop it."

"Fine. But I'm going." My voice had more defiance than intended, but I let the jab stand.

That night I did go to the rally with Charles, and many more nights after that. He would pick me up in his government car, exchange pleasantries with Patrick. The quintessential Catholic Good Girl all my life, bravado had a tinge of sweetness, tempering my anger at Patrick for not being emotionally available. The poor guy was doing his job and, right now, that took everything he had. But his words had lodged in the recesses of my mind. Emotional distance revived them. *Maybe you should go home. Mary. Go home. Blend in.*

Attending political rallies with Charles wasn't exactly blending in; no other diplomatic spouses did such things. I didn't care. And Patrick didn't forbid me. It wasn't about blending in, we both knew that. I suspect Patrick empathized with me. He wasn't the only one who had come to South Africa to be part of this moment in history. Stuck in an office with township visits off limits, I sensed my opportunities slipping away. Rallies with Charles were easy enough to rationalize—Patrick thought nothing of weekly pick-up basketball games with the guys, regular poker dates. He needed those outlets. I needed outlets too, beyond Girls' Night Out. At local rallies I would be in the thick of it.

Rallies with Charles became a weekly thing. I would tell Patrick about them, excluding how much fun I'd had. After a while I stopped saying much. And he didn't ask. No wonder half of all Foreign Service marriages ended in divorce—the stress, the fishbowl existence, myriad restrictions, lack of down time, loneliness, the mission itself—there were countless factors that chipped away at a relationship, at our relationship. The great adventure that was supposed to launch our marriage into a life of exotic travel had become a crucible testing our mettle. I wasn't the only one feeling the heat.

Patrick had his moods too, which translated as withdrawal from me. Sometimes it was as if I had been carried to some distant country on a fast-moving train and left on my own. It was hard to find my way, keep any balance. Half the time I was angry, the other half sad. If Patrick had those same feelings, he kept them locked in that emotional vault of his. At least I was free to express mine, had I someone to express them to. The roller coaster of emotions wore on us, leaving us ragged around the edges, snapping at each other.

To make matters worse, I had my own jealousy issues over a very flirtatious woman, another officer, who would mosey into Patrick's office unannounced, all giggly and touchy-feely, flicking her hair back. From what I saw, he sure didn't seem to mind the interruption. At diplomatic parties this same Jezebel would hone in the moment I wandered away from my husband's side, her head on his shoulder, laughing. I wanted to scream. So let him think about Charles.

Funny how these instances of balancing the emotional books are delicious in the moment, but over time, drive the wedge between you further apart. Hurting Patrick was the last thing I wanted to do. Danger, not my husband, was the source of restrictions. His work, not his feelings for me, made him emotionally distant. But like David back home and Peter from *Woman of Desire*, part of me wanted Patrick to be jealous of Charles. I was human and couldn't help relishing my power, however fleeting.

As the weeks drifted deeper into winter of '93, Patrick and I drifted further apart. I had experienced the pain of jealousy, understood I was using it now to cope with my needs. What an ironic twist that being here with him in South Africa, I missed Patrick more than I had back home. Maybe *because* I was with him. There's nothing lonelier than the loneliness you feel when you're with someone. As long as we were in South Africa there would be a wall, his work as formidable a barrier between the two of us as Table Mountain was between the Cape Basin and the township flats.

Two marriages at our post were in trouble. A sliver of anxiety set in as I worried about how Patrick and I would ever close the widening gap at the end of our two years, revert back to that loving couple who stepped off the plane in Johannesburg fresh from their honeymoon. I had to do something. The longer we ignored it, the worse it would get. There's no way I would let that happen. I needed a plan.

Except for my rally outings with Charles, which were practically work related, I resolved not to put any demands on Patrick—no complaining about basketball, poker, late nights at the office. I focused on my work at the embassy, the standing tennis match with Helen, Girl's Night Out with Beverly and friends, aerobics classes at the club. The Wildlife Rescue needed volunteers. I signed up for two shifts a month. At the Botanical Gardens, I led visitor tours one morning a week. Staying busy helped me feel less lonely, kept me from asking Patrick for time he couldn't give. But keeping the peace wasn't enough. We needed to find each other again.

Not long after this epiphany, I launched my plan. The timing was bad, but when was the timing good? Patrick had worked late, then met the guys for basketball. Exhausted when he walked in the door, he still had to shower and change. By the time he threw his shorts in the washer, dinner was on the kitchen table.

I poured us each a glass of wine. My stomach tightened. "You know, hon, you've been under so much pressure. I wish there was something I could do."

"I'm fine. Don't worry about it."

"But you're *not* fine, Patrick. You're stressed out. We barely see each other—"

"Mary, don't start."

I turned away biting my lip. "No, that came out wrong. I'm not asking you for anything. Well, I mean, I am." It was coming out all wrong. "I think we should take a break."

"Makes sense. You can go home on early R & R."

It was a sucker punch to the gut. My back hit the chair, the heat of anger flushing my face. *Maybe you should go home, Mary.* Did he want me to leave so badly that that was the first thing he thought of? I waited a moment, then leaned forward again, close to him.

"That's not what I meant." Deep breath. "I was thinking you need a break, just a short one. I thought we could get away." He opened his mouth to cut me off. "Wait. Just listen for a minute. I keep thinking about all the places you went in '87, the beautiful places you told me about. We really haven't been out of Cape Town, except to visit the Donovans."

"It's not a good time."

I bent low, struggling to make eye contact, my voice soft. "It's exactly the right time, hon. Look, there isn't even a date set for the election yet. It's not going to happen tomorrow. You could leave for a few days and everything would still be here when you got back. If you keep working at this pace you'll drop dead of a heart attack before you ever see a democratic South Africa."

"Is that meant to be funny?"

"I'm dead serious. And my guess is that Ambassador Lyman would be the first person to encourage you to take a few days off."

Silence. I waited.

He mumbled into his plate. "You might have a point. I guess I could use a breather. But not here. It would have to be somewhere else."

"How does Kruger Park sound?"

He looked at me for the first time since he walked in the door. As he put two and two together, a smile began to form. "You're not asking out of the blue. You planned this."

I jumped up to get brochures from the kitchen drawer. Suddenly I was in the air. Patrick let out a guttural howl, grabbing me around the waist, twirling me around to face him.

"Mary Byron, you *are* the smartest girl in the room." It was a toothy kiss through his big smile.

"Never underestimate the power of a woman in love."

"I should've known." He whispered in my hair. "Mary, I *do* need you."

It didn't come across as the romantic epiphany of a soul mate acknowledging the weight of his good fortune as much as a mechanic realizing he *did* have the part he needed to fix the car. Still, it took some of the sting out of the *go-home* memory.

"First thing tomorrow, I'll talk to Princeton. Any sign of hesitation, and that's it, end-of-discussion."

Patrick locked up early. I lit candles in the bedroom. That night we started down the path to finding each other again.

Ambassador Lyman, more than anyone, understood the pressure Patrick was under. He didn't skip a beat with his encouragement. The consul general agreed. Travel dates proved difficult. It's not as if Patrick's job could be done by anyone. We narrowed our window to accommodate his coverage. Five days—five glorious days, just the two of us, away from civilization in one of the most untouched places on earth. Patrick and I shared a love of animals and nature. This would be perfect.

As a reserve, Kruger Park represented the Real Africa—seventy-five hundred square miles of big game and small, windswept plains, deep forests—the part that really was true to movies like *Out of Africa, Gorillas in the Mist, Born Free,* the South Africa as I had imagined it when clueless. Kruger was located in what was called the Lowveld, a low-lying section in the northeastern part of the country with a subtropical climate, part of the Kruger Canyons Biosphere designated by the United Nations as an Educational, Scientific and Cultural reserve.

Equal in size to Wales or Belgium or New Jersey, each area in Kruger has its distinct flora, fauna and wildlife with wilderness trails through the bush in each. The part we chose was relatively safe, the qualifying adverb denoting the amount of danger required by my husband to qualify as worthwhile. The possibility of danger thrilled me too, as long as it stayed this side of scary. Risk of danger had been part of our lives since stepping off the plane in Joburg six months earlier. Tracking wildlife was self-imposed, preferable to living in the constant residue of political unrest.

Like everyone else, the Big Five topped our list—elephant, lion, buffalo, leopard, rhino. Four weeks, that's how long I had to plan. Camps ranged from luxurious guest houses to cottages to huts. Moving through the park, we would need a selection. The next decision would be the most important—go in a safari vehicle as part of a small group, on foot with an armed guide, or in a rented vehicle on our own. Take-charge man that my husband is by nature and training, he wasn't about to hand our trip over to a guide. Patrick would be armed. And he was familiar with the park. Team Byron and McGhee would navigate the wilderness as the indomitable team we were.

A ferocious predator was not our biggest concern, but a tiny insect—a mosquito. Malaria prevention included proper clothing, insect sprays, plus the option of anti-malaria medication to minimize the impact if we did get bitten. Stories of those infected were enough for Patrick and me to choose the combo. Three weeks before leaving the flat, we took our first dose of chloroquine. By the time we arrived in Kruger the chemical protectant was well established in our blood.

The actual trip would be five days, but the weeks leading up to it worked its magic. Now, when Patrick came home we went over my research and talked about preparation, a topic which had nothing to do with what we always talked about—our pressure cooker existence—or with all the things we couldn't. The change in him was immediate. Time together was still scarce, given his long hours, including weekends, but what time we had was tension-free. At last.

The Day of Departure, following a two-hour flight from Cape Town to Joburg, we were in our rental car, a Range Rover. Patrick's shoulders visibly dropped the further we got from the city, past the townships into the wide plains. Four hours later we reached the west park entrance and followed the map to our first lodging, a *rondavel*—a small hut with thatched roof and a door. The thatched roof looked surprisingly like stacked wheat just waiting for a herd of wildebeest. With flirtatious energy Patrick teased me when I asked him to lock the door, pointing out that big game lack opposable thumbs to unlatch it, that if they wanted to barge in, they would. Still, the eponymous scene from *Elephant Walk* stayed in my head.

Somewhere in that hypnotic state between sleep and wake, I listened to the sounds—laughing hyenas, a lion's roar, the half-hearted crackle of a dying fire. No fear. The darkness, the unfamiliar sounds, the fresh smells, all of it was magical, Mother Nature's lullaby. I pulled the sheet over my shoulder and drifted off.

The next morning I woke feeling I'd had the best night's sleep since our honeymoon in Ireland. It wasn't actually morning as I know it, but sunrise. Minnesota winters had been like that—go to bed early and wake at first light, a natural rhythm sidelined long ago for a world that lived by the clock. If Patrick and I were to spot wildlife at all, it would be on their schedule.

Provisions on board, including Patrick's scope and high-powered binoculars, we climbed into the Range Rover, making our way to the nearest waterhole. Early morning was best for seeing animals headed for the plentiful water of the Sabie River and a breakfast of grass. In stealth motion, we drove at a crawl. Patrick nudged the car into a cluster of trees. He cut the ignition. It was so quiet, birds waking with loud chirps the only sound. We didn't speak. It was enough to sit next to each other in the car, participants in a scene that would be emblazoned in our memories—the stillness, just him and me in the wild.

To wake in a world so different from the one we'd left behind refueled our weary souls. Without the tension, closeness between us resurfaced, stress supplanted by life's grandeur and transience. Death here was part of life, killing the result of a well-honed genetic program designed to save the species, not murder as an outcome of violence. Biology, not ideology.

Patrick squeezed my arm. He handed me the binoculars. An impala crouched through a grassy knoll toward the water. We watched in rapt attention as the animal drank from a stream. Thirty minutes later a small herd of zebra came and went. Intent on spotting our next find, Patrick surveyed the landscape in slow motion. As the African sun rose high, its heat sent us clambering for shelter along with the wildebeests and Cape buffalo.

And so it went as we worked our way through the park, traveling mid-day when wildlife nestled in the shade, our movements in sync with game whose sole focus was to eat and sleep, to survive another day. It slowed us into forced relaxation, our own biorhythms attuned to Mother Earth where all you hear is the sound of your own breath. Conversation flowed in the comfortable leisurely way borne of few distractions, where you actually listen to each other.

A few days into the trip, I forgot all about government goons. No one spied on us, such mental luxury. Tangible luxury came in the form of meals cooked by locals in the camp we shared with other nature enthusiasts. Each night hired cooks prepared special dishes with exotic veggies and fruits. They had their favorites of *bobotie*, curries, meat pies, and of course, Cape wines to end the night. Dinner was an event in itself.

As we settled into a relaxed focused existence, our long days of patient waiting paid off. One morning we spotted a herd of elephant yanking branches from tall trees until they got their fill, a lone giraffe eyeing us with indifference as he ate and we snapped photos. One early evening we happened upon a herd of water buffalo at least three hundred strong. Patrick cut the engine. From the car we engaged in a stare down with what appeared to be the lead buffalo while he scoped us out with impassive curiosity.

Plenty of springbok, impala, and guinea fowl came close, as well as a family of warthogs, cute and clumsy. One day we came across elephants and their babies rolled on their backs in the mud, trunks spraying water over their bellies and heads.

It was such a joyful scene, the biggest land animals on earth frolicking like puppies. That night we drove to a waterhole. A hippo lumbered out of the water right before our eyes. What a sight.

The best moment came during a night drive in an open game-viewing truck. We had stopped to listen to the sounds of the plains under a full moon. Our mouths dropped open at the same time. A lion stepped from behind a bush in plain sight. He swaggered toward us, inspecting the foreign species. We made not a sound as the big cat lumbered forward in all his muscular glory, nose twitching in the breeze at our scent. Patrick and I squeezed each other's arms, holding our breath lest we disturb him. My heart jumped in awe at such a thrill.

I moved not a muscle. Park officials had instructed us to keep our arms and hands inside the truck. I had the powerful urge to duck out of sight of the magnificent beast. And lock the door. Nervous tension almost burst forth in a giggle at the memory of our exchange about locking the door to our hut.

The lion stared at us, then raised his head, as if about to roar. Master of deceit that he is, rather than make noise that might alert prey to his presence, he bared his teeth to get the message across. A moment later he was next to the truck, veering past us into the bush. Unable to squelch our exuberance, we broke into cries of amazement, reliving the tense meeting, the physical rush of proximity to the king of the jungle. What a glorious moment under the light of a full moon, Patrick and I hearing the same sounds, smelling the same smells as bushmen had thousands of years ago. A shiver ran through me. Indeed, adrenaline seared through me for hours after our adventure.

Sharing such a special moment in the trip of a lifetime was levitating. Months of tension melted away as if they had never been there. I loved Patrick with all my heart. And I finally loved the country he so badly wanted me to love, understood in a visceral way why South Africans would fight for it—die for it, blacks and whites alike—die for the right to self-determination.

This extraordinary land from which humanity evolved was in their blood—Zulus, Dutch-descended Afrikaners, native South Africans, each group staking its claim on the land, and the land on them.

In the Range Rover that night overlooking the countryside, South Africa staked its claim on me, right there in Kruger Park where Patrick and I had found our way back to each other.

Twelve
A Rose by Any Other Name

March 1993

"Helen, the place is crawling with agents tonight. There must be something special on the agenda...?" She looked at me with smiling eyes but didn't give me the scoop. Playing it close to the vest was as much a part of her role as it was Patrick's. It wasn't about trust. It was about protocol. Pushing aside my frustration, I assumed security had been heightened just as it had at the embassy with the recent violence in Cape Town.

Riots in Joburg were replicated across the land, even reaching our idyllic enclave in Sea Point. The morning *Argus* had reported another carjacking at a city bowl stop light the previous night, this time a young man. He got away unhurt. The violence was tension-driven with uncertainty about the elections. Local newspapers were sketchy reporting the incidents. Friends and family at home in the States often included clippings in their letters from the *New York Times* or *The Washington Post*, or we would hear about the township violence from Azisa—robberies, rapes, heavy-handed police overreacting at peaceful demonstrations with beatings, shootings.

The Commonwealth Observer —a fifteen-member team which consisted of police, military, legal and political experts— concluded that the country was "one of the most violent" in the world, based on its homicide rate. It was about this time that our fair city got the nickname "Cape Town, Rape Town. " Experts recommended that South Africa's best hope for containing the violence was for parties to move speedily toward democratic elections.

Nothing about negotiations went speedily. And so we waited as Mandela and De Klerk pounded out the details of a new constitution while Buthelezi threatened war if election plans proceeded without meeting his demand for a separate Zulu nation. The town was on tenterhooks. At the embassy I continued to help organize diplomatic events, both congressional visits from the States and embassy gatherings. One in particular remains in my memory to this day in vivid Technicolor—the event that was "crawling with agents."

Ambassador Lyman and Helen hosted the diplomatic reception at their home. I loved visiting the Lyman residence for my weekly tennis matches with Helen. For this particular event, I had not seen the guest list, which was unusual.

The day of the reception Patrick seemed distant. Once again, I chalked it up to concern about security for the evening—that, on top of heavy pressure at work. I knew better than to ask. Protocol dictated these events, from who was invited to the order of the reception line and other tradition-bound considerations.

That night I wore a fancy emerald green cocktail dress cinched at the waist with a deep V-neck. Other women wore scrumptious dresses as well. The opportunity to get decked out proved a welcome diversion, the chance to pretend the world outside our doors was life as usual. Helen was the consummate host. If she had ever doubted she was the perfect emissary to represent our country, as she later claimed in her memoir, *Not to the Manor Born*, you would never have known it by the grace with which she pulled it off. Warm, unassuming, friendly, Helen could have been hosting a fundraiser for disadvantaged children in Washington, D.C. rather than a diplomatic reception during civil unrest. But she was the engine driving these important social events—part of her husband's behind-the-scenes efforts for the three stubborn political parties to agree on an interim constitution.

Attention to detail was paramount for this particular evening, as for any of these diplomatic events—hors d'oeuvres drawn from local fare, excellent local wines. After dinner we were invited to move into the main room. Silence fell over the group as our Political Officer, Charles Monroe, introduced Ambassador Lyman. Like Helen, Princeton Lyman was effective in groups with his warm, open manner, just as he had been with me. Guests, as well as disparate party leaders, understood this man to be a straight shooter, a man you could take at his word. This was a major asset in touchy diplomatic situations. It also helped build a sense of camaraderie at the embassy with everybody's nerves on edge.

Ambassador Lyman, though youthful in middle age, had a fatherly quality, a reassuring confidence that in his hands all would be okay. It was easy to imagine his using the same warm manner to meet with Zulu Chief Buthelezi, whose hair-trigger temper was legendary. Our ambassador was a calm voice in the contentious din of Buthelezi's opposition to a united South Africa.

As guests assembled to hear Ambassador Lyman speak, I grabbed my camera with hopes of getting a group shot for the newsletter. The room was packed. It wasn't easy to move. Camera in position, I stepped back for the wide angle. I bumped into someone. Whoever it was stepped back. I quickly snapped the photo. Ready to offer an apologetic smile, I turned around.

My mouth dropped open. The room became a blur, everyone disappearing but the one who now stood inches away, face-to-face with me. Our eyes met. Breathing stopped. At first I didn't recognize him. He looked nothing like he did on TV or in the newspaper, dressed in ethnic garb, all feathers and skins and lion's teeth necklaces. In a business suit with silk tie and matching pocket square, the man before me was well-groomed, distinguished looking. He could have been any politician or diplomat. But he wasn't.

I was staring into the eyes of Zulu Chief Buthelezi.

Stunned, I remained motionless. The chief nodded at me in acceptance of what he must have been sure was an incipient apology. Words wouldn't come, but I did manage to close my mouth. Reflexively, I nodded in return, certain my face was sickly green from the summersaults in my stomach. The ambassador began to speak. The room hushed, all eyes focused on him.

Heart in my throat, I began to inch away from the Zulu chief, bumping into several guests in my retreat toward the rear. Was he armed? Was he there to assassinate Ambassador Lyman? Images of bloodshed from the recent deaths of sixty-three peaceful ANC marchers in KwaZulu, Chief Buthelezi's homeland, screamed through my mind. The attack had been nothing short of mass slaughter. How could one person orchestrate such senseless murder of unarmed men and women? My thoughts ran wild.

Ambassador Lyman's words were muffled, indecipherable with the pounding in my ears. Where was Patrick? Could he see Buthelezi? Was he ready if the warrior pulled out a gun? A wine tray floated above guests' heads in my direction. My hands shook so much I nearly knocked the glasses over as I plucked one. Too queasy to drink it, the glass was my effort to look normal as I calculated the fastest way to distance myself from Chief Buthelezi in the crowded room. But no one moved.

Lightheaded, unaware I had been holding my breath, I teetered. The wine threatened to spill. The room spun as I edged toward fainting. *Gather your wits, Mary.* With a deep breath I steadied myself. Inch by inch I worked my way to the side of the room, cutting a path through the throng, mouthing my apology for momentarily blocking guests' views. The wall was in sight. Finally I broke free of the pack, collapsing against the wall, my wine sloshing to the tip of the glass.

The wall was the first half of my goal—to get out of there. This event was the perfect set up for an assassination attempt. In tiny steps I continued shuffling toward the back of the room, each move increasing the distance between me and Chief Buthelezi. Patrick and the security detail must be close, positioned at the back. I spotted him. He came forward.

"You're white as a sheet, hon. Everything okay?"

Instead of collapsing in his arms as my impulse dictated, I managed a half smile. "Yeah. I'm just…not feeling all that great."

"You can leave early. It's okay." Another agent stood nearby.

How could I tell Patrick without crumbling that I had been face to face with the murderous leader of the Zulu nation? My hands still shook. No, leaving the event meant leaving without my husband. What if warlords were lying in wait, surrounding the property beyond the fence in position for an ambush?

"I'll be okay. I just need a minute." His whole body told me he wanted to hug me. That alone helped. With a squeeze of his hand I moved toward the crowd, but stayed in back near Patrick, far from Buthelezi.

When the event ended, I waited for Patrick to wrap up his detail. On the drive home I told him all about it, still shaken up. Encountering Buthelezi up close made him all the more real, not just someone I had heard or read about, but a real warlord with brutal means for achieving his end. Of course that explained the heightened security. Patrick had seen the guest list. If ever I hated being in the dark, that night was it.

The events of that evening took me to a new level of anxiety. Danger lurked everywhere, with no way to know where or when it might erupt. My body was weighted with dread. Nowhere would I feel safe again. Instead of my favorite haunts in Sea Point, I would stick closer to home.

The entire next week, unless I was at the embassy, I stayed in the flat. It was too much. Stir crazy, I pushed aside my anxiety—after all, the event at Ambassador Lyman's had turned out to be peaceful—and gave in to my urge for American fries at the Hard Rock Café on Victoria and Albert Highway. It wasn't far from the flat. Fresh sea air always cleared my head, and the promenade was my happy place. The fifteen-minute walk would do me good.

The café was busy with most tables taken. I stood inside the doorway scanning the room for a place to sit.

BANG!

I staggered sideways into a table of equally shocked patrons. They bolted for the door. Mugs of hot coffee sloshed back and forth, spilling all over the floor. Everyone was screaming, shouting. Ears ringing from the noise, I couldn't quite get what was happening. I had regained my balance when a second blast sent me reeling off kilter in the opposite direction. This time I collided with a table tipped over on its side, which is all that kept me from falling. The ground rumbled; the floor shook. Patrons shoved me aside on their way out the door. Stunned, I couldn't move. Someone was smoking. No, not smoking. Smoke.

The ringing in my ears made it impossible to make sense of what everyone was shouting. But the terror on their faces was unmistakable. Dazed, I felt as much as heard the wall of glass shatter behind me. Smoke that had wafted in trails now poured into the room.

A bomb! *Mary, get out!*

Pushing through smoke and debris, hand over mouth, squinting, I followed the others as we stepped over food and dishes scattered across the floor.

Fresh air.

People were screaming, running in all directions. Flames shot up from the barbershop window next door and found the opening that two minutes earlier had been the front wall of the café. Fire swallowed the doorway I had just walked through. All I wanted was to get away from there.

The flat. It was close.

Mouth covered, I power-walked toward the ocean, toward clean air. At the embassy we had prepared for an explosion, had protocol for what to do. I kept walking. Sirens wailed in the distance. Gunshots rang out somewhere behind me. I turned around. Smoke clouded the scene. It was impossible to know where the shots had come from. A man yelled. Then another. The yelling got closer. I picked up my pace. More men joined in the yelling. Glancing over my shoulder I broke into a jog.

Four black men, two with rifles, two waving spears, ran toward me. Were they after me? No. The official embassy compound where diplomats' families lived, that's where they were headed. More men merged from side streets into what was quickly growing into a mob. Our flat was closer than the compound. If only I could get there before the mob caught up.

Yanking off my flip-flops, I ran as fast as my legs would carry me until I reached the building. The outer gate was locked. Shaking it, I called out.

"Mr. Khumalo!"

He didn't come. My hand shook, flailing through my purse for keys. More shots rang out. Neighbors across the street rushed inside their homes from the pool area in back, kids and moms dripping wet. Mr. Khumalo was nowhere to be found. I found my keys. The lock was broken. The mob was closing in on the neighborhood. All I heard was the heartbeat in my ears.

Pressing through the front gate, I ran to the entrance of the building, also unlocked. The lift would be too slow. Taking the stairs two at a time, I sprinted the six flights. Inside the flat I threw the deadbolt. It made a reassuring thud. Patrick. He would be at the embassy. The last few days of mayhem on the streets—carjackings, muggings—it had been impossible to reach him. Struggling to keep the panic from rising in my chest, I rushed to the table next to Patrick's chair. The gun. I felt for the magnetic key holder taped to the frame underneath the sofa. Those hours of training at the shooting range as a precaution suddenly meant survival.

I unlocked the drawer. With a deep breath, I exhaled the shakiness out of my mind. With the Smith and Wesson tight in both hands, I assumed the proper stance, then faced the door. The sound of breaking glass made me turn around. Men shouted from below, outside the garden wall. With caution I slid the glass door open and peered over the deck rail. Men threw bricks at the windows of flats on the ground floor. One must have smashed. In a unified effort, a throng of black men pushed against the gate. It clanked as they banged it back and forth.

One last push and the gate gave way. Men poured through, shouting anti-white slurs. "One settler, one bullet" they cried. No one looked up at me. On tiptoes I retreated inside and resumed my stance, waiting for them to barge through the door. A different sound overpowered the shouting. The vibrating thwack of a helicopter shook the building. The windows rattled in protest.

I waited. Every fiber of my being was poised for attack. A mechanical-sounding voice came through a loudspeaker. Adrenaline coursing through my veins drowned out the words

Sirens blared. They got louder. The flat stopped shaking as the helicopter sound retreated in the distance.

How long I had been standing there poised with the gun was impossible to say. The street got quiet. I waited several minutes before opening the slider. The sound of crashing waves rose to the deck. No shouting. The crowd must have dispersed. Inside, I stood numb, unable to think. The gun dropped to the floor.

Patrick, come home

But he couldn't. He had prepared me for this moment. And I had done exactly what the moment called for. I was prepared to shoot. Prepared to kill. But I didn't feel strong, or sure. I was more alone than I had been in my entire life. If the mob had caught me on the street or broken into the flat, I would have died alone. Absolutely alone. The chair caught me as I collapsed, shaking uncontrollably. Mom. I wanted my mom, my dad, home. To feel safe.

The gun lay at my feet. After a moment, my basic training took over. I emptied the bullets, wrapped the gun in its cloth, returned it to the drawer and locked it. Then I replaced the key in its spot on the sofa frame. Protocol. Going through the motions brought calmness to my body, a sense of control to my mind.

Someone was shaking my shoulder. "Mary, Mary, wake up."

In a fog, I opened my eyes. It was daylight outside. Patrick sat on the couch next to me, stroking my hair. "Hey, that's some bad dream you were having."

Dripping with sweat, it took me a moment to get oriented. Had it really been a dream? But the bomb; the yells; the helicopter. I couldn't speak. Terror consumed me. In spite of Patrick holding me all night, I fought sleep. It had been so real, the fear so visceral.

Twenty-four hours later my dream became reality. In my office working on the newsletter, tense chatter filled the hallway. The words "Hard Rock Café" drifted through the transom. I went to the door to listen.

In broad daylight on the Victoria and Albert Waterfront, the Hard Rock Café had been bombed. My knees buckled. I struggled to keep from hyperventilating.

That afternoon it was déjà vu in the meeting Patrick called to instruct Americans to be hyper vigilant in observing their surroundings. The mission organized a telephone-tree line with a list of names and contacts so people could spread the word in case of emergency. Imagine this task without cell phones for group texting. Phone calls started with the first person on the list, who called the next person, who called the one after him, and so on until everyone was notified.

Embassy security was heightened. Barbed-wire fences topped with razor wire went up around the building. Additional cameras and alarms were installed. High-wattage bulbs lit up the parking garage. Patrick continued to work closely with the Marines at post to prepare for internal defense against a direct attack. Evacuation and lockdown drills became more frequent, most of them at unexpected times.

Patrick and the Gunny Sergeant created a repertoire of drill scenarios to guard against complacency. Mail was inspected for anthrax, among other dangerous chemicals. It was surreal, like preparing for war, which I guess we were. In security briefings, all of us were warned to practice "extreme caution" inside and outside the embassy—check under our vehicle for explosive devices before getting in; vary our route to and from work; keep windows up in our cars, doors locked; vary our lunch routine; no travel after dark.

A huge concern was the growing incidence of carjackings said to be the work of a syndicate in major cities, including Cape Town. We were instructed that if stopped, not to resist, to hand over possessions and money. These bandits would kill for one rand. Homes were broken into, muggings on the street a common occurrence. White Afrikaners and ex-pats hastily put up fencing to deter hoodlums from home invasions that were on the rise. Incidents of rape gave our beloved Mother City the nickname "Rape Town."

Now when I walked to the Pick-n-Pay I noticed white women scurry to the other side of the street to avoid a black man approaching in their direction. Inside the grocery store I didn't get the usual greeting, nor was there casual conversation between the white check-out girls and the blacks stocking shelves. The promenade was quiet, streets deserted except for the random kombi slowing down to drop off workers and pick others up before speeding away to the next stop. Tension permeated the air in our little paradise by the sea.

Groceries in hand, I had just left the store when I saw our neighbor's maid, Hadiya. She kept her head down and pushed past me. I called out, not in Afrikaans, but in English to ask how she was doing. She stopped.

The young woman smiled nervously. "Okay, Lady."

"Hadiya, it's me, Mrs. McGhee, Mary."

She nodded but didn't look up. I bent down on one knee to play with the toddler. "We're all friends, aren't we?" The little girl let out a squeal of delight. Hadiya and I laughed. It hurt that she had ignored me. It hurt her too, sadness written on her face. All the same, she could not afford to be seen chatting with a white woman.

Hadiya started to leave. I grabbed her hand, pressed it. She pressed mine back.

In all my worries of impending war, the discomfort of racial tension, nothing compared with the sadness playing out in our sidewalk tableau as each of us took our place along the color divide. It wasn't loneliness anymore that hollowed me. It was loss. For the first time I realized how grateful I had been for Azisa, Mr. Swandie, the building maids and gardeners, all those who had peopled my world in the early days. It had been more than just sharing pleasantries, my news of home—they loved the pictures, couldn't imagine living in such a cold place. They told me about their families as well, their kids and parents, the trials of life in the townships.

With a heavy heart, I wondered if now they would shun me. Patrick was gone when I woke up. Another early meeting.

A bump under the covers with little furry ears stuck out. Teddy. Today he had a yellow post-it on his chest. "I couldn't *bear* to wake my sleeping princess, A & F, Moi." I smiled. It had been eight months since our wedding day. Patrick's affectionate signature—a reference to our wedding day with my friend David singing a favorite Luther Vandross song, *Always and Forever*— warmed me. It had been such a perfect day, a lifetime ago. I refused to be blue.

Azisa had the day off. Patrick would be with the ambassador until late evening. My plan for burning off excess energy without leaving the flat was to spend the morning cleaning house. For me it was therapy, cranking up the music to an ungodly decibel. Mrs. Osborne across the hall was hard of hearing. The people below were on holiday. Blasting upbeat music, moving, dancing, loosened the knots in my shoulders that came with the extra level of anxiety now weighing on us daily, plus whatever tension Patrick brought home that he no longer recognized as stress.

Channeling Tom Cruise singing *Old Time Rock n' Roll* in *Risky Business*, I danced across the hardwood floor to my favorite tunes by Madonna; Prince; Earth, Wind, and Fire. I sang for both me and Patrick, full-tilt boogie driven by the feelings we had rediscovered in Kruger. I mopped the kitchen floor, washed the sheets, vacuumed, dusted, ironed Patrick's shirts, dancing my way through the chores, oblivious to my surroundings for a few blissful hours.

Dancing. We both loved it. As homecoming king in high school, Patrick had polished his take on the most popular moves, including the Swing. A man who liked to dance and actually *could* was as rare in the adult world as it had been in high school. At embassy dinner dances, the other diplomats watched Patrick with a mix of envy and derision, as if he were showing them that He-men—officials and diplomats doing serious work—could actually relax and have fun without feeling foolish. He and I made quite a pair out on the floor, pure joy radiating from both of us.

Such moments were welcome respite, as those of us at the embassy, along with all South Africans—in fact the whole world—waited for the new constitution. Between De Klerk and Mandela butting heads over policy and Buthelezi's demand for a separate Zulu nation, it was a miracle the talks continued at all.

   If anyplace was in need of a miracle, it was South Africa in 1993.

Thirteen
Revelations to a Friend

April 1993

Excitement boosted my energy level. Jane, my dear girlfriend back home, was due to arrive for a ten-day visit. That's all I could think about, all that mattered as we moved into spring. Politically, there were signs of progress. On April 2, party leaders met at the World Trade Centre in Kempton Park. But in protest at the perceived sidelining of the Inkatha Freedom Party, Buthelezi backed out of negotiations.

In addition to President de Klerk and Mandela, another key figure stood out in the negotiations. Cyril Ramaphosa was a seasoned negotiator in industrial conflicts, a leader who drove a hard bargain but was able to break stalemates and find consensus, in the process earning the respect of his opponents. Following his role as visiting Professor of Law at Stanford University, Ramaphosa was elected Secretary-General of the ANC.

At that time seats in the whites-only parliament had always been elected by a winner-take-all system. That system would clearly favor the black majority in any election. But the ANC did not opt for this course. Mandela understood long before the election the disparities in a winner-take-all method would destabilize the country with the likelihood of civil war. It had to be a more equitable outcome. How ironic if the country were to avoid civil war on the way to its first nonracial election, only to have everything fall apart afterward.

Instead of winner-take-all, negotiators decided the configuration of parliament would be based on the proportional representation system—whatever party won more votes would have a seat in parliament. This was an integral part of the five-year executive power-sharing strategy in the new constitution, which Mandela understood would be crucial to creating an atmosphere of inclusiveness and reconciliation, the best way to hold the country together. The white parliament was all for proportional representation in place of being shut out altogether if they'd gone with a winner-take-all, which no one doubted would lead to the black majority winning all the in parliament.

Nelson Mandela showed his wisdom in myriad ways.

At the embassy we had our hands full. As the political landscape intensified, the number and frequency of U.S. congressional delegations visiting South Africa shot up. These official trips required careful planning in maneuvering safely around Cape Town for meetings and events, all done through the embassy. Ambassador Lyman was the key person involved, which meant Patrick was right there with him.

The routine was familiar to us. Delegates would make a stop in Pretoria, then find their way to Cape Town, the beautiful Mother City. Most wanted an audience with Mandela. If they were lucky, they got a photo. We worked long hours, the logistics a Rubik's Cube of schedules and agendas that had to mesh. Our limited staff pulled together with plenty of late nights. No one talked about the turmoil around us as interest in the election peaked across the globe, but an underlying sense of unease filled the air. We kept our noses to the grindstone and pushed ahead.

A successful congressional visit meant no security issues. It took everyone working together to pull one off. "Wheels-up Parties" became a major coping strategy. No one needed that break more than Patrick. He and I took the lead more than once, card games a welcome way to let off steam. Poker topped his list. After a particularly difficult congressional visit that spring, Patrick suggested we host a poker party at our flat. Southwest American cuisine would go nicely with Texas Hold 'Em, the headliner, followed by Dealer's Choice. Luck was on my side when the American Store had tortilla chips and canned green chilies.

The RSVPs came in from everyone on the list—Ambassador and Mrs. Lyman; Political Officer Charles Monroe; Admin Officer, Bev; Marine Gunny Sergeant and other of Patrick's colleagues; and for me, one very special guest—Jane. Her timing was perfect.

We had ample reason to celebrate. The party was a huge success. After a late night of poker and countless pitchers of skinny margaritas, Jane and I stayed in our jammies most of the morning drinking coffee on the deck. Stunned by the view, she asked about the tiny lump of land off the coast. Robben Island seemed too small, inconsequential for the famous prisoner who had put it on the map. Unlike Alcatraz in California, Robben Island, at that time, was not open to the public. But I had contacts who could help. Jane and I made plans to visit the place Mandela had lived out eighteen of his twenty-seven years doing hard labor.

With the same charm and dignity I had witnessed at the convention center two years earlier, Mandela had won over the most brutal guards, the most punishing wardens. He was defiant in oppression, but he had honed his natural capacity for leadership, his innate charisma, into a powerful political tool. Once he succeeded gaining access to the prison library for all black inmates, he taught himself the Afrikaans language, as well as the history of early Dutch settlers, their path from the Boer Wars through World War II to the present.

Mandela wanted to get inside the Afrikaner mind, understand their motivation, more specifically their fears. Only then could he determine a course of action that would win their trust. One man at a time, Mandela changed from a terrorist to be feared into a politician with whom they could sit down at the table and talk about the country's future.

Jane and I noted the parallels between South Africa and the United States—the fight for freedom here and our Civil Rights movement of the 1960s, with the big difference that blacks were the minority at home. Racism, sexism, oppression—from American Indians to African Americans—our country had blood on its hands, the same as Afrikaners had on theirs.

Reuniting with a girlfriend from home brought me the comfort I had longed for, the familiarity of shared history. I had indeed made friends with Helen, Michele, Beverly. But Patrick's admonition not to trust anyone, even other embassy families, had held me back. To these women, I was Patrick's wife, the "+ 1" that spouses inevitably become in the mission hierarchy. With Jane I was me.

Girlfriends have always been a mainstay of my coping. Holding back was not in my nature. In a household of ten there were few secrets. After leaving home, girlfriends had become my pack, Jane one of our tight knit group of ten. Like a Midwest sisterhood we had supported each other through the years. No wonder the adjustment to South Africa had been brutal. The American community here shared a special bond. But protocol dictated the need to report every outside contact, regardless of social context. That doesn't exactly breed trust.

In my eagerness to show Jane everything, we started with an outing to the wine country, a one-hour drive from Sea Point. I told her what Richard Donovan had told me—South Africa's wine country was comparable typographically and in climate to that of France and Italy, adding my sense that the gently rolling hills looked like the wine country in California.

Our first stop was Delheim Wine Estate for a tour and to sample the Pinotage Rosé, which was lovely. From there we were on to Historic Boschendal, a 300-year-old farm in the Franschhoek Valley where French wines were grown by Huguenot refugees given land by the Dutch. Jane and I shared a Vintner's platter with a variety of cheeses, olives, veggies. Our first toast was to the Dutch for giving the Huguenots land to grow grapes for such fine wine.

The second toast of Shiraz was from Jane to the State Department for our assignment to Cape Town so she could drink the fine wine under the oaks with me. Raising my glass for a third toast, my mouth quivered. Whether it was the wine or the comfort and trust of being with an old friend, I can't be sure, but I let it go, all the tension built up over a year.

Through tears, I told her how stressed Patrick had been, was; how I couldn't talk to him, or to anyone; how I was trailed and watched by government goons. I left out the part about the flat being bugged to save her from horror and put an end to future conversation. Loneliness, living with chronic anxiety from social unrest, to say nothing of continual reports of violence and murder—I blurted it all out.

Worst of all, I confessed my abject failure as a diplomatic spouse who had buckled under the pressure. In the beginning I had been so determined to be strong, prove I could handle it. As evidence that Patrick also thought I had failed, I told her about the terrible argument after the dinner at Ambassador Lyman's, Patrick's accusation of my not blending in, his telling me to go home. It all poured out in jagged sobs.

Jane listened until I stopped. "Mary, it was an argument. Married couples fight. It doesn't mean he really believes that. What I see watching you and Patrick is, first, how much he adores you, but beyond that, how proud he is of you—your work at the Embassy, your involvement in the American community, in Cape Town itself. Right now you're down on yourself, so maybe you can't see clearly. But I can."

"Really?"

"Of course. If anyone could pull this off, it's you, girlfriend. You *do* have a lot of pressure, you're under constant scrutiny because you're foreign…foreign and in government. So yes, being a diplomat's spouse has a downside. But you'll look back on this and be so glad you stuck it out. Look at you, an officer in Foreign Service yourself. My God, woman, you get to be part of this moment in history."

I sniffled with a half-hearted nod. "You're right. It's hard to keep perspective. And Patrick can be so distant."

"In his job he has to be. But that's not the Patrick I see. The man I see looks happy…and very much in love with his wife."

"Poker and scotch tend to have that effect."

She swatted me with her napkin. "This is sophomore slump. You'll pull out of it."

Jane's feedback did give me the perspective I needed, the feedback no one here could give me. Sometimes it's so hard to see things clearly without someone else's eyes, someone you trust completely. I didn't want to tell her my brush with depression was more than sophomore slump. But she was right. Patrick did love me.

Girlfriend time with Jane had been a tonic. I had desperately needed familiarity and a confidant. But when she left, homesickness returned. Work at the embassy gave me focus and plenty of contact with people, but that was part-time. With security tighter than ever, any freedom I did have was limited. I was back to waiting—waiting for Patrick to come home from work, to have time off, to decide it was a good time to get pregnant. If we couldn't talk about my loneliness, what were the odds there would be time for The Talk?

These were extraordinary times, I understood that. But living by his schedule was one more way my independence had been thwarted, along with the emotional isolation of trusting no one and watching my back—two psychological constraints that chipped away at marriage. A good marriage. Any marriage. As much as we were in love, the constant pressure posed a counterweight that pulled us apart. Old insecurities reared their heads. Kruger Park, the closeness we had re-awakened, faded under the stress of low-grade war.

The post was a perfect breeding ground for jealousy. Patrick had had a girlfriend on his last mission here. Was he seeing her, confiding in her during what I thought were basketball games and poker nights? My insecurity drove me to work late the nights Patrick did, the nights many staff did. I stayed late as much for companionship as any suspicion about an old girlfriend, which was silly, crazy.

It was well after 7 pm.
WOOOONKKK. WOOOONKKK.
An announcement came over the PA system.
"ATTENTION. THE EMBASSY IS ON FIRE. LOCKDOWN."

My heart pounded as I looked out the office door. Coworkers ran down the hall to their offices. By now, the lockdown drill was familiar. Then someone yelled something about a dirty bomb. I locked the door, then stayed down. The phone, it was close. Should I call Post One?

Who would answer? Who would know what was going on? Patrick was aware of most political protests beforehand through his intelligence sources. In general, these were orderly demonstrations. This had obviously taken everyone by surprise.

The wait was endless. The building was quiet. I crouched at the window for a peek. Nothing. No smoke, no fire. No protesters. No heat under the door. What was going on? It must have been minutes. Then the announcement: "THIS HAS BEEN A DRILL."

Relief! Patrick had ordered it. Protocol demanded I remain in my office until the process was finished, at which point a Marine would swing open one door after the next with the "All Clear" announcement. Patrick, in full RSO mode, came to my door with the carry-on message. My husband was all business like the true leader he was.

The exercise put an end to my day. I shut down my computer. The phone rang. Patrick said he would stay late for the detachment debrief. That was fine with me. My head was still spinning, the inevitable "what ifs" refusing to abate. The adrenaline surge had been a visceral reminder that danger was very real, not that I needed reminding after the Hard Rock Café bombing. The drill had been frightening. I opened my drawer for stationery.

"Dear Mom & Dad,
I hope you are both well and enjoying the grandkids. Things are fine here. I just wanted to tell you both how very much I love you and..." I choked up... *"and if anything should happen to me, please be assured that I died knowing how much you loved me..."*

How I wanted to tell them the truth. But my entire existence was based on a triple life—the one I lived on the outside, my emotional life on the inside, and the Disneyland version of both that I described to my parents. The crumpled paper hit the rim of the trashcan.

This wasn't the first Final Moments letter I had written Mom and Dad. Soppy emotions wouldn't help anything. But after every drill, whether in my head or on paper, writing the letter had served as a way to cope. Patrick was doing a masterful job of keeping us safe with endless preparation like the drill. That's who he was. No one in the diplomatic community doubted my husband would keep us safe. He alone ran the Regional Security Office at the Cape Town Mission, the group within the embassy responsible for supporting the process of moving toward a fair, non-racial election. There were other RSOs in Pretoria he could call, but the reality was that in the immediate aftermath of an attack, we would be on our own.

The stress took its toll on him, on me. Neither of us slept well anymore. And the election was still a year away.

The roar of a motorcycle drew me to the window. It was not a familiar sound in our neighborhood. The biker outside revved his engine again. Pulling his helmet off, he shook the mass of blonde hair. Charles. Patrick met him at the door. "What's with the wheels?"

"Meet Clyde, my speedy bike."

"Is that how you plan to get to the rally?" He turned to me. "As your husband and security agent, I advise against this." Charles agreed. The Honda replaced Clyde. As always, Patrick declined the offer to join us.

The ANC rally was on the University of Cape Town campus. As political officer, Charles would observe and write his report.

Even though this wasn't my first rally with Charles nerves gripped me. It's not as if we were heading into the rural areas where big rallies had been plagued with violence. This would be a small one with a heavy police presence. Still, if I had learned anything from Patrick, it was that crowds could turn bad quickly.

We exited the highway onto City Road. The place was a madhouse. Cars lined the street on both sides. People scurried in every direction. What was supposed to be a small rally had grown. A ball of lead formed in my stomach. We parked and walked toward the university quad. It was pure mayhem, so loud we couldn't speak without shouting. Charles grabbed my hand as we wound our way through the mob toward the center stage well behind the front row. Patrick told me to always stay on the periphery, away from the center of the pack in case of a bomb or outbreak of panic.

The crowd was electrified with energy—old people, young people, blacks, whites, some dancing the tribal Toyi-Toyi chanting, *Madiba—(Mandela) for President*. Homemade election posters in green and gold showed a black fist holding a flag, the shield of hope. A man at the microphone strained over the cacophony to announce the speaker. We could hardly hear. Charles scribbled notes on a pad.

A hush came over the crowd as Allan Boesak, a lead spokesman for the ANC took the stage. As he spoke about the end of apartheid and a new democratic South Africa, the crowd went crazy, overwhelming the speaker with cheers. The buzz of energy, the intensity of it, ran through me until I broke out in goose bumps. How I wished Patrick was next to me in the jubilant frenzy. More people joined in dancing the Toyi-Toyi, hands waving in the air. It was contagious. Before long I was dancing right along with them.

Charles watched me. His body twitched to join the throng. But he was on the clock. A diplomat could not express a position either way. I danced for both of us, for Patrick and for Beverly and for all those who would dance for joy if they could. The din and dance undulated as the crowd stopped long enough to hear the speaker before breaking into a new crescendo of cheers.

Police milled around the edges, ready, but everyone remained on good behavior. I looked at the throng, jubilant faces all. And I was with them, giving my heart to the ideal of freedom for which Nelson Mandela had been prepared to die. A sob grew in my chest. Back home, Patrick and I had talked about the opportunity to witness history. I understood the significance of it, but in my head, as a concept.

That night, dancing the Toyi-Toyi under the stars, shouting at the top of my lungs, *Mandela, Mandela*, feeling the thrum of frenetic energy in my veins, it was no longer a concept. I wasn't witnessing. I was participating—a living, dancing, shouting, waving part of humanity clamoring for freedom. In that very moment, I was one with South Africa. And South Africa was one with me. In all I lived through there, nothing compared with the pulsing jubilation of that moment.

The rally remained peaceful to the end, no small feat in the midst of such an impassioned crowd. Charles and I shimmied our way toward the street for a quick getaway. It was tricky with the crowd dispersing, the energy still high. Once again, Charles grabbed my hand as we zigzagged through the pack. All I could see was the back of his coat.

The Honda appeared. Rally-goers were thick in the street, still ramped up, singing, and shouting chants. We finally made it to the car. Charles started the engine. We couldn't move. Even in their cars, rally-goers continued the celebratory mood. Honking horns became voices of cheer, shouts for Mandela, for freedom. Even at concerts back in the States I had never come close to anything like the party atmosphere of that rally. More and more, it looked like there really would be something to celebrate.

Slowly the crammed pack began moving. We inched forward. People on their way to the bus or kombi moved to let cars pass, the lingering high spirit bringing good will to all. On the highway back to Sea Point it was quiet. My ears still rang. Back at the flat, fighting tears of high emotion, I thanked Charles. Off he rode on Clyde. I couldn't wait to tell Patrick everything.

The minute I walked in, he jumped up from the sofa and threw his arms around me, grinning and swaying us side to side. Between clips on the news and updates on the radio, he had followed it all. On the sofa we sat facing each other as I told him about the craziness, the noise, but mostly, the power of feeling like part of it, part of struggle for freedom on a real gut level, the joy of it. He took in every word.

When I had no more to tell, Patrick pulled me over to him with a kiss. My left knee missed the sofa. We rolled onto the floor, laughing and kissing, adrenaline still thrumming through my body as we made love.

Fourteen
Deadly Spring

April 1993

The Pick-N-Pay was deserted for a Saturday morning. I stood in front of the chocolates selection. Dark, that's his favorite. A few groceries and I would be out the door with the goods stuffed in my backpack. The next day would be Easter, our first as a married couple. At nearly 30, I still loved the traditions—lilies, chocolates, marshmallow bunnies in my basket. There would be no bunnies in Patrick's, but he loved chocolate.

Chocolate didn't sound appealing at the moment after a Saturday morning bike ride to our favorite café on the Victoria and Albert Waterfront where they had a yummy local version of Eggs Benedict with Cape Salmon. Patrick had a rare day off. Ambassador Lyman was taking an even rarer day off to hike with Helen, which meant Patrick was free on a gorgeous Saturday.

Outside the Pick-N-Pay, Patrick had a frown on his face.

"Weather's coming. Let's go." A long cloud hung low over Table Mountain like a tablecloth ready to drop into place, just as Richard had described it the first time we met. Patrick was a closet meteorologist, tracking weather patterns on the Cape.

"Sorry, there was a long queue."

"No worries." He sped off on his bike. I caught up, unsure about the frown on his face.

"What's up, all good?"

He motioned me to pull over on the bike trail. Something was definitely wrong.

"I got a page to call Post One."

"The consul general? What is it? What's happened?"

Patrick looked toward the ocean, then at me. "Holten said Chris Hani was assassinated this morning."

I stared at him, trying to grasp the news. "Hani? When?"

"About an hour ago. I'll know more soon. Princeton's called an emergency meeting."

In silence we sped back to the flat. After Mandela, Chris Hani was the most popular leader in the ANC, beloved by the party youth. He had been exiled like Mandela, was a stalwart leader like Mandela, feared and hated by Afrikaners. But to blacks and other non-whites he was a hero.

Patrick showered, dressed, then left for a briefing at the embassy before an official meeting at the Mount Nelson Hotel. Still in disbelief, I turned on the radio. Hani had been shot dead in the driveway of his home in a multiracial suburb, killed by a white assassin. It was unbelievable, a key African National Congress negotiator and hugely popular black leader murdered in broad daylight.

Oh my God, what would this do to negotiations? Would this be the end?

When the news of Hani's murder broke, absolute mayhem erupted. TV images of the fallen hero in a pool of blood sparked demonstrations across the land—torched cars, roadside bombs. In response, armored police trucks outfitted with machine guns appeared, police in riot gear with rifles. Black protesters had every right to be outraged and think that Mandela's peaceful negotiations with the white government were hopelessly naive. They were ready for war, hungry for it with this latest move to hobble the ANC and start all-out war.

It was nearly dinnertime when Patrick got home, still in shock. We both were. He dropped on the sofa. I brought him tea.

"How did it go? You look exhausted."

"I am. But there's so much work to be done. Hani's assassination is a huge set-back, not to mention a deplorable act and major loss to the party."

Patrick spoke in a monotone, his voice distant, energy depleted. "His wife was away for the Easter holiday. He was supposed to have a quiet weekend after days of speaking at rallies." He rubbed his forehead. "There's so much to investigate."

"What's going to happen now? He is…was…so popular. He seemed to be the only voice of reason that youth vigilantes would listen to. And they're getting more and more dangerous." Patrick didn't answer my rhetorical question; he couldn't. No one could. But we sensed the reaction would be bad. I made an easy pasta dish for dinner. We ate in the kitchen with the TV on. State television interrupted its programming. Mr. Mandela appeared on the screen. It was an unprecedented move that underscored the government's eagerness to defuse tensions from the killing. Mandela offered a brief tribute to Chris Hani. We left the TV on and went to bed.

The next morning, Easter Sunday, Patrick's basket was still in the closet, where it would remain all day. The headlines that morning read:

VIOLENCE ERUPTS IN WAKE OF HANI ASSASSINATION

At least two black protesters were killed in clashes with police and two whites were burned to death yesterday as the nation reeled from the assassination of Chris Hani, one of the heroes of the black liberation movement. A third white man was beaten and had part of his tongue cut out, police said.

As the country faces the prospect of a much larger explosion of violence, the ANC, its political allies and the government urged calm and said Mr. Hani's death should not derail their negotiations aimed at achieving black equality.

Nelson Mandela and other African National Congress leaders decided on Easter Sunday to press ahead vigorously with constitutional negotiations, rejecting calls from militants for a suspension of those talks in protest. The ANC, meeting in emergency session with its Communist Party and labor union allies, concluded that the killing of Hani by a white gunman was designed to derail black-white talks.

The assassination, along with the fact that the alleged assassin himself was a member of the radical white nationalist group AWB nearly plunged the country into a race war. Gun sales shot up as nervous whites panicked.

The all-night vigil held for Hani at the First National Bank stadium outside Soweto ended in carnage with mobs of black youths setting fire to nearby houses and attacking passing cars. At least two people died in these disturbances, which resulted in riot police intervention. One of the white men who burned to death in a house set aflame turned out to be a member of the white AWB that had orchestrated the hit.

Radical AWB leader Terre' Blanche took advantage of the resultant turmoil in the country and more than once during his public meetings at that time told his audiences that if "Hani had not been shot, then if there was a state of war, I would have done it myself!" Violence broke out in Natal and all over South Africa. Nearly every major city center in South Africa was ransacked by enraged mobs. It was nothing short of mass hysteria.

Mandela was crushed at the news of Hani's death. He had great personal affection for the younger man, saw him as the future of the ANC. But Mandela had no time to mourn. He had to act, calm the masses. If he didn't do something quick, violent outrage, not an election, could determine the fate of South Africa. If ever a single moment in Mandela's life called for his powers of persuasion, this was it.

He lost no time. Monday was declared a National Day of Mourning in an effort to quell violence, appease the masses. In a dangerously over packed Jubalani amphitheater in Soweto, a large black township of five million, Mandela addressed the nation. But by the time he arrived, there were already ominous undertones. According to news sources, young men waved sticks and spears, a few carried guns. The rally was clearly intended to transform the anger into political energy focused on Mandela, dressed in a presidential-looking charcoal suit. But with more than ten thousand people overwhelming a facility built for half that number, thousands more pushing at the entry gates, the organizers got Mr. Mandela to the microphone as quickly as possible.

"I understand your anger," he said. The crowd could not be calmed. People surged against the stage and rumbled impatiently throughout his speech. His remarks were interrupted by the pop-pop of firecrackers meant to simulate gunfire and by jeers when Mr. Mandela mentioned his bargaining partners in De Klerk's National Party.

"We can see he's too old and doesn't want to fight," shouted Raseleti Komane, an unemployed thirty-eight-year-old woman.

But Mandela had to reach them. Instead of responding with outrage at the murder, he spoke in the tone of a father who had lost his son. He appealed to the nation to use Hani's death to affirm the man's strategy of peaceful means to achieve a united democratic South Africa for which he fought. Mandela's quiet dignified manner and voice of reason worked. The crowd settled down. If their great leader was willing to keep his anger in check for the long term good of the people, they must do the same.

Never was Mandela's power as the leader of the nation put to such a test.

What happened next was unthinkable. Mandela dismissed the multitude for a peaceful march to the police station. According to journalists and other witnesses at the police station, the crowd was ready to disperse when an armored police vehicle came around the corner, then roared back and forth through the crowd. Another vehicle followed.

When a few young men showered stones on the vehicles, a line of thirty police, most of them white, opened fire with tear gas, shotguns, and pistols. The police later claimed they had been attacked and were forced to open fire. Mandela was beyond outraged.

The national protest that erupted was one of the most violent in months, reflected deep-seated anger over Hani's assassination and growing discontent with the slow pace of negotiations in townships still beset by crippling poverty and hungry for change. Marches countrywide were marred by widespread looting and the killing of four protesters by police
in Soweto.

President de Klerk vowed to crack down on the rioting, promising to send three thousand police and army reinforcements to join the twenty-three thousand-strong force already deployed to halt the escalating violence as millions mourned the black leader. "What happened in South Africa today cannot be tolerated in any civilized country," he declared.

Cape Town hysteria continued all week. I drove with Patrick to and from the embassy each day and stayed in for lunch. A sense of gloom filled the hallways. Across the country, crowd-control marshals deployed by the African National Congress struggled to hold angry youth in check and often failed. In Cape Town, rallies turned into rampages of looting, burning, clashes with the police. "No peace! War! War!" rioters chanted. Two people were killed and a train derailed. The scores of Capetonians injured included a prominent black leader who was punched in the face as he tried to restrain rioters.

At home I kept the radio on full-time as news of the funeral dominated airtime. There were plans to have two memorial services for Hani, one for the Diplomatic Corp to take place in Johannesburg following the first one at a football field in Soweto. Danger was imminent.

All of us at the embassy were on edge. I was very nervous for the ambassador and Helen, who had decided to attend both memorials. Even with the bodyguards and extra security, the funeral day in Soweto would be dangerous. Jesse Jackson would also be there, as well as Muhammed Ali. He and Mandela went way back, the ANC leader himself an amateur boxer back in the day.

Ali, fifty-one, visited the embassy with his photographer to meet with the ambassador. Princeton invited us to join the informal meeting. There were a handful of us, Patrick and I included. Ali, impeccably dressed, actually did a few tricks, juggling three balls, recited a few rhyming poems with his photographer snapping photos. It seemed rehearsed, yet we enjoyed some joking. As he departed at the elevator, he turned to me with a grin. "Is it really true blondes have more fun?" I'll never forget my shock, complete with blushing. Yet I admit it was sort of cool to be noticed, complimented. He was on his way to a banquet at the nearby civic center held in his honor for raising funds for boxing gymnasiums in Khayelitsha and Langa townships.

Chris Hani's funeral was a major event, televised live. In a stadium built to accommodate eighty thousand, more than a hundred thousand mourners crammed in. Helen told me later she was increasingly fearful on arrival with the angry shouts of young men walking to the service. Fires were set, rocks thrown at the steel military and police vehicles along the road. Overflow crowds stood on the rooftops of small buildings surrounding the stadium.

As Helen and the ambassador reached the entrance of the football field, two white faces among thousands of agitated ANC and communist mourners, four additional bodyguards met them. Very unceremoniously, two of the hefty men took hold of the ambassador under his arms and lifted him off the ground, literally carrying him through the crowd. The other two carried Helen across the length of the stadium to the platform where they were to stay for the service.

The white government and the African National Congress, which had begun the week with an extraordinary show of concerted action aimed at heading off violence, ended the day with an exchange of bitter recriminations. Helen said her heart rate was going through the roof as she listened through increasingly irate speeches. Even Nelson Mandela seemed in danger of losing control of the crowd. He did manage to quiet people though his well-thought-out words and passion for peace.

"Black lives are cheap and will remain so as long as apartheid continues to exist," he said, contending that police had treated right-wing extremists with kid gloves. "We want a police force that is there to serve our communities, to protect our lives and property, to respect us as citizens. That is our right."

"Only then can we begin to change the culture in the police force and army that says the people are the enemy." President De Klerk's actions since the assassination of Chris Hani are the best demonstration of this attitude. He deployed 23,000 more troops, telling white South Africans that they had enough troops for them to feel secure. But why deploy troops against mourners?

"Our people continue to die in violence on the trains, in massacres, and by assassination. The killing must stop! We want the immediate installation of a Transitional Executive Council with one purpose: to ensure that free and fair elections are held in the shortest possible time. Above all, we want an agreed election date to be announced."

"When we leave here today, let us do so with the pride and dignity of our nation. Let us not be provoked. The struggle is far from over. You are our soldiers of peace, our army for the elections that will transform this country. Go back to your homes, your regions, and organize as never before. Together, we are invincible."

Spellbound, we watched the speech live on TV at the embassy, hearing it along with the rest of the world. Nelson Mandela accused President F.W. de Klerk of outright corruption, of condoning legal murder. It was his strongest indictment yet of the state police, of De Klerk himself. Mandela had to use the tragic event of Chris Hani's death to push the president to set a date for the elections. Without one, the people would lose faith and the killing between blacks and police would continue.

It worked.

A few days later President F.W. de Klerk announced that one year from now, on April 27, 1994, South Africa would hold its first nonracial election in 300 years. The whole nation, the entire world, had been waiting for this announcement. It was met with a range of emotions. The reality for white Afrikaners brought a sense of desperation. Radical groups on both sides vowed not to give up their drive to prevent the election. No one doubted it would be a rocky road.

One year. It was an eternity.

In the chaotic days following the funeral, I saw little of Patrick, who was holed up with the ambassador at the Mount Nelson Hotel, the historic landmark in a historic city. His role was never more crucial than in this unstable period. At home we didn't talk about it, both of us more than aware of what was at stake, along with the increased pressure that came with it. At the embassy we were warned that Hani's death might not be the last tragedy, to expect vigilante activity to continue from those with a stake in apartheid power.

It became public knowledge that there were more names on Chris Hani's assassin's hit list—ANC leader Joe Slavo, former South African President Pik Botha, Judge Richard Goldstone of the Goldstone Commission that exposed white government support of Chief Buthelezi's party to generate black-on-black violence to derail negotiations.

But the biggest scare was the name at the top of the assassin's list—Nelson Mandela.

After months of bitterness, De Klerk's National Party finally won Mandela back to the table by agreeing to several concessions, which included the release of 500 prisoners convicted of murder and other serious crimes in the guerrilla war on apartheid.

Stress took its toll on Patrick in unexpected ways. One night in late May while playing basketball with the Marines at the University of Cape Town, he broke his tibia plateau—a saddle bone at the top of his tibia which supports the femur. Four days later he was in surgery, but not before preparing for a demonstration, a sit-in, at the embassy. He may have been hobbled, but the State, First Wife, would not be denied. By the end of May he was back at work, leg in a brace. Until then, he had the added frustration of limited mobility, which didn't help the situation at work. Or at home.

It had been another sleepless night, Patrick's cast was like a steel beam that swung my way every time he turned. Caffeine before my first meeting was the first order of the day at work. Bev came down the hall in my direction. Rather than her usual gregarious greeting, she mumbled a hello with eyes downcast as she walked past the coffee room. I didn't take it personally. Bev had a lot on her plate running the consul general's office, as any good administrative assistant does, especially during those uncertain days.

The Consul General, Donald Holten, was in charge of the U.S. Embassy, including visa applications, administrative duties, and communications. He had a packed schedule speaking at events to move diplomatic relations along. With the election looming, his office had been in high gear, many expats on edge about the future of their estates, their future in South Africa.

Like Americans, most Afrikaners, Brits and French were concerned about their properties and businesses under black majority rule, which accounted for the overtone of anxiety. The pressure was tremendous, diplomatic relations prickly, violence erupting every day, especially since Chris Hani's murder. Lots of people were in a hurry to leave the country. South Africans and expats alike were calling in favors for visas to the U.S. It was Bev who handled the brunt of incoming calls from worried Americans. She also handled those from U.S. officials requesting delegation visits, which required excruciatingly detailed planning.

The tension was getting to all of us. Bev ducked inside the ladies room. Either she needed space or a friend. The black pumps gave her away. Bev came out of the stall, blue eye shadow smeared across her lids, mascara down her face in runny black blotches. She clenched a wad of tissue and leaned against the sink next to me. A shudder of sobs came out in one giant exhale.

The consul general had gone into the township for a meeting. Patrick, as Regional Security Officer, had advised us not to go into any of the slums. Political violence wasn't personal these days. It was directed at anyone who happened to be in the wrong place at the wrong time. But my husband couldn't prevent someone from going into the townships; he could advise and warn. And he had. Consul General Holten was confident he would be fine with his driver, a black embassy employee who spoke Xhosa. As consul general, Holten had important work with black leaders in the township.

The memory of my visit to Mrs. Tambala flashed to mind, how even with Mr. Swandie we had barely gotten out safely. When Donald Holten and his driver were en route through the area, locals took notice of the shiny black Mercedes. And the white man in the backseat. A group of teens got riled up, hurling rocks and bricks at the car. Vehicles in the embassy fleet were not armored, except the ambassador's. The driver revved the engine and sped away around a corner. No one got hurt. But a brick cracked the back window, leaving spider-like veins on the glass. Rocks dented the hood. And thugs chased after Holten shouting the racial slur, "One settler, one bullet"—death to whites.

"Oh, Bev. How awful. I know how fond you are of Donald and his family. That's so upsetting." Something told me it wasn't just that. Bev was such a positive person, always happy, humming her way through the day. If she had inner turmoil, I never saw it, even on our Girl's Night Out. Like Patrick, maybe like most officials at the embassy, Bev kept her emotions in check. This episode with Donald might have been the last straw in what had been a particularly volatile month since Chris Hani' murder.

"Every day I get news about a maid who didn't show up, or another girl who's been raped, or someone else from the office getting carjacked. This morning a woman called to report that she was followed home from the market by two black men who made slurs. With all the rapes lately, she was terrified and wanted to know what the embassy could do."

Bev's shoulders shook as she leaned forward with her hands over her face. A big trash container was near the sink. Pushing it to the door, I blocked the entrance.

"Tell me what's wrong, Bev." With a deep breath, she told me about the official State Department email she received stating she was eligible for a retirement seminar in Washington.

"Can you imagine, a retirement seminar? Why don't they just boot me out tomorrow?"

It wasn't just the job Bev loved. It was Cape Town. It was South Africa. She loved it like a native born Afrikaner, considered it her home.

"But this isn't…forced retirement?"

Yanking a roll of toilet paper from an open stall, she had a good nose blow, then scoffed. "No. But the writing's on the wall—'either you do it, or we will.' Not today, not tomorrow. But—" She leaned over the sink and threw cold water on her face. "Oh, I know it's protocol, not personal. But I'm barely fifty-five. Now all of a sudden I'm useless."

Helen had told me this was one of the hardest parts of Foreign Service—the end of a post. You spend two years getting used to a place, a job, a city, a situation, then it's time to move on. Only Bev wouldn't be moving on to another post. A shudder went through me. This is what would be in store for me one day in the not-too-distant future.

"I'm facing reentry to civilian life at this ripe old age. Can you imagine?" She wiped her face dry with a paper towel. "Even prisons help inmates transition to the outside. You'd think the State Department could at least do the same."

"Maybe that's what the retirement seminar is."

"Are you kidding? It'll be all about how to protect the government by not spilling any sensitive beans. They probably use cult-programming techniques."

I stifled a grin. "Oh Bev…"

A downward smile emerged. The paper towel had left red streaks on her face in place of the messy make-up. "Well, anyway, what do you say we meet for a Sundowner's later?"

"A Sundowner's"—Bev's special brand of unwinding—meant a few bottles of Cape Blanc de Blanc and a front row seat where we could watch the glorious South African sun melt into the sea.

"I'll let you in on the juicy tell-all I'm going to write about the cult-induced exit counseling after my 'retirement seminar.'"

A set date for the election was too good to be true. The next morning, the *Cape Times* headlines yelled out:

MASS VIOLENCE ERUPTS WITH BOMB IN EASTERN CAPE

White violence had been a major concern the closer we got to the election. This one had been orchestrated by the radical right-wing AWB led by Terre Blanche, a white supremacist and Afrikaner nationalist group affiliated with Chris Hani's assassin. My stomach flip-flopped at the headline. Will this ever stop? I folded the newspaper and went to get dressed for work. When Patrick and I first arrived in South Africa, the big concern was black-on-black violence, black-on-white violence. At that time, most of the brutality happened in Joburg or the townships. Now it could happen anywhere. Patrick and I had been reviewing our evacuation plan more frequently in case of a possible "drawdown."

That very week of the bomb, Embassy Security—Patrick's team—was highly considering the drawdown order, which would mean all non-essentials evacuating the country first—spouses, dependents, embassy staff, myself included. Next up, USAID, Trade and so on until the embassy was cut down to a skeleton staff of Security (Patrick), Political (Charles Monroe), the new Consul General (Bismarck Myrick), the Deputy Chief of Mission, Ambassador Lyman. It was drilled into our heads to be ready for action at a moment's notice. I would have to leave South Africa along with the other dependents. My duffle bag with evacuation essentials and a small suitcase stood in the corner, always at the ready if and when that drawdown order came.

As community liaison officer, I kept one list in the office and a copy at home with information on all staff—spouse and dependent names, telephone numbers, addresses with priority highlighted in yellow, spouses and dependents first. We had the telephone tree in place, but this was my back-up. All this ran through my head at the *Cape Times* headline. I didn't want to leave the flat that day. Had violence gotten out of control? Patrick hadn't left a note that morning. He hadn't had breakfast. I called Bev. She was getting ready for work. Yes, we were to report to the embassy today.

Two months later, on June 25th, negotiations were dramatically interrupted. Approximately three thousand members of the Afrikaner Volksfront (AVF), Afrikaner Weerstandsbeweging (Terry Blanche's AWB) and other ultra white right-wing paramilitary groups stormed the World Trade Center in Kempton Park near Johannesburg where negotiations were being held.

A peaceful protest led by the AVF and AWB had been scheduled for that day outside the negotiation venue. Reports said the mood had begun as a festive one with AWB supporters bringing their families, even provisions to barbeque. The mood changed when right-wingers began rocking the cars of Kempton Park employees and negotiators. A Viper armored vehicle was used to crash through the windows of the building, allowing protesters in who carried firearms and chanted "AWB."

Police attempted to form a cordon to prevent invasion of the negotiations conference room. They couldn't hold protesters back. Once inside, they were effectively left in control while the multi-party delegates took cover in meeting rooms. The protesters painted slogans on the walls, urinated over furniture, harassed delegates. Police did eventually get control by agreeing that no protesters would be arrested. They made a peaceful exit.

Violence would continue throughout June. According to public records, deaths from political violence for that month shot up to six hundred and five from the previous month's figure of two hundred sixty-seven. The violence was particularly severe in the homeland of Kwa-Zulu—Buthelezi Land—where supporters of Mandela and those of Chief Buthelezi were still essentially at war.

But negotiations did move forward, albeit in jumps and starts. President de Klerk's National Party finally agreed to a power-sharing Transitional Executive Council, at last. The final obstacles to peace were the Afrikaner extremists and Zulu nationalists.

And Chief Buthelezi's demand for a separate nation in his homeland.

That summer my work on USAID projects slowed to a halt. I was banned by the Regional Security Officer, Patrick, from travel to the townships to assess projects. The best I could do was put those projects on the back-burner and focus on other responsibilities. My Secret clearance finally came through. It was a big deal. I was now legitimate. It should have been a moment of victory. But along with everyone else, I was on tenterhooks waiting for the other shoe to drop.

In management meetings we discussed how to build morale through more social gatherings and local events. The most patriotic of all holidays was right around the corner — the 4th of July. The consul general offered to host a celebration at his home. Timing was perfect, giving us a way to channel our energies. Everyone got on board. I always looked forward to the Marine Honor Guard — the processional entrance, our standing at attention followed by the "Star Spangled Banner." At home in the States, I would get choked up at our national anthem. What would I feel like here, now, at this moment in time?

July Fourth, I was at Consul General Holton's home early to help get ready. Two years up, this would be his last event before moving on to the next post. Unable to suppress my public relations/event planning pedigree, I offered to share hosting duties. By now, anyone at the embassy charged with organizing an event turned to me for at least a consult if not a plea to run the thing. Acknowledgement of my professional background boosted my confidence. The work itself was a joy, especially this year.

As the Marine Honor Guard began their procession, a ball of emotion built in my chest. Images of home ran through my head—Independence Day barbecues with my parents, siblings, neighbors, kids running around, hamburgers and potato salad, ice cream, night time fireworks at the park. Patrick sensed my nostalgia. As the Honor Guard began the national anthem, he squeezed my hand, in part as support but also to remind me this was not the place to break down.

I flipped into work mode. As the crowd dispersed after the song, I focused on introducing the consul general to some of our guests. We did the whole traditional bash, a good old American celebration with burgers, brats, beer. Just as we'd hoped, the patriotic celebration gave us the boost of belief and courage to push forward in what promised to be an unpredictable nine months.

Monday morning at the office, I grabbed a cup of lukewarm coffee. As it did every Monday, the mail pouch had arrived in my office. Now it's unimaginable to think about life before the internet. But in 1993, communication still came in the form of paper, including letters from home. U.S. mail arrived weekly in a secure pouch, which is how I sent my correspondence once it was cleared. Letters sent through the regular mail were rumored to be censored.

First, I sorted through my inbox, which consisted of internal memos, local tour and restaurant brochures, story ideas for my embassy *Cape Pointer* newsletter. Then I grabbed Patrick's mail as well as mine. A flyer handwritten in black caught my eye. *Suicide Gorge*. What was this? Some kind of threat? For Patrick? Me? I closed the door to read it.

Sunday, May 2nd, 0500hr.

The second page was written in English and Afrikaans, the third was a map showing a starting point and milestones along the way. Was this a joke? No name was on the flyer. My mind raced.

"It's a dare. The Marines do this every year to challenge macho staffers."

I slumped in the chair across from Patrick, who seemed amused. Suicide Gorge, aptly named for its death-defying jumps between cliffs that ranged from three and twenty meters, was one of South Africa's most thrilling hikes, a gauntlet thrown down for the young and ultra-fit. "Experienced Kloofers only." The nine-hour trek wound in a circle with blood-curdling challenges such as Commitment Jump, Thread-the-Needle Rock, Waterfall Jump, and the end point, the ultimate kloof—Suicide Kloof, the gorge-jump in which, as one kloofer put it, "You look death in the eye."

Stunned, I stared at my husband across his desk. "Since when do Marines have something to prove? Isn't there enough danger as it is?"

"Actually, it's a great diversion, like the Super Bowl." He grinned.

"Tell me you're not going."

His answer came with a slight tilt of his head and a smirk. Of course he would be going. Mr. Potato Head would definitely have a missing body part next to the note I would leave for Patrick by the coffee pot the morning of the hike. Back in my office, I reminded myself that that was who I married, a jock who would never pass up the challenge of competition. It was times like these that made me glad I was a woman, childbirth better than war. Or jumping a gorge.

The mail pouch slumped on the floor. There had better be something upbeat in here after that announcement of suicidal intent. There was. Mom and Dad wrote every other week with news from their world. Reaching inside the pouch, my hand stopped on a heavy envelope. That wouldn't be it. They wrote on tissue-thin air mail stationary.

Addressed to me, the handwriting in blue ink was feminine, different from Mom's. I thought about our first formal invitation in Cape Town—dinner at the ambassador's home. That seemed like years ago, before the break-ins, before Somalia, before Chris Hani's murder.

The letter opener slid through the envelope. Carefully, I teased the paper out as if it might be a letter from Nelson Mandela himself. Better. An elegant wedding invitation announced my sister Kathy's wedding in August, three months away. August would also mark the one year anniversary of my arrival in South Africa at twenty-nine years old. All the clichés about turning thirty and becoming an adult proved true in my case, or at least becoming a mature adult. Some days I was forty, at least a decade older than the bubbly naïve young woman who stepped off that plane.

My little sister, getting married. My eyes tears up. I cried easily these days. Living with anxiety every day threatened to morph into full-on depression. According to the medical book at the embassy, I had several clinical signs—jitters, poor sleep, lack of appetite, low energy. When the list grew to include spontaneous crying, it was time to get help.

The embassy doctor assured me it was a situational depression brought on by the very real pressures of the mission, a common occurrence among those in high-risk posts. It was good to know I wasn't actually going crazy, that my crying and anxiety were both appropriate reactions to our current reality. Still, I felt lousy. And the situation was likely to get worse before it got better.

I did my best to keep the dark moods from Patrick, who had all he could handle without worrying about a depressed wife. On some level he had to know, but in our coded language, we made a tacit agreement to pretend I was coping. As treatment, the doctor advised me to increase my exercise, which would help with jitters and anxiety. It would stimulate my appetite as well, improve sleep, and boost my energy.

Daily workouts became an obsession. My beefed up routine included a nightly bike ride. After work I would get out on the promenade. With the focus of a lion stalking prey, I would race to the end of the waterway, by that time, free of tourists and nannies, basking in the glorious view of the setting sun. On the return trip I got the light reflecting on Lion's Head. Such beauty.

The additional exercise, including weekly aerobics classes, did help with anxiety. Work sustained me through the day, adrenaline and coffee rather than sleep the source of my energy. But at home, I dragged, depleted. Whenever I would start to feel better about the political situation, something else would hit me—the lack of emotional intimacy with Patrick. Around each other we walked on eggshells. I steered clear of anything that might be construed as a demand. He forced himself not to act too distant. When we had time together, that is.

In July, still in his cast, Patrick was due to go back to the States on R & R for a class reunion. When he returned, I would leave. I replayed my time on the *Woman of Desire* set, working nights, crawling into bed half an hour before he had to get ready for work. The old "ships in the night" cliché hadn't applied. I had been happy, excited to be working, which spilled over as welcome energy between us.

R & R would be different. Back-to-back leaves would mean two months apart, a temporal wedge added to the emotional one driving us apart. It was a dismal prospect. Maybe time apart would have the old "absence makes the heart grow fonder" effect. With mixed emotions, I booked my flight.

Tragedy struck a second time before July was out. Four black terrorists from the militant arm of the Pan African Congress attacked congregants at St. James Church in Cape Town during Sunday evening service on July 25th. With automatic weapons and grenades, they killed eleven white worshippers and wounded another fifty-eight. Gcinikhaya Makoma was arrested ten days later and convicted of eleven murders. Violence had crept into Cape Town already, but the Saint James massacre rocked our world. A pall fell over the city.

And that was before what happened next.

Fifteen

Closer to Home

August 1993

My visit home came none too soon. If I had been anxious before the St. James massacre, afterward I was an edgy, tearful mess. On the way to the airport, my body tightened as we passed the outskirts of Khayelitsha. Warm memories of the visit to Mrs. Tambala were overshadowed by more recent events— bombings, carjackings, house burnings, people torching anyone suspected of alliance with the white government. Kids were getting killed, women, innocent bystanders who wanted no part of the bloodbath. Eyes locked on the road ahead, I tried to remember to breathe.

At the gate Patrick and I faced each other and hugged tight. What if something happened to him? Should I stay? We kissed, then parted in opposite directions, both of us turning around for a final wave and air kiss—our own protocol. Patrick was so handsome with his big smile in one of those now-rare moments when his face was free of tension. An urge came over me to run into his arms and go back to the flat. Instead, I boarded the plane.

It wasn't until we were in the air that it hit me—flying away from South Africa was the first time I had felt safe since the flat was broken into a year earlier. I closed my eyes and began the long journey home.

Kathy's wedding was everything she wanted it to be. I struggled. My head was back in Cape Town. Images floated in and out of consciousness like movie scenes. Instead of the church where the ceremony took place, another church popped into my mind—St. James—the massacre. Instead of a ballroom with family and friends congratulating the wedding couple, knife-wielding men surrounded a government informant to necklace him. The high-pitched laughter of jubilant guests became the screams of women and children. Candlelight on the head table was fire in the Hard Rock Café.

Stuck in some netherworld of in-between-dom, I was neither here nor in South Africa. The twenty-four hours of travel had catapulted me out of one world into another too fast. The time warp cut me off from the joy for my sister that lay nascent somewhere inside. Snippets of conversation drifted by, talk of dress shopping and gift choices. It was a bizarre feeling, me as an alien from another planet. The music sounded off, all wrong for the Toyi-Toyi. One minute I wanted to scream at the guests to open their eyes to what was going on in South Africa. The next I wanted to hold my little sister, protect her from everything bad in the world.

It was exhausting trying to stay focused. I needed rest, familiarity. Mom and Dad. How good it was to be home. The apartment over our funeral home looked just as it had when I left. How could time stand still in one place and not another? The three of us spent hours catching up. Mom and I covered the locals, my high school friends, St. John's parish, and their volunteer work at the Senior Center. It was hard to imagine Mom with enough time to volunteer. A trip to Alaska was in the works. Mom smiled more than I remembered. Dad too.

How could I have been critical? What a good life they had — safe, secure, a world where they went to sleep knowing what tomorrow might bring. With all of us kids gone, they had time to talk, eat together, watch TV—reap the rewards of raising a family. In them, I could see the majesty of a long marriage, the mutual respect, the easy comfort, the tiny tender signs of affection between them—fifty years of their own coded language. Growing up, I had seen only parents. Now I saw a couple, a team.

For all the insistence that my life be different than Mom's, a feeling of envy came over me in the presence of two people who simply enjoyed each other's company, basked in the satisfaction that they had delivered eight responsible, compassionate citizens into the world. Would Patrick and I ever have this? Would I look back on my life with satisfaction? I had gone to the other side of the planet to change the world. My parents had done that right here in Lakeside, Minnesota.

"Mary?"

"Sorry, Mom. What did you say?"

She laughed. How I loved that laugh. "I said you're daydreaming again." Mom pushed her chair back and picked up plates.

"Let me do that. You have no idea how I've missed your cooking." Over dirty dishes, we gossiped and giggled and enjoyed being together as if no time at all had passed. Tea towels folded, we looked at the clock, then each other. In unison we said, "Frazier." Just as we had countless nights at nine o'clock, we plunked on the sofa with coffee and Mom's gooey brownies. American TV—how I'd missed it.

Over the next week I got reacquainted with the current pooches—Babe, a Springer Spaniel; Muffie, a toy Poodle. In warm reminiscence we recounted funny stories about the four-leggeds who had been in our lives—dogs, cats, turtles, birds, and one very peculiar guinea pig, Henry. Dad let me use his office and typewriter for a new trade project I'd brought from the embassy. A Richard Clayderman CD played on his sound system. We both loved this French pianist's easy listening arrangements. Dad often played his music during memorials. That was Dad, nothing fake about him. He shared with his client families the same music he enjoyed in his personal life, the music that soothed him.

The office was a quiet room, well-organized as any good business man's would be, full of mementos from grateful families whose loved one's burial he had arranged. What a gift, to have worked in one place long enough to earn the respect of your community. Dad was my mentor. We had talked about his owning his own business, the possibility that I might work for him. It wasn't the first time the possibility crossed my mind. But a summer stint as a radio DJ was all it took to give me a taste of a completely different life. No funeral parlor for me. My future would be in some branch of entertainment or hospitality—glam. It didn't take long to dream of one day owning my own public relations firm.

The house phone rang. Mom yelled from upstairs. "Mary, its Patrick. Hurry. It's long distance."

Patrick? Why would Patrick call? My visit was winding down, but I still had eight days left. I wasn't ready to come home. Not yet. I picked up the phone in the kitchen.

His voice was low, forced. "Mary, something's happened."

My throat caught. "Are you okay?"

"I'm fine. Now listen, I don't have much time. Something bad has happened to an American here…a young woman." He stopped.

"Hello? Hon, are you there?"

He cleared his throat, forcing the words out. "She's been murdered."

I dragged a kitchen chair over and dropped in it. "My God, Patrick. What happened?"

"Amy Biehl, a twenty-six-year-old American was stabbed and stoned to death by a mob outside Cape Town." He paused. I could hear him struggling for control. "I can't go into details now. I've spoken with her parents in California. They're booked on a flight to Cape Town. I changed your ticket to be on that flight with them."

"What can I do to help?"

"Mary, when you land, there's going to be officials and media everywhere. It'll be chaos. I need you to be with Mr. and Mrs. Biehl. Do what you can to get them through the airport as quickly as possible. I'll be there to pick you up."

"Yes, of course, I will." My mind reeled. Murder. Parents. Airport. Media. "Hon, are you okay?"

No answer.

"Patrick? Are you there?"

"I went…to the morgue…to identify her body." A small gasp followed his words.

My poor Patrick—for all his steely resolve at work, he was so sensitive, compassionate. I remembered the first day we drove together to the embassy, the kids waiting for the snack bars he'd been giving them. I'll never forget the tender smile on his face. That same compassion led him to spare this young women's parents the torture of viewing their daughter's mutilated body. Patrick—always the protector. It was his job to identify Amy, talk to the coroner. It was Patrick who went to Amy's apartment to pack her personal belongings, talk with her roommate. My heart broke for him. On some level I had no doubt he blamed himself for failing Amy, though he had never met her. But that was who he was.

Our conversation was cut short. Patrick was needed. Lightheaded, dazed, I sat motionless in the chair, trying to process his news.

Amy had been murdered in Gugulethu, a township like Khayelitsha where I visited Mrs. Tambala, where the angry mob had harassed me and Mr. Swandie. Amy, blonde, blue-eyed, four years younger—we could have been sisters. I tried to stop the thought. It broke though anyway. That could've been me. The trembling started, first in my hands, then my torso, down through my whole body. I startled when someone touched my shoulder.

"Mary, you're shaking. You've lost all your color." Mom pulled a chair over. My eyes stayed downcast. How could I tell her? How could I not? It would be all over the news. I opened my mouth to speak, but what came out was a wrenching groan followed by tears. Mom would have to know. She and Dad would be scared for me. Worse, they would know I was scared for myself. There would be no White Lies Dance this time.

I looked at Dad and saw Patrick, standing at a morgue, as Dad had done hundreds of times in his career; Patrick never had. My whole body ached for him, for Amy's parents, for the racial hatred rocking South Africa. Part of me wanted to stay put, not go back. But how many times in our marriage had Patrick turned to me for help? He needed me to be strong. It was Somalia all over again. But I had made it through Patrick's mission without collapsing in a heap of emotion. Now I would draw on that history, be there for Amy's parents on this unimaginable trip to have their daughter's remains cremated. I would not let my husband down.

After a sleepless night, I packed my luggage. Mom fixed me and Dad omelets, the last of her cooking I would have for another year. She clutched pooch Muffie between us as I hugged her long and hard, holding back tears. Still in her robe, she waved us off. Whether it was lack of sleep, nerves, or the weight of what lay ahead, I struggled to hold it together. At the airport Dad hugged me tight. "We love you Mary, always remember that."

I boarded the plan and asked for help finding the Biehls. They weren't aboard. At the last minute they had delayed their flight.

Patrick met me at the airport, as did the media circus he had warned me about. He and I exchanged a quick glance, his eyes expressing gratitude for my coming home early on the flight that he expected would also contain Amy's family. Two days later at the same airport, a plane would take off for California. Amy would have been on that flight. An airline ticket was among the belongings Patrick boxed up. Amy Biehl was scheduled to go home two days after she was murdered.

The embassy had jumped in right away in the aftermath. Security was a nightmare. The ambassador needed up-to-the minute briefings. The American community was in shock. My fear of violence in Cape Town deepened as Amy's story came out. The Stanford graduate and Fulbright Scholar had come to South Africa to study women's issues and help with the election. The afternoon of her murder she had been at the University of Cape Town with friends preparing educational materials for voters.

Two of the black women needed a ride home to their township. At a church in Gugulethu a political rally had just ended. Riled up with excess energy, people spilled into the street with loud cheers, singing in Xhosa, dancing the traditional Toyi-Toyi.

In her yellow Mazda, Amy turned the corner onto the crowded street. Men began shouting, "One Settler, One Bullet," the war cry to kill white Afrikaners. Someone threw a brick at her car. The windshield shattered.

The crowd cheered, blocking the Mazda. Angry men pulled Amy out of the car. She tried to explain she was an anti-apartheid activist. Her friends tried to stop the melee. Their words were drowned out by shouts from the mob, "Kill her! Kill her!"

Amy managed to break free. She ran. The men gave chase. A fence blocked her way. Trapped, she slumped against the fence, begging for her life as three men stabbed and stoned her to death.

Patrick went to the morgue, to her apartment, called her parents. The consul general's officer asked me to be with the family, assist with logistics during their stay. Patrick would continue to investigate, collect evidence, meet with Prosecutor Niehaus. The Biehls were grateful to both of us. Investigators would find the three militant thugs responsible for Amy's death. There would be a trial. But that would come later. In the meantime, we mourned at the embassy. All of Cape Town did too.

I felt a personal connection to Amy the moment I met Linda and Peter Biehl. A few months later, the consul general asked me to accompany them during the preliminary hearings. That was one of the hardest tasks of my tenure in South Africa—to witness the heartbreak Amy's parents and sister had to endure to bring her killers to justice. Until I sat with them in that courtroom, hate had been a foreign emotion. But when I looked at the killers, the sick smirks on their faces, it was all I could do to stay in my seat.

Bishop Desmond Tutu had been a huge support to the Biehls. He met with them before the proceedings, encouraged them to speak from the heart. To this day I cannot imagine how awful it must have been for them to address the court. It was awful for me and Patrick to watch them suffer, as it was for the American community, which also grieved with them, for them.

Patrick and I both came to know Linda and Peter well. Somehow that made it more real, unlike the countless murders taking place every day that I read about in the paper.

I suppose we all have the capacity to numb ourselves to horror. The brutality of Amy's death, the irony of her efforts in helping blacks have a voice, the devastation her family suffered, all of it was personal, touched my life, our lives, in a deep way. I still have letters the Biehls sent us during that awful time, expressing their gratitude for all we did.

It's funny how you don't know which experiences will change your life—Nelson Mandela's speech in Washington, D.C.; my work at the embassy; the visit to Mrs. Tambala; the terror of escaping the township; the bombing of the Hard Rock Cafe; coping with Patrick's mission in Somalia; my growing fear of being a white woman in an angry black world.

It wasn't one single thing that shaped me. It was everything, good and bad, including Amy's murder. Life became more precious, more fragile. Joy tasted sweeter. Death loomed closer. But I was still here, still listening to Beverly sing Broadway tunes, still riding my bike, still meeting the Donovans for dinner at their favorite Greek restaurant, still climbing into bed every night with Patrick, holding him close.

The world became bigger, my place in it clearer. Patrick and I were no different than other husbands and wives—be it in Khayelitsha, Cape Town, or Kwa Zulu Natal—who wanted to end the day with the one they loved, to sleep among angels and wake to see another day. In losing a young woman I had never met, my heart broke for wives across the land who had lost their husbands to violence. For them, as for the Biehls, as for me and Patrick, the price of freedom was very personal.

That fall, Mandela, De Klerk, and leaders in both parties were hard at work forging a new constitution. Sticking points included minority rights, property rights. As talks stalled, the culture of intolerance continued in party rivalry as radical factions on both sides did their best to undermine the negotiation process. The three-way tug-o-war played out between De Klerk's Nationalists, the ANC, and Buthelezi's Zulu Inkatha Freedom Party.

Making it to the actual election was still very much touch-and-go that fall of '93, the country as torn as ever. The outskirts of Joburg had turned into a patchwork of no-go areas. Pressure was growing on Mandela from blacks for him to move forward to the election before the country imploded into chaos.

Preparation for violence was our best defense, both at the embassy and at home. We reviewed evacuation routes, planned for lockdown. My "bug-out" kit consisted of a duffle bag filled with stash—bottled water, two-way radios, batteries, poncho, candles, matches, dry foods—including my guilty pleasure, Pop Tarts—cash, flashlight, copies of I.D., maps, pain meds.

Patrick and I rarely ate a meal together anymore, but oddly enough now that danger had permeated peaceful Sea Point, I was no longer on the sidelines of Patrick's world. I was closer to him than ever, in part because of Amy's death, in part because I had renewed purpose in my work and better understood Patrick's commitment to his own. South Africa's suffering touched me in a very real way. Change had to come. I would be part of the process. Had I died right then, my life would have mattered. That gave me deep satisfaction.

Protests had become regular events. Some were planned, announced, some not. On a Monday morning, I was anxious to get to the embassy for one that was to check for staff alerts. The mail pouch was in my office when I arrived. A quick check found no cards or letters from home. My in-box did have new memos and a package that had been badly squished in transport. Memos had become became part of our daily incoming mail, mostly security alerts. The top memo referred to the protest that would happen today: SUBJECT: Access during protests—instructions for staff. Elevators would be locked, no access to the parking garage, and so forth.

These alerts were hardly routine for me. Unlike seasoned staff, my nerves were jangled with the emergency prep. Diversion was welcome at such times. That morning I had a good one—the first class in Microsoft training.

Like most organizations, the State Department was switching over to computers, new PCs to replace the antiquated Wangs. Our instructor was my dear friend Helen. I was fortunate in getting into her class of six, as much to spend time with her as to learn the new software system.

Helen hadn't been working at the embassy. She was recruited to teach the computer classes. Her explanation that she had been a first grade teacher at the American school in Ethiopia and knew nothing about computers fell flat. The recruiting officer clapped his hands and said, "Exactly. That's why we need you," a reference to the collective resistance of State Department officials in learning the new technology.

The white minority government in South Africa was way ahead of Americans. It was two decades later that I learned the extent of computer use in South Africa, the real reason the Reagan administration had been reluctant to impose economic sanctions. American computers were in widespread use with seventy-five percent purchased from American corporations. Computer technology was used in virtually every governmental agency—including the police and military—responsible for contributing to maintaining the apartheid system.

Software from the U.S. provided an electronic population register for twenty-five million blacks, passbook records with data on racial classification—name, sex, date of birth, residence, photo, marital status, driver's license, dates of departure from and return to the country, place of work or study, fingerprints—all to keep track of the black population. The Department of the Interior maintained files on the other seven million citizens classified as non-blacks using an IBM hardware system.

Such technology gave police remarkable power. Seemingly innocuous software could be applied to disastrous ends. Given the mission of the private police industry, its allegiance to the military and other state departments, and given the complete lack of procedural rights and safeguards for non-whites, it would be naive to assume that U.S. security and surveillance gear sold in South Africa was not used as a tool of repression. In this way, we were complicit.

The embassy computer room was near the "Grand Canyon," code name for Post One, the Marine post. From our computers, we had a front row seat of the comings and goings, could catch a few words over their short wave radios. That Monday morning as class got under way, a few Marines walked by, then Patrick, followed by Charles. Their movement told me the protest had begun. If it went bad, we would know soon enough.

With the new Excel program open on my screen, I struggled to concentrate. Someone yelled through a bullhorn. We all looked up from our computers. It was hard to make out the words. I excused myself to use the restroom. On my way down the hall, I looked through the barred window. A sea of colorfully clad people had gathered in the street below. Banners with slogans and flag replicas waved in the breeze. Some protesters danced. It seemed pretty calm. I returned to class.

"BUFFALO BILL!" A voice blared over the speaker system. It was Patrick's. Every one of us froze.

"Go ahead, Bam Bam," must have been some code for the Gunny Sergeant. "We've got a Dirty Harry in the fourth floor elevator bank."

An intruder? A trespassing visitor?

"LOCKDOWN!"

A Marine burst into the classroom with the order to retreat to our respective offices. His radio cracked but the message was clear, "We've got ourselves a Kojak."

The crowd had grown in number and energy, the formula for a mob situation. I locked my office door, prepared to wait it out. Screams and scuffles from the street drifted up. Then it was quiet. No one announced the "all clear." It felt like an hour that I had been hunkering down with no word, though it could've been fifteen minutes. My stomach rumbled. I mentally kicked myself for eating the last of the Pop Tarts in my emergency duffle bag two days ago in the midst of a sweet tooth attack.

The squished package from the morning mail pouch lay on my desk unopened. Turning sideways, I read the words stamped on the side: "American goods." What relief. New pop tarts I ordered weeks ago. In the middle of a squished untoasted pop tart, the "All clear" announcement came over the PA. I crept to the window for a look. The crowd had thinned. Smoke hung in the air. Tear gas. Local police working with the embassy, with Patrick, lined the chain link fence between the embassy and the dispersing crowd. My mind raced. I slipped into the hallway, hoping someone would know what happened. Officer Brown came out of her office.

"What was this all about?"

"A peaceful protest, freedom march, pro-Mandela. It wasn't us."

A peaceful protest? Not us? But why the tear gas? My mind scrambled to make sense of it. Amy's murder had shaken us to the core, left a dark cloud over the American community. No one was immune to the violence. And nowhere was completely safe—not home, not the streets, not the embassy. Peaceful protests could very quickly turn bad in the edgy environment with political nail-biting, racial tension. But the trauma of Amy's murder still had a hold on all of us, on Patrick especially, the task of keeping us safe heavy on his shoulders. He wasn't about to take a chance.

Sixteen

Mothers, Fathers, Sisters, Brothers

October/November 1993

Linda, Peter and Molly Biehl returned to Cape Town two months after Amy's murder for the preliminary hearings. Patrick and I, along with Ambassador and Helen Lyman, joined them at a Memorial Mass at St. Gabriel's Church in Gugulethu, the black township where Amy was murdered. More than three hundred people attended the Mass—several speakers reminding us all that it had been Amy's dream to be in South Africa after graduating from Stanford to promote the election that would make South Africans citizens in their own country again. That's what I tried to remember to comfort my own mind. My heart was not so easy.

All of us stayed strong for the family with hopes our compassion, our tears, would offer some small bit of comfort. Their daughter had been loved in Cape Town by all who crossed her path. Patrick and I had only in death, yet we had come to love her, too. One night after I returned from R & R with the Biehls, Patrick told me how hard it had been for him, how he cried in Amy's flat as he boxed her things to ship home—keepsakes and letters, clothes, books, records, photos of her new friends wedged into the frame of her mirror—the normal things of any young woman living a fully engaged life.

After the service the family wanted to visit the location where Amy had fought for her life, took her final breath when she couldn't escape her killers. On the drive from church my stomach tightened. The Mass was one thing, but I dreaded the site visit, struggled to understand. It were as if Linda and Peter wanted their daughter to know they hadn't left the country without acknowledging her final moments, how terrified she must have been as she ran from the mob.

At the field the Biehls walked first to the fence Amy had clung to as she died. The cold lump in my gut turned to stone, it's weight pressed against my chest. My feet resisted each step the closer we got to the fence. Voices became muffled, distorting the words I struggled to follow. It was warm out, the sun was high, yet a shiver ran through me.

Amy's parents and sister locked hands at the fence. The image of men attacking Amy made my stomach turn. Did her family dare to imagine the scene, wonder about Amy's last thoughts as she faced death?

I turned away, but the comparison had already formed—what if it had been my parents, my sisters and brothers standing there? Khayelitsha flashed through my mind, the escape with Mr. Swandie. I stepped backward toward the car with a powerful urge to jump in and lock the door. Standing in the field with our small group that day, it was hard believe such sadness could take hold of one heart.

The Biehls returned to their hotel, Patrick and the ambassador to the embassy. Helen stepped over to me. "Mary, come back to the house with me. I'll have Maarit fix us a nice lunch."

Dear, sweet Helen, always sensitive to others. But I didn't want to fall apart on Helen's patio. My guess is after one glass of wine that's exactly what would happen, just as it had with Jane. This was something I had to process on my own, as if comfort might cancel everything bottled up in my aching heart, the feelings I had for Amy, for her family. Part of me didn't want the pain to go away, another part wished there were some escape. Helen was offering it—friendship, solace.

"Thanks, Helen. I need to go home. Let's make it another time. I appreciate your offer." We hugged. She understood.

At home I sat on the couch in stillness, staring at the vast Atlantic. The powerful emotions bludgeoning me at Amy's murder site were gone, my body rigid, eyes locked in trance, mind a vacuum.

A mechanical thrum cut the silence. In the vast sky a plane appeared over the ocean making a slow U-turn. Through some tiny crack in my numbness, a thought emerged in slow motion, then clutched my insides—a plane just like that one would take the Biehls home the next day, without Amy. A small gasp escaped. Armor that had protected me all day long, all these months long, gave way. The floodgates opened. With an anguished cry, I let the deluge come.

My body ached with sadness, not just for Amy, but for every South African whose death I had turned away from on the news, in the paper, afraid to imagine what those mothers must have felt losing a child. Countless images flooded my mind—once-blurred faces of angry young men suddenly came into focus, each one loved by someone; formless shapes lying in the street became the human bodies they were. I saw crying women, frightened children. The massacres, the marches, the brutality of renegade police—all of it filled my head in harsh, unrelenting scenes of death.

I cringed in pain, imagining the blow of a police baton, the smothering feel of tear gas, guns and knives and spears and machetes. A teenager necklaced—a petrol-drenched tire around his neck as he burned to death; little kids blown apart in the blast of a grenade, or hit by shrapnel. Death, so much death.

In great sobs of despair I fell sideways on the couch and cried like a grieving child, cried for them all—sons and daughters and husbands and wives and sisters who had died for a freedom they would never experience. All the anguish I had denied for months burst forth, overwhelming my defenses. There was nowhere to go except with it. Feel it. Mourn for Amy, mourn for all the Amys, men and women alike.

My body broke out in a cold sweat. I wasn't ready to die for my ideals. I had never suffered like they had. Maybe I couldn't begin to know a life of oppression at the hands of another. Maybe I was a coward. But I didn't want to die.

It was dusk when I woke up. Patrick wasn't home yet. My head ached. My stomach rumbled. A banana would keep me upright until dinner. Wrapped in a throw blanket, I suddenly remembered it was Mom's birthday. There was still time to call, nine in the morning her time.

"Mary?" Mom inhaled deeply. "Mary! What a surprise. Honey, is something wrong? You sound like you've been crying."

There was a second click. The government goons. "Hi, Mom. Tail end of a cold." I forced a tone of gaiety. "Happy Fiftieth Birthday!" It was her sixty-second.

She giggled. "How are you, Mary?"

Oh, Mom. My heart is broken. Today I watched a mother face the unthinkable. I wish you could hold me, hug me tight, never let go.

A sob threatened. I held my breath until it passed.

"I'm fine, Mom, really. Is Dad taking you out for your birthday? Bowling?" I loved seeing my parents act silly and outright affectionate when they bowled, showing glimpses of what they must have been like in their twenties, young and in love. Dad couldn't resist Mom's laugh any more than any of us could, a warm, reassuring sound that said all was right with the world. It had been so easy to believe that as a child. If only it were true this moment.

I closed my eyes, pretended Mom was in the living room with me, felt the familiarity of her presence.

"Dad has another burial today, then we may go to the Supper Club for prime rib." Prime rib at the little restaurant on the edge of town was Mom's favorite. Her voice softened. "Mary, Dad and I saw the news about another bombing. Are you sure you're safe?"

"My Special Agent man is by my side day and night." I faked a giggle with hope of a like response. "You know how the news exaggerates everything."

Mom didn't giggle back. Silence told me she knew I was lying. If I had told her the truth, it would have been the last good night's sleep she would have until we got home. I maneuvered the conversation to my younger sister Kathy, the last in our line of eight, about to have a baby.

"I'm going to write stories for my new niece, share my time living abroad. When she's older she'll appreciate it and, who knows, maybe go into Foreign Service someday herself." I regretted the words the moment they left my mouth, the image of Amy's body tumbling out with them. If only I could go home. But then what would I write for my unborn niece? That her aunt had let a gang of thugs rob her of ideals because she was too afraid to stay in a country struggling to free itself? That she went home with her tail between her legs?

The phone clicked again. Goons. I kept the conversation short and turned the focus to Mom's excitement about our growing clan, as Dad referred to our ever-expanding family. I was able to keep it together long enough to say our goodbyes. The line went dead.

I scoffed. What a fool. It hadn't been me protecting Mom. It was the other way around. By accepting my little white lies, Mom let me step back into a world where people bowled and ate prime rib at the corner restaurant and went to bed at night feeling safe in their beds. From half a world away she was doing whatever she could to support me. If white lies made me feel I was shielding her from reality, then she would go along. It's what moms do.

Guilt. Shame—the old familiar feelings emerged in the wake of our call. For a good Catholic girl, guilt and shame were easier to deal with than the horror of violent death still fresh in my mind. As the child who had moved away at nineteen and rarely came home, I understood South Africa was an unimaginably foreign place to Mom. Of course she was worried.

I *would* write those stories for my niece—not as the aunt who turned away from belief in a better world, but as one who fought for the same ideal Amy had died for, that all the Amys had died for. She would stay with me forever, a powerful reminder that a life without belief in a better future for all is a life without meaning. My commitment to the mission took on new weight because I *could* die, because I *wouldn't* run.

Because in her absence from the world, Amy Biehl would be present in me.

In death Amy helped me find my strength, Amy and her mother. Linda Biehl taught me that you can indeed survive that which you think will break you. Maybe I couldn't survive what she had gone through, what thousands of South African mothers had gone through. I'll never know. But that day in Gugulethu township, Linda Biehl showed me she could go on, embrace what her daughter had died for rather than yield to bitterness in its wake, go beyond forgiveness with the unbelievable generosity of spirit she would show down the road in a story that tests the bounds of credulity. But that would come later.

By late fall, fear in the weeks leading up to adoption of the interim constitution was tangible. It was in the air, even in Cape Town, even in Sea Point. Phrases like "hacked to death with a *panga,*" and "*shot with an AK-47,*" or "*burned to death in her house,*" had become common, almost cliché. Killings of blacks, coloreds, non-white and whites—anyone and everyone was at risk. Assassinations and executions in the homelands and hostels (where temporary workers lived) were a weekly occurrence, with barely a mention in the newspaper. Whites caught in the fray got news coverage.

Threat of an armed insurrection was real, said an article in *Business Day*. Both the right wing Freedom Alliance and Buthelezi's Inkatha Freedom Party still refused to negotiate. In the cities, commuters were thrown off the trains. People were mugged, robbed at gunpoint.

Mandela continued his accusation of President de Klerk of conjuring the violence to prevent the election, even as they worked together on the interim constitution. Negotiations teetered on the brink of collapse as Mandela grew angrier and De Klerk held firm to denial. The entire country—including the military and police—would be thrown into a state of total chaos had the talks come to a halt. Each morning brought a new round of uncertainty.

Then one day the tide turned.

In the early hours of November 18, 1993, a Monday morning, negotiators —Mandela, President de Klerk and the Multi-party National Federation—ratified the Interim Constitution and put into place a Transitional Executive Council to oversee the government during the run-up to a democratic election. Mandela and De Klerk had finally met in the middle.

That day was a turning point for South Africa. There was no going back. There would be months of conflict and bloodletting ahead, but the deal was sealed. Negotiators agreed that the country would be ruled by a government of shared unity (De Klerk and Mandela) after the election, but it was unclear how the cabinet would function. De Klerk's National Party wanted decisions made by consensus. Mandela wanted the president to be in charge. They compromised. The president would have final say after hearing from the other parties.

This process was a familiar one for Mandela. The future president had grown up in the bush as the son of a king, encouraged to play and work together in groups, an early introduction to the value of collective effort. After his father's death, Nelson was sent to the royal palace to be raised by a regent. He had a privileged upbringing, including the best university education. As a boy hovering around when the regent held court and dealt with disputes in the tribal community, Nelson learned to listen to every side of an argument before offering his own opinion, then find the best solution for all concerned. It was an approach to problem solving that continued throughout his life.

Once the interim constitution was ratified, there was a collective sigh of relief at the embassy. The other good news that fall was that the United States lifted economic sanctions. President Clinton asked Commerce Secretary Ronald Brown to lead a South African mission to explore trade and investment opportunities. President Bush had earlier issued an executive order lifting virtually all bans against doing business with South Africa. But the Transitional Constitution was solid proof that De Klerk and Mandela could find their way to a democratic model of government and political stability.

A sense of renewed optimism took hold. The end was near. The election would happen. In the meantime we had to get from one event to the next. Our optimism spilled out in good ways. The new consul general, Bismarck Myrick, with his ever-enthusiastic diplomacy, suggested we hold a Thanksgiving dinner for the families of the townships. He had an embassy list of eighty men, women and children to invite. I volunteered to help plan, along with the other spouses.

We would pre-order turkeys from France, which was faster than shipping from the States, and find locally grown cranberries. Using protocol, I made arrangements for transportation from the townships to Bishopscourt, recalling from my own trip into Khayelitsha the length of time, taking into account where there would be a change of vehicles to get to this neighborhood. The buffet dinner and games would be hosted in Consul General Myrick's immense backyard. Diplomatic spouses with kids who were familiar with games for a wide age range, took care of that part of the agenda.

Celebrating Thanksgiving with our traditional American menu and the added energy of games helped all of us feel connected to home. Since South Africans didn't get the big deal about Thanksgiving, we considered telling them our story of the Pilgrim's landing. A metaphorical slap in the face brought us to our senses. Our belief in Manifest Destiny—divine ordination that white man should control the land from sea to shining sea—rang a similar bell to Calvinist Christianity. We'd skip the share.

It was a wonderful afternoon with kids playing rugby, families visiting, friends catching up, Patrick and I enjoying our part. For one afternoon there was no politics, no violence, and no tension. If I live to be a hundred, that's one Thanksgiving I will never forget.

Ambassador Lyman was well acquainted with the ever-present pitfall of low morale in a difficult and dangerous post. He encouraged me to continue planning events and activities that would carry us through to the election, still five months away. As a major tourist attraction, it surprised me the number of colleagues who had never hiked Table Mountain, or even ridden the tram. In the upcoming issue of the embassy newsletter, *The Cape Pointer*, I would write about the mountain, its history and significance over time, followed by an organized field trip up one side with a tram ride back.

Though I loved publishing the newsletter, it was an intense process getting it out the first of each month. The embassy PR department—U.S. Information Services—was aware of my background in the States. For PR we teamed up. Their staff and I worked together on many of the same projects and helped each other at events courting journalists, providing story ideas, spin on publicity for added optimism to boost morale. That helped.

"I expect your nose is buried in this month's newsletter. Or are you working on the delegation visit?" Bev and I often ran into each other at the coffee counter.

"Newsletter then delegation. I need to book hotel accommodations, so let me know of any date changes." We looked at each other and laughed. Things were always in flux until wheels down on the tarmac. More and more congressional delegations were visiting the closer we got to the election, with scheduled visits in Pretoria before heading to Cape Town. Admin Officer Sands approached me with a memo.

U.S. Commerce Secretary Brown and his delegation would be arriving on a trade mission with touchdown in two weeks. This was major. More than another congressional delegation, this visit had weighted significance because of what it meant for South Africa's future economy. Our staff was already stretched to the max, Cape Town overrun with officials visiting from the States. So it was no surprise that tasks in planning landed on my desk. Managing the logistics of these complicated visits with large numbers of delegates, coordinating their movements as well as concurrent meetings and events was right up my PR alley—hotel accommodations, transportation to meetings, dinners—all of it had to be coordinated.

Patrick would be planning primary, as well as alternate routes, working with U.S. Special Agents as well as South African police on Secretary Brown's detail. Schedules were likely to change at the last minute, as well as numbers of officials attending an event or meeting. Problem-solving and quick thinking were paramount. I lost no time getting started.

It was almost six-thirty when Bev popped her head in my office.

"Hey, I'm going through my closet tonight. How 'bout joining me for a sorting party?"

As a fellow clotheshorse, Bev and I had started an informal clothing drive. It had grown over the summer months with staff turnover—foreign service workers ending or beginning an assignment, families moving in or out—which meant new closets to plumb. There would be another drive near winter as warmer weather came on strong. Each time Bev and I chose a new organization as recipient of our donation, from St. James Church to a township school.

It was Patrick's basketball night. He dropped me off at home, then headed to the university courts. A quick change into jeans, and I walked to Bev's with a bottle of her favorite wine in hand—Boschendal Blanc de Blanc. The doorman buzzed me in, as familiar with me as Mr. Khumalo was with Bev. The smell of curry hit me. Bev had gotten take-out. A bottle of wine chilled in the fridge.

The flat had two bedrooms. Closets in both were stuffed. I sat on the bed in the master with a glass of wine. Bev had already started three piles—donate, save, tailor. It was like shopping in a closet. We toasted our mutual love of haute couture. Her closet reflected a long career in diplomatic service—beautiful tailored suits, tasteful dresses—most in navy, typical of conservative work attire. But she had another side to her.

"Oh, if these clothes could talk." She held up a devilishly sexy dress with a deep V-neck. She handed me a cashmere sweater in coconut, saying the color was better suited to my blonde hair than her brunette. For those few hours I had an older sister again. In a family of eight, with four sisters, I was the beneficiary of hand-me-downs from fast-growing older siblings. I didn't care that they weren't new. Each of my sisters had her own style, including me. Sharing clothes challenged each of us to come up with an innovative look.

I watched Bev hold up this blouse and that pair of pants, this sweater and that suit, as we conferred about which pile to assign. She reached in the closet, then twirled around, holding a floral ruffled number against her body. "This is a doozy. I wore it on a date a million years ago. I can't bear to part with it. I'm designating it as 'closet art.' A new category is born."

Like my sister Marcy, Bev loved to regale me with stories about her boyfriends. She had never found The One. It wasn't for lack of smarts, beauty or charm. Between the two of us, Bev was the consummate Mary Richards in the Tyler Moore show, a career woman to the core who treasured her long, productive tenure in Foreign Service with the State Department. She loved travel, new cultures, the challenge in high-risk posts, noble causes.

Neither of us brought up the retirement cloud hanging over her head. As the evening wore on, we drank wine, ate curry, played music, and got silly. Scarves and hats became props for mimicking celebrities. Bev belted out her favorite Rodgers and Hammerstein tunes when particular outfits tapped into her Broadway musical repertoire.

Across the way lights went on in our flat. Patrick was home. With a Tupperware of curry, Bev sent me on my way, aware that time with my husband was precious. "Next time, your closet," she said with a hug.

An orange glow lit up Lion's Head. Inside I was glowing too. Friendship is therapy for women. How different things would be for men if they could be silly, share problems, let down their guard with each other. With a smile I hummed the tune from South Pacific Bev had sung, "I enjoy being a girl."

Once word was out that he was going to South Africa, with the possibility of a handshake or even a photo op with Mandela, the list of visiting delegates in Secretary Brown's delegation grew, with more officials on board. As names were added, hotel and transportation logistics were adjusted accordingly. Schedules changed. I rolled with it.

There were a million details to cover in making it easy and safe for Secretary Brown and his burgeoning delegation.

Patrick focused on both Secretary Brown and Ambassador Lyman, their myriad meetings and events in the Western Cape. He was immersed in planning sessions with Secretary Brown's security team, with the South African security and police, briefing the mission and the marine detachment.

It took the effort of all of us, the whole crew to pull these visits off without a hitch, but at home I liked to kid Patrick that it was Team McGhee and Byron. We were back on the dance floor, in perfect sync. The hours were long. Most mornings we got up early, grabbed a coffee and headed directly to the embassy. November in South Africa meant late spring, which meant long days, late sunsets. Even so, most often we got home after dark. But how the time flew.

Delegation visits might have been a lot of work, but there was a huge upside. They infused the embassy with a special energy, as if we were offering our visitors a preview of the miracle to come. Had there been tee shirts that said "South Africa Spring 1994," some vendor could've made a fortune. Congressional visits had a collateral effect as well. As optimism grew in the global community, it became increasingly clear to President de Klerk's National Party that Mandela's presidency was undeniable.

The whole world was watching, waiting for the inevitable transition of power from single to multi-party rule. Any collusion that had gone on between De Klerk and Chief Buthelezi to derail negotiations and prevent an election had come to naught—so far, anyway. The curtain had been pulled back on Oz. Now we just had to make it to April 27, 1994.

Optimism was welcome. It had been a difficult spring and summer with the deaths of Chris Hani, Amy Biehl, the St. James Massacre. My busy schedule at work helped keep me focused on the future, the mission taking on new life as the dream began taking shape into reality. Not since Kruger Park had I been this happy. Sometimes I was close to Patrick, sometimes he seemed a million miles away.

But I had begun to understand that marriage, at least for us, meant the waxing and waning of emotional intimacy.

The trick was to be patient during the waning times—weeks, even months—and hold tight to belief the feelings would return, that we would reconnect. And that's the way it happened. Patrick and I always found our way back to each other. As I had with our trip to Kruger, when I sensed us drifting apart, I waited it out, then found a way around the waxing and waning to center— a full moon. I figured that if our marriage was based on a deep love and respect, this was the natural rhythm of two individuals trying to live their lives in sync. Add stress to that, and it wasn't hard to understand wreckage left in the wake of life in the foreign service.

By the time Commerce Secretary Brown arrived on November 28th, the number of congressional delegates had grown to fifty, the trip extended from two days to four. Secretary Brown's mission was the first of its kind to help construct a new non-racial society based on political and economic justice. Secretary Brown arrived first in Johannesburg, where he met business leaders, blacks in particular, before heading to Cape Town to meet Mandela, President de Klerk and Finance Minister Derek Keys.

The Saturday of arrival we were ready for the red-carpet welcome from government and African National Congress officials. Optimism filled the air. Secretary Brown had said there was a good chance the United States and South Africa would sign an Overseas Private Investment Corporation agreement, giving U.S. federal government backing to investment, which raised the confidence of U.S. investors.

Monday morning Ambassador Lyman hosted breakfast at his home in Bishopscourt for Nelson Mandela and Secretary Brown. For the next four days we transferred dozens of delegates around the Cape like puzzle pieces, all needing to fit in the right place before it was scrambled again for the next thing. As if the formal and informal meetings weren't enough to keep all the pieces in place, delegates also wanted downtime in Cape Town's high-end shopping district.

That meant more coordinating of transportation, booking lunches, juggling free time in their schedules. And of course, the delegates all looked forward to the main event—a chance to meet Mandela.

They got their wish. Mandela said he would speak to the group in a brief informal gathering before the official private meeting limited to U.S. Secretary Brown, ANC Allan Boesak, and a few others at the ambassador's home. Patrick was there, awaiting the arrival of Mandela and U.S. Secretary Brown, who traveled separately from the hotel to the ambassador's residence. My job was to meet the rest of the delegation at the hotel and escort them to the ambassador's home, their briefing docs in hand. We arrived twenty minutes late. The mini bus had to pass through levels of security at designated access points before arriving at its final staging position in the lower parking area at Ambassador Lyman's residence to await further instructions.

Patrick and local security police covered the home. As anxious delegates waited in the bus, Patrick appeared. He walked toward us with Ambassador Lyman, escorting Nelson Mandela to the lower parking lot where we waited. Laying eyes on Patrick was my sign to begin forming a meet-and-greet reception line. Slowly I invited the high level U.S. officials off the bus. There was no pushing or shoving, of course, but excitement filled the air. A busload of wide-eyed kids about to meet Santa Claus himself could not have been more eager.

Mandela approached with his trademark warm smile. In a crush of enthusiastic mayors and congressmen surrounding the future president of South Africa, the formal meet-and-greet line broke down. Pushy officials elbowed their way closer, easing the ambassador and me to the sidelines. The newspaper photographer clicked away, one handshake to the next. Mr. Mandela was his usual gracious self, eloquent in speech and manner, as he expressed his gratitude to the delegates as representatives of the U.S. for supporting the future of South Africa's economy.

It was a moving moment, being in the presence of this dignified man who was both noble icon and wily politician. The delegates stood in awe, great big grins on their faces. It was impossible not to feel the special weight of the moment. Had smart phones been around in 1993, photos on social media would have flooded the internet, a very different encounter from the one we had where pure excitement held center stage, rather than the recording of it. We were free to bask in the moment of what would become a very special memory.

Patrick stayed on with Ambassador Lyman. I returned with the U.S. delegates to the hotel, as each had other meetings or alternate plans. For shopping, I took a group to the city center for local art and curios, like a schoolteacher on a field trip. It was a heady feeling, anticipation of the election dominating conversation. I never lost sight of my own presence at this moment in history.

The days were a blur of activity. Before my groove had worn a path, the congressional visit was over. I joined the delegation en route to the airport, which took us past Khayelitsha Township. In hushed tones the delegates discussed the abject poverty of the townships, the significance of the now-lifted economic sanctions for recovery and future growth. A few delegates spoke of plans for a future visit, the way most people did who came to South Africa, diplomatic families included.

Patrick and his security team had arrived at the airport in advance of departure. The delegation got a warm send-off. Then they were on the U.S. Air Force jet from Cape Town back to Johannesburg and from there to the U.S. Our gang on the ground let out a collective sigh of relief. The trip had come off without a hitch.

Seventeen
Rhinos Bearing Gifts

December 1993

"Hon, you are a man of many talents. Travel agent is not one of them."

Patrick tossed his shirt at me as I leaned in the doorway of the bedroom while he changed into jeans. I caught it with one hand. "Listen to how this travel magazine describes this 'vacation destination,' as you refer to it. And not to bring up your track record, but where have I heard that before? Here's what *Exotic Travel* says."

"The SKELETON COAST IS DUBBED THE HELL GATE IN NAMIBIA. SEPARATED FROM THE OUTSIDE WORLD BY SWAMPS AND RIVERS, THE AREA IS NEARLY INACCESSIBLE, THE BARREN DESERT ONE OF THE MOST DANGEROUS REGIONS IN AFRICA, UNTOUCHED BY HUMANS. Are you hearing this? It's not exactly the Amalfi Coast."

He answered with a kiss as he walked by. I kept reading.

"IN ADDITION TO DIFFICULT ACCESS, THE AREA IS BARREN AND DRY, FULL OF SKULLS. IT'S HARD TO GET WATER AND RAINFALL IS RARE. THE BUSHMEN WHO FIRST INHABITED IT IN THE FIFTEENTH CENTURY CALLED IT THE LAND CREATED WHEN GOD WAS ANGRY."

"And yet…here it is, featured in a Travel Magazine."

"Even the name is creepy. Skulls and Shipwrecks as the highlight attraction?"

Grabbing the magazine from me, Patrick rolled it into a cylinder and tapped me on the head with it. "Trust me, Mar. I wouldn't lead you astray. Not like that, anyway."

His devilish grin made it impossible to argue. I didn't care where we went, as long as we were away from the stress of work for a few days.

Twelve hours alone in the car worked its magic. The further we got from Cape Town, the more relaxed I became, tension blowing out the window like so much hot air.

Stress lines on Patrick's face smoothed out with every passing mile. Our first stop would be the Fish River Canyon in southern Namibia, the largest in Africa, Namibia's own Grand Canyon. Never having seen our version in the States, I was excited to visit this one.

My heart rate ratcheted up a notch as we reached the border between South Africa and Namibia. The country had been independent since 1990. Three years earlier this would have been German Southwest Africa, reflecting its European colonization. Passports in hand, Patrick slowed as we approached the crossing. A beefy border guard peered in the window. Patrick started to lower it to hand him our ID, but he waved us through. It might have been the diplomatic plates, or maybe Namibians welcome newcomers. The travel magazine might have equated "deserted" with "exotic," to entice tour companies to book their Jeep tours, but my guess was that Namibia needed all the inhabitants it could get.

The border in our rearview mirror, I reached behind the seat into my backpack for ostrich biltong—beef jerky—and handed a piece to Patrick. The road was deserted, like the countryside. We drove for hours without passing another car, as if we were the only two people on earth. The place was appropriately named, "namib" meaning "vast land." Four hours into our trip, and the turmoil in South Africa was a million miles away.

December had been the perfect time for a quick getaway after the success of Secretary Brown's congressional delegation visit and before the next group arrived in time to meet Mandela before the election. Except for a long weekend here and there, Patrick and I hadn't been away since Kruger Park nearly a year earlier. Decompressing was important.

More than that, we badly needed to reconnect. The job required everything of Patrick. He had to stay focused around the clock. Vast open space and distance from Cape Town erased years from his face, his focus intent on the unpeopled landscape. One week. That's all we had. I would make sure it was enough.

The car was loaded with camping gear, our response to stories of travelers stranded in the desert. An inhospitable place brought its own danger. In Cape Town we had grown used to violence taking place all around us. Death from the elements—lost in the Namib Desert—hadn't sounded as daunting as it otherwise might have. The quiet was seductive. At home in Minnesota we had big empty spaces where you would be in trouble if stranded. But I had grown up with snow, took measures to stay safe. Hypothermia as a mode of death was more appealing than dehydration, a peaceful drift into sleep with little suffering. Here a cruel end awaited. A sense of forbidding washed over me. I began wishing for some sign of humanity.

Thirty minutes later my wish came true. In the distance a form took shape, growing bigger as we approached. Our B & B. Bright sunlight created something of a mirage in the empty landscape. Patrick smiled at me. "Good thing there's only one road through the desert. This must be our place."

The home was a lodge-type structure with a wraparound porch and wooden posts. An assortment of chairs sat empty as the sun bore down at that five o'clock hour. An older couple greeted us with cold tea and cookies, then showed us to our room. The four-poster bed invited us to collapse into it. Windows offered views in every direction, the unspoiled plains an incomprehensible expanse.

At eight o'clock we met in the dining room with four other lodgers, one a couple from the Eastern Cape. It was lovely to talk about Cape Town as "home" and to hear about the other side of the country over a meal fit for royalty. After dinner Patrick and I retreated to our room, where we headed to the patio. Darkness softened the environment. A double swing against the wall looked neglected. Patrick pulled it out far enough to rock gently back and forth. In silence we stared into the night sky, an atmospheric version of the vastness below.

The environment had softened in darkness. The stars were close enough we might reach out and touch them. Instead of waiting to catch one shoot across the sky, countless implosions created a virtual fireworks extravaganza for our entertainment. A background symphony of crickets played in unison with the creaking swing.

In utter contentment, we tried to decipher other sounds. Lulled by the swing and the infinite majesty of the night sky, hours melted into morning, the Namib Desert working its way into our souls. What a magical evening.

Sunlight shot across the room in large unencumbered swaths, a reminder that our sleep-wake pattern was indeed dictated by the primitive rhythm of darkness and light. At our request, our hosts had prepared a sack lunch of bread, fruit, and juice ready for us to eat on our way to the Fish River Canyon for a hike. After a short trek to Hell's Bend, we stopped for a drink of water and to take in the panoramic view of the canyon, the enormity below ground in the canyon as vast as that above. The Fish River itself is very deep in the canyon. There's little water. The land is arid and the canyon brown and dusty, just like it said in the travel magazine. They failed to mention the primordial beauty of a barren expanse.

It was an eerie quiet, the two of us the only living souls in the canyon. Patrick reminded me to watch my footing on the trail and keep an eye out for snakes, my worst fear. Pounding my trekking sticks into the dirt harder than necessary for balance, I hoped it would announce my presence to any reptiles lurking in my path. The steep hike required total focus. I didn't look down, but kept my eyes on Patrick ahead of me, his shoulders relaxed, as were mine.

Our footsteps were the only sound on earth in this inordinately peaceful place, my singular focus on the next step. No political tension. No civil unrest. Nothing but cloud formations, dessert plants, spiders, the constant buzz of flies— an external tinnitus to punctuate the solitude.

After another night of conversation and spectacular stargazing, we headed to Windhoek, the capital. Hours passed on the road without another car in sight, and no road signs. Day turned into night, our headlights and the brilliant sky illuminating the road. We should have been at our next lodging before nightfall.

"Patrick, do you think we took a wrong tur—"

The car swerved left in a violent jerk. I steadied myself with the door handle. A car barreled toward us in the dark with no headlights. Patrick's quick reaction prevented us from getting sideswiped.

"Oh my God! What was that?"

"Someone obviously didn't want to be seen." Visibly shaken, he pulled over. We turned around. Darkness had swallowed the car.

"Could be poachers, diamond smugglers."

"Jeeez. We're out in the middle of nowhere, sharing the road with criminals?"

"Yeah, let's get out of here." On the road Patrick picked up speed. The stars were so close it seemed they might hit the windshield. In the distance two tiny lights flickered. There was nothing around, no structures. Another pair of lights appeared as bright as the first. Then another. And another. As we got closer Patrick slowed to a crawl. Both of us gasped at once. Little springbok deer, dozens of them, stood eating in a field, some bouncing excitedly as we approached. At five miles per hour, Patrick carefully inched through the herd, little springbok bounding to one side or the other to make way. Once past them, we spotted a rustic farmhouse inn, our accommodations for the night.

It was a strange place with no other dwelling for miles. Yellow lamplight welcomed us to stop. All I wanted to do was shower and go to bed. Patrick met the hosts to get our key. In no time we hit the sack for the night. The next morning it wasn't the sun that woke us, but dogs barking in the distance. Patrick hadn't stirred all night. Cuddling against him, I felt closer to him than I had in months in this enormous empty space. If the power of his being My Only Person on this side of the planet had been strong in Cape Town, in Namibia we were Adam and Eve, the only two beings in the world, lovers without the garden.

A sleepy kiss started our day. Drawing me into his arms, Patrick mumbled with his eyes still closed. "We're in total silence for three days then wake up to barking dogs. I think we should stay in bed in case they're wild. They might be Namibian dingoes." He yanked the duvet over our heads. The garden may have been absent but we were definitely channeling Adam and Eve.

On our way to breakfast the commotion revealed itself. Two Borders Collies on the plain herded sheep into a fenced area near the farmhouse. Leaning against the rail, we watched as the dogs barked orders to "get in line" while the sheep dashed this way and that until they funneled and made their way into the paddock.

"Good workers, huh?" Our Namibian host handed us each a cup of tea. The three of us watched the dogs go 'round and 'round, closing in on the livestock. It was quite a sight, those Border Collies as bossy as any schoolyard bully. Laughing, we followed the man into the farmhouse for breakfast. Something nudged me from behind. Quickly I turned around to face the biggest ostrich I had ever seen. The thing was huge, and tall. Our host lunged toward it, waving it off with his hat. "Their eggs are grand but they can be pesky buggers."

By mid-morning we were halfway to the famous sand dunes of the Namib Desert. At home as a kid I was known for my daredevil sledding. As we drove alongside the dunes, it was all I could do to restrain myself. They were stunning, some mounds the size of stadiums.

Perfectly shaped formations as if manmade, the flaming orange shapes filled the landscape as far as the eye could see. Whoever had set foot here before us was a mystery. Wind erased any trace of human presence, leaving untouched perfection.

What I had imagined a barren landscape was an artist's atelier, the windswept mounds a constant work in progress. Had I been an artist, I would have been joyfully doomed trying to capture on canvas the power of such geography.

When the car stopped, I made a mad dash for the tallest dune. Patrick was hot on my trail. Screaming and giggling, we raced up the mountain, stopping at the top long enough to exchange a glance that needed no words. With complete abandon the two of us started downhill, our feet sinking deep in the sand. Three steps into it, Patrick fell forward, his buried feet knocking him off kilter as he rolled and tumbled to the bottom. Laughing at the sight of him from above, I lost my balance too. In a flurry of sand and sky, the world rushed by in a blur until I bumped right into him, still lying where he had come to a stop. Again we raced to the top, yelling in glee, not a human within miles of earshot. On our third run we figured out the art of sand duning. On ascent you keep your legs flexed in a sort of lunge so you're close to the ground for balance. Gravity takes care of the downhill trip. Run after run we flung ourselves forward like barrels over Niagara Falls, but with a soft landing. My face hurt from laughing. Patrick's voice dried to a croak. But we didn't stop.

In a contest by turns we each marked our landing spot, measuring who could go furthest. Fifty pounds of extra weight made it obvious who had the advantage. It didn't matter. Testing himself was my husband's version of fun. It wasn't lost on me that even in a deserted world, he craved competition, the game a sport in which he must push himself to excel. No wonder he carried the weight of the world on the job. An injury to anyone in the American diplomatic community would be seen as a personal failure. He tested himself on that mountain every single day at the embassy.

Exhausted, exhilarated, finally we were spent. I held open the Ziploc bag while Patrick poured in a scoop of sand, our bit of the Namib Desert. The sight of Patrick giggling and tumbling down that dune would stay with me forever.

For a while we had been two eight-year-olds at Disneyland in the Namibian Desert.

After tending our blistered feet and sunburned skin, we got back on the road and continued our four-hour drive to Etosha National Park, wildlife tracking at its best in Namibia. The black rhino topped Patrick's list. As we approached the park, he stopped the car.

"Mar, look." He cut the engine. "To the right of the third low bush."

Pressing the binoculars against my face, I spotted the rhino. Next to it was a baby. The mom nearly tripped on it as she nudged the baby toward the watering hole, looking in every direction to check for predators. Amazed to have come upon such a special sight, neither Patrick nor I moved. I'm not sure we breathed. Mama rhino didn't seem to notice our presence. The baby was her sole focus. I tried to imagine the primitive instinct of such protective behavior, the difference between life and death in the wild. My heart swelled. I wanted to feel the power of that maternal drive with my own offspring in this crazy world.

Conversations about having a baby had been theoretical. I hadn't pushed too hard. Foreign Service in a dangerous post was no time for a baby. As a kid, I had loved every pet I ever cared for. That Mama rhino with her baby stirred a different feeling. The quiet scene awakened in me desire for the mother-baby bond we had witnessed in wild game at watering holes in Kruger Park, with moms and kids living in township shacks, mothers and children on the beaches in Cape Town where families came to play on the weekends. It was no longer theoretical. Desire for a child overwhelmed me with a force I had yet to know.

Patrick squeezed my shoulder. I turned to him, peered into his moist eyes. How I loved him. When we turned to the window for a final glimpse, the black beasts had disappeared into the bush.

An unexpected sight, the rhinos had given us back our

deep connection in one of the most tender experiences of our two years in Africa. Three days later, we left Etosha National Park after sightings of zebras, giraffes with babies—countless wildlife—each sighting a thrill. The infamous Skeleton Coast was the final leg of our trip. Heading out the next day, we once again found ourselves alone on the road. The camp guide had given us directions, but the map showed no roads. It was disorienting, the driving, endless without signage or landmarks.

By late afternoon we were concerned. At the side of the road Patrick reversed the binoculars for the magnifying effect. He zoomed in. A smile emerged. He handed me the glasses. Along the ocean a strip of land appeared, covered in purple sand. I adjusted the binoculars. Individual grains sparkled in the sun. No. This wasn't sand. The entire length and width of the beach was a purple haze—gemstones. Garnets.

I handed the glasses back. Patrick looked again. "Any prospector would tell you garnets are one of the better indicators that you're in diamond country. Makes sense. This the richest diamond producing region in the world."

And there we stood, in this forbidden region, a short distance from where we parked the car. "It's entirely possible that among the billions of pebbles below our feet is a diamond created three billion years ago." We looked at each other in awe.

On the drive back to Cape Town, we stopped at a petrol station for fuel and snacks. When I came out of the restroom, Patrick was nowhere to be found.

I said it nonchalantly so he would agree with my reasoning. "Hon, there's no way this will work. Our car is too small."

The look on Patrick's face told me it was no use. He had already fallen in love with the sculpture. For the remainder of the trip home, Namutoni, the six-foot tall giraffe, rode in the back seat of our Honda, long neck sticking out one window, feet out the other, his tail riding high above the roof.

Eighteen
New Assignment

December 1993

News of our next assignment loomed on the horizon. Patrick hadn't said much about it, perhaps not wanting to remind himself that one day in the not-too-distant future we would leave South Africa. At the embassy we had been so immersed in the thick of things that it was easy to forget this wasn't a personal quest—that we were still working for the U.S. State Department. It had become personal for me, for all of us I think. Leaving was unthinkable.

Patrick had gone through this parting ritual once before in Cape Town. He knew how to prepare emotionally. In spite of the progress, or maybe because of it, pressure on the job had been unrelenting. As much as he loved South Africa, or any country he was assigned, it probably helped knowing it would end. Departure would bring respite. He gave me gentle reminders of our timeframe—five months until the election, then another four months before we would leave for a new place in a new country.

It seemed we had just filled out the paperwork in D.C., though it had been eighteen months earlier. I was stunned at my reaction to leaving. Not only had I *not* been a trailing spouse, I had become my own person with my own work, my own connection to the mission, a seasoned member of the Foreign Service. It had been a once-in-a-lifetime experience. This time the task of choosing six possible posts hadn't been as daunting as the first time. Patrick and I reviewed the choices and filled in the blanks—Bangladesh, Sierra Leone, Tajikistan. Then we waited.

Two weeks later, Patrick waved a big manila envelope as he walked through the door—our new assignment. My stomach did a flip-flop. He had never sat down before changing from his suit into jeans. That night he did. I tried to decipher some hint on his face. No dice.

One leg tucked under me, I plopped on the couch next to him as he ripped open the envelope. The cable was long.

I followed his eyes as he scanned the first page, then the second, racing through State Department jargon. He stopped at the bottom of page three.

Our first choice was out, that was clear from the look on his face. Ditto for the second was my guess. I prepared myself. With a devilish grin, Patrick looked at me. I leaned forward, arms open in question.

"Well, it's not Burundi. It's not Chad. That's something anyway, right?"

"C'mon, out with it." He didn't answer. I lunged for the cable. He held it over his head. I grabbed again. He held it higher. "Hon, don't torture me."

Tapping his cheek, he turned his eyes toward the ceiling as if in deep thought.

"Hmmm, let's see...how to tell you." I sat back on my heels, not amused. In one svelte move he jumped up from the couch, his back to me. In a dramatic twirl-around, he grabbed an invisible microphone out of the air. Eyes closed in deep emotion like a soppy crooner, body and microphone at a strong diagonal, he burst into song.

"I left...my heaaaart...in San Francisco—"

"What?" This time I snatched the cable from his hands. He kept singing.

"Above the bluuuuue...and windy sea...."

"You're kidding!" I skimmed the page. There it was at the bottom. *You have been assigned to the San Francisco Field Office...to report on August 1, 1994.*

"Back to the States? But why? Have we done something wrong?"

Patrick stopped his lounge act, his whole face a grin. "Mar...you do recall that most of the post choices weren't exactly Shangri-la."

I leaned back. "I know." My voice was barely audible. "I just thought somewhere in Africa. And after such a difficult and dangerous post, I thought we'd get one of our choices. But San Francisco?"

"Maybe that's exactly *why* San Francisco instead of any place on our list. Think of it as payback, a reward."

I stared at the cable, trying to wrap my mind around it. "I don't understand why we can't stay in South Africa. I mean, you're the best person for the job after doing it for two years."

With a huff of frustration, he headed to the bedroom to change. His voice echoed in the hall. "Nah, that's not the way it works. We talked about this, Mar."

I stared out the window. Sunlight sparkled on the water. I had finally gotten used to the long days, sun shining without remorse until ten at night. Those long days had slipped by so quickly while I was busy doing other things, good things, hard things. I followed Patrick, his voice still loud enough to hear in the living room until he saw me.

"The State Department doesn't want anyone getting too cozy in one place. It tends to make people territorial. We go where the country needs us to go. That's the deal in Foreign Service." His balled up shirt flew by me on its way to the dirty clothes basket. Plopped on the bed, hands behind his head, he stared at the ceiling with a dreamy look on his face.

I sat down next to him on edge of the bed. "Patrick, I'm not ready to go. This is our home. We can't just up and leave."

He lifted his head with a grin. "Yes. We can. Up-and-leave is exactly what we'll do."

"But...well...what if I didn't? Maybe you could go and I could come later."

This time the grin was gone. He rolled sideways and leaned on one elbow. "You're kidding, right?"

The pained look on my face said I wasn't.

"Hold on, Mar." His chuckle had a tinge of sarcasm. "First, you knew this was only two years. Did you really think if we liked it we could just stay?"

"No...but—"

"Second, you make it sound like we're being punished. San Francisco's a dream post. Third, we're not leaving tomorrow, or next week. We have until August. Eight months."

"I know."

How could Patrick be excited about leaving? In a flash he pulled me down to his chest. With his hands he held my hair back. I tried not to look at him, not ready to accept.

"Hon, Cape Town will always be special as our first post together, your first post. And that's the hardest one to give up. I know you feel like the rug's been pulled out from under you. But we have lots of time to get used to the idea. San Francisco's a fantastic city. By the time August comes around, you'll be chomping at the bit to go stateside."

"So just like that I'm supposed to be happy about a new post?" It sounded more like a pout than I'd intended.

"That's the whole reason they tell you so early. They know it's tough to change from one assignment to another after you've gotten used to a place. But that's the way the system works."

"It's a stupid system."

Nibbling my neck he teased. "I'll be sure to convey your sentiment to the Secretary of State next time he asks my opinion on how to improve the Foreign Service program."

"You're patronizing me."

He dropped back on the bed. Mary, I'm not patronizing you. I'm reminding you this is how it works. That's why only big kids get to play on the State Department playground—because change is hard. Giving up control is hard."

"Not for you. You're just switching embassies. What about a third year, like Bev did?"

"What, are you trying to kill me?" He laughed out loud.

"I'm just trying to wrap my mind around it. I can't imagine leaving."

Rolling me onto my back, he nibbled again. "As your Regional Security Officer, it's my duty to console you in your moment of distress." I offered no resistance when he kissed me my face—forehead, each cheek, nose, and finally my lips.

Of course, he was right. Patrick loved South Africa as much as I did, maybe more. My emotional reaction had forced him into his Reasonable Adult mode. I kicked myself for not going with his playful mood when he first walked in from work. Once again, I had pushed us into our respective corners of Reason versus Emotion in the face of a loaded topic.

We had gotten better—I had gotten better—at recognizing unhealthy patterns in our communication. I supposed our current supine position on the bed a fitting correction and joined Patrick finding our way to neutral ground.

Wide awake, I lay with his arm thrown across my chest. Gently lifting it, I scooted to my side of the bed. San Francisco. It wasn't even foreign. In the early days, I would've paid to get Patrick re-assigned to the States. Now I had work. I had friends. South Africa was home. Maybe it was even more of a home than any other because the adjustment had been so difficult.

In D.C. we didn't have much of a social life. Here we had friends as a couple, entertained them in our flat. We got together for Greek food with the Donovans, knew their kids' activities, their dogs' latest antics. At the embassy I knew dozens of people, including the drivers, knew the building staff at the flat; cashiers at the Pick n' Pay, was a regular at the spice market where I bought fresh curry for Patrick's favorite dish. I knew the mechanic who serviced our Honda, the owner of the dry cleaners where I took Patrick's and my suits, the party rental company I used for diplomatic events, directors of the nonprofits where Bev and I donated the goods from our clothing drives.

I had been with the same hairdresser from the start, knew the manicurist at the salon, the aerobics instructor at the gym. At the University of Cape Town, I had audited classes in English literature, was granted a temporary student pass in the music department where I could play the piano for a few lazy hours, had a direct line to the Around Town editor at the *Argus* who gave me scoops on local events for the embassy newsletter.

Friday Girl's Night Out was a given on my schedule. Saturdays when Patrick was busy I went shopping with Bev. Helen and I had a standing weekly tennis date.

From Azisa I had learned phrases in Xhosa, several in Afrikaans from Mr. Khumalo. I was a regular at political rallies with Charles on this side of the mountain, had evaluated dozens of applications for the USAID program, met with local women outside the townships who needed guidance on the application process.

I had planned dozens of diplomatic social gatherings—baby showers, birthdays, anniversaries, departure parties, welcome teas, staff hikes, picnics, even an Easter egg hunt in the park for the children of embassy employees. One morning a month I volunteered at the wildlife rescue, another as a stand-in docent for student tours at the botanical gardens. I had initiated a recycle program in our building.

In Cape Town I was more involved in the community than I ever was back home as a career-oriented single woman. Patrick and I had been at his condo less than a year before coming to South Africa. Hometown reentry was a non-issue—we hadn't established community ties; in fact, had no real home to go back to, no picking up where we left off. Returning to D.C. now, I would feel as new and out of place as I would in San Francisco, as I had when we first arrived in Cape Town.

It was hard to imagine two years from now I would be severing my ties in San Francisco for another unfamiliar place somewhere on the globe. Maybe I wasn't cut out for a life in Foreign Service. Helen Lyman had done it, found a way to love this life. But I was no Helen Lyman, not yet, not at thirty. It was not in my nature to come and go. After college and moving a few times in my twenties, I needed continuity, roots.

Most of my girlfriends I'd had since high school, our loyalty to each other beyond reproach. Part of me was defined by those relationships, connections that tethered me to a history. Without that context, my life would be a series of two-year episodes—waiting for a tanker to bring our photos and personal items, settling in, making friends, starting jobs, then packing up for the next post, leaving it all behind.

Travel was part of what had drawn me and Patrick together. But it appealed to me because I had a home base.

Adventure and travel are extraordinary because they're not a way of life. Familiarity is not dull, but comforting. I still cooked with pots and pans my mom gave me after college, still had clothes from my sisters that I had no intention of giving up, even if they never got worn. Attachment is not easily explained, much less justified. Those pots and pans still connected me to Mom. Each sweater and scarf carried some small part of my sisters, whoever had worn it last. My dad's Minnesota Twins cap, the same.

These associations didn't come to me as conscious thought, but a comforting sense of the past bumping into the present, one long continuum of relationships that meant something to me. When Patrick and I had talked about a life in Foreign Service, the side of the ledger with adventure outweighed the price of impermanence. Context and history are incompatible with transience. In committing to a life in Foreign Service, I had committed to the feeling of sadness at the end of each post, the ability to nurture long-term friendships, the satisfaction of a consistent career. What I said to Patrick was true—he would be switching one embassy for another, like transferring to a new job location within the same company. But I would be starting from scratch. Every time.

In the beginning we had been so in love. Patrick was the only home I needed. I hadn't planned on getting attached to South Africa, hadn't planned on meaningful work at the Embassy, hadn't planned on Helen, Bev, Michele as wonderful friends. After Cape Town it was unlikely we would cross paths again. Patrick had known from the start not to get too attached to Cape Town, just as he had known not to invest in real friendships, people in his world reduced to coworkers in the background of his career. The Donovans were the one exception, non-embassy friends who would remain at some fixed point where he could find them from time to time as he orbited the sun.

Patrick had scoffed months ago when I brought up the idea of our staying to go into business with Richard Donovan. How could Patrick be so nonchalant about leaving? I replayed last night's argument.

What if you hate your new post, investigating counterterrorism, tracking the paper trail of some lowlife fugitive? You might as well go back to being a trial lawyer if you want to be stuck in an office all day. You'll be bored to death without the threat of doom hanging over you.

He'd laughed. *In the dead of night I'll scoop you away to Mount Tamalpais. We'll wear night vision goggles and hide behind trees to negotiate a truce before the imminent destruction of the world. I'll be Ambassador Lyman. You can be Buthelezi. A monster crocodile with Botha's face will slither into the city to knock down buildings and drive people into the San Francisco Bay. Doomsday. My assignment will be to save civilization.*

Humor was a favorite way to deflect conflict. Patrick would rather sidetrack a conversation in which we would be pitted against one another than work through a disagreement. My parents never argued in front of us kids, but with eight children, there's no way they had been conflict-free. And their marriage survived, even thrived after we were gone. Maybe that was because of what they had built together, because of their strength as a team.

If that was the secret to a lasting marriage, Patrick and I were in trouble. He had his career, I had mine. Before Cape Town I had agreed to wait these two years with the understanding that I would start my own business at home, where we would revert to being two single people who were married. He would be gone half the time on State Department assignments. I would stay put, the anti-trailing spouse.

Patrick's fanciful scenario about the excitement of his new job was truer than he'd realized. Indeed, I did feel like Buthelezi advocating for a homeland, preserving tribal identity through tradition, permanence. And Patrick did seem like Princeton Lyman, always ready to swoop into the fray to prevent disaster, get the country back on its feet, always with his eye toward the future, the next disaster in the next post in the next country.

Thirty years from now I would be looking back at a string of address changes—twelve assignments in a thirty-year career. *Where should we send your Christmas card this year, Mary?*

My first impression of Patrick had been that of a selfless man, willing to sacrifice home and hearth to serve those in need. But maybe it was something else that drove my husband into public service. Maybe he needed Foreign Service as much as it needed him. A regular job in one town with kids and dogs and an annual two-week vacation would never be enough for Patrick. He hadn't changed since that first date. It was I who hadn't listened.

The man I loved would never be ordinary, never live an ordinary life. To him, that would be torture. But I had watched my parents weather the joys and sorrows of the everyday. From them I learned that ordinary grounding so that one could experience the full range of life, good and bad, without having to watch out for your footing all the time on unfamiliar landscape.

In that way, the ordinary life became extraordinary—events and people and experiences adding context until you could look down as if from a mountaintop and finally see the shape of your life. Maybe I would never get that view, limited to bits and pieces from ground level where people and events and places were strung together with no shape at all, the meaning of my life elusive.

As much as I loved my husband, we were very different people, wanted very different things. In eight months we would leave Cape Town. That wouldn't make the problem go away. It would be waiting for us in San Francisco, and in every post after that.

A loud snort from Patrick jarred me. The clock said three-thirty. *Mary, go to sleep. Stop thinking.* I nuzzled up against him, then began repeating the one mantra that had served me well my entire life. Eyes closed, I mentally began reciting the *Our Father* until I drifted into a deep and dreamless sleep.

The window air conditioner rattled with a terrible racket. It was hard to concentrate, but better a rickety A/C inside than high nineties out. December meant summer, a scorcher this week, a perfect Clifton Beach day. Layers of Coppertone already had me smelling like a coconut just walking to the office from the car. I was happy to stay inside for lunch.

Last night's pasta microwaved would have to do, along with my favorite little Simba curry potato chips from the vending machine. The mechanical vendor had become my lunchtime friend, though it was often out of chips and cookies, which drove me to stash pop tarts in my office in case of a sweet tooth attack. A lot of staffers ate lunch at their desks. Work schedules were crammed full.

A string of restaurants were within walking distance of the embassy. When the work load wasn't so high, Patrick and I tried to keep our weekly lunch date at a little place across the street— our hidden gem we called it—with such regular patronage the owner actually named a sandwich after Patrick. The McGhee Special with its chopped chicken and onion on a fresh Panini roll slathered in barbeque sauce was a favorite among Foreign Service officers. My husband was nuts for barbeque sauce, would put the stuff on anything from eggs to salads.

The restaurant owner and eventual friend, James, made his own version. At the end of our meal, James would drop by a wrapped sandwich with a wink. He had caught on to us ordering one to go for the disabled kid who hung out under the big shade tree in front of the restaurant. Patrick liked to say the McGhee Special was his legacy to South Africa.

Summer heat and heightened security warnings gave added appeal to leftover pasta in my office. The newsletter for our American community sat unfinished on my desk. And I had to catch up on debrief notes from Secretary Brown's visit. The success of the visit had given us a momentary boost in morale, but within a few weeks, collective anxiety filled the hallways in our countdown to April 27.

Also on my agenda for the day, probably most important, was to draft a memo on the Neighbor Watch Program, a new project introduced by the State Department and monitored by the Regional Security Officer, Patrick. It would prove to be one of the most effective weapons against residential crime, the new reality even in Sea Point. These programs—neighbors helping neighbors—were a novel concept back then. U.S. citizens and South Africans alike signed up to receive a placard, attend neighborhood meetings and social gatherings. It turned out to be the perfect strategy for adding a sense of security as well as bringing people together. And that always boosted morale.

I certainly benefited from it. The long days of summer were perfect for getting out at night to watch the sunset, walk the promenade, and swim under a dipping sun. Bev and I would head to our favorite spot on the beach under Lion's Head peak. It was an upbeat way to escape the tension all around us. When the kombi of workers headed back to the townships, we took our cue to go home.

"I have cherished the ideal of a democratic and free society in which all persons live together in harmony and with equal opportunities. It is an ideal which I hope to live for and to achieve. But if need be, it is an ideal for which I am willing to die."

Nelson Mandela spoke those words at the sentencing hearing that would send him to prison for twenty-seven years for treason. Thirty years later, in December 1993, he was awarded the Nobel Peace Prize, along with President F.W. de Klerk for their work in bringing apartheid to an end, though popular consensus was that Mandela's efforts over decades really did it.

The words he spoke in court that day as a young man were deeply embedded in my mind. With his release from prison, Mandela had the means, the power, the justification to avenge generations of institutionalized oppression. No one would've blamed him. But that's not what he did. It's not who he was.

He chose not only to forgive, but to actively seek reconciliation at the national level, something almost unheard of in politics, especially South African politics. Nelson Mandela knew it could be no other way. Oppression bred resentment in blacks. It would do the same in whites—undermine the future he dreamed of for South Africa. His generosity of spirit was validation of the larger ideal he had expressed decades earlier—equal opportunity for all. The son of a tribal chief far from his homeland in the bush, Nelson Mandela carried the future of the country on his shoulders like the royalty he was.

The more the world tuned in to South Africa, the more the stakes ratcheted up among right and left wing radical groups. But the heightened attention brought good things too. Artists for a New South Africa (ANSA) was founded in 1989 by Alfre Woodard, Danny Glover, Mary Steenburgen, Blair Underwood, CCH Pounder and friends to support the quest to end apartheid. They were coming to visit Cape Town in the countdown to Election Day. For us at the embassy, that meant we would have these artists as a big draw at events.

Hoopla and fanfare marked their arrival at the Peninsula Hotel. Ambassador Lyman and Helen hosted the group along with special officials at their home in Bishopscourt. As Community Liaison Officer and PR Person Extraordinaire, as Patrick called me, I managed logistics, which included meeting with Danny Glover and his wife Assante at the hotel before our trip to the ambassador's home.

In Bishopscourt our visitors were caught off guard as we progressed through each security post. If nothing else impressed upon them the climate of danger surrounding the election, the security checkpoints did, by the looks on their faces. Speeches kicked off the evening, many centered on growing concern over the HIV/AIDS epidemic. I was eager to learn more as a former colleague had recently passed away from AIDS. In the early '90s, people knew about HIV/AIDS, but nowhere near to the extent in the next decade. It was still a mysterious disease with no united effort to fight it. USAID had launched programs to help educate.

The highest HIV infection rates in South Africa were in KwaZulu Natal, yet Buthelezi's IFP turned a blind eye, refusing to acknowledge the epidemic, which exacerbated the key obstacles to prevention and control. Education, Information and Counseling Centers located in cities weren't much help for those in the rural homelands where need was most acute and access to healthcare poor. ANSA celebrities like these trailblazers worked hard to promote awareness across the globe.

That evening after photo ops, in the waning hours of the night, I made my way to Assante Glover to check on how she was doing. My guess was she didn't like the limelight as much as her husband, actor Danny Glover. She and I had clicked right away. She asked me about life in the Foreign Service and how long I would stay in South Africa. Assante and Danny lived in San Francisco, knew the city well. She was more than eager to give me excellent suggestions on where to live—Russian Hill, an affluent neighborhood was filled with unusual boutiques, antique shops, trendy restaurants and nightspots.

Assante was a visual artist, a painter. I promised to visit her gallery when we got settled. It was lovely to talk about art, beauty, the creative drive, no mention of violence or politics or disease. It was food for the soul. Alfre Woodard, co-founder of ANSA, and actress Alexandra Paul of Baywatch joined us in the living room as conversation turned to politics and women.

The morning headline had Winnie Mandela on the front page as head of the ANC's Women's League. Her marriage to Nelson had collapsed under the weight of decades of imprisonment along with Winnie's misguided involvement with radicals who used violence to promote the cause of freedom. She had found her way back to the pursuit of peaceful means, which was good for the party, but too late for the marriage.

But it was clearly a new era. The four of us, two black women, two white—Assante, Alfre, Alexandra and I–talked excitedly about women in politics, gender and racial equality. Back in the States, Madeleine Albright had been appointed by President Clinton as U.S. Ambassador to the United Nations.

And California became the first state to be represented in the Senate by two women elected concurrently—Dianne Feinstein and Barbara Boxer. South Africa seemed light years behind. I shared my stories about the USAID township projects—the grants given to women's start-ups.

If only we could have harnessed the collective energy we generated with our ideas, each of us revved up discussing new possibilities for involvement. My emotions climbed to a major high, momentary respite from the plummeting feeling of vulnerability in the latest spate of violence.

By the time I bade goodbye to everyone that night—Assante Glover last—the idea of moving to San Francisco wasn't so bad. I had already made a friend at our new post.

The morning of December 30, I woke up feeling unsettled. It had been almost one year since our flat had been broken into that New Year's Eve. As we had come to understand, celebrations often morphed into mob chaos with passion turning into aggression with little time for transition. Thanks to Patrick, I was aware of the no-go areas around our home.

The heartbeat in Cape Town was the university where Amy Biehl had studied and where Patrick played basketball every week in the gym. Observatory, a suburb near campus, was one of the few areas where all races could live together. On the evening of December 30th, three men entered a popular student hangout, Heidelberg Tavern on Station Road—the very road Charles and I had taken to the rally—and opened fire, killing four people and injuring another five students. The news was crushing.

It was moments like these that gave me pause about whether the election would really happen or if the country would collapse into civil war. The Azanian People's Liberation Army claimed responsibility for the Heidelberg Tavern Massacre. Ballistic tests indicated the weapons used were the same as in the St. James Massacre the previous July.

Trepidation surrounded the approach of the New Year. Maintaining a positive outlook would be a tough resolution, but that was my top priority.

Nineteen
White Flight

January/February/March 1994

My conversation with Assante Glover was a huge factor in adjusting to the idea of our return to the States. It was still months away, but Patrick helped too. He talked about "disengagement"—the term diplomats use to describe the psychological process of preparation for leaving a post. He suggested I call my parents or one of my sisters every week as a way to reconnect with my old life as I transitioned into my new one. It was a practical strategy, though disengaging from South Africa seemed impossible.

The New Year rang in without incident after the December massacre at Heidelberg Tavern two days earlier. That's what things had come to—one day at a time, always waiting for the other shoe to drop. Anxiety had become a way of life. We dealt with tragedy the best we could and tried to move forward, keep our eyes on the prize.

That morning Patrick and I stayed in bed long after our second cup of coffee. Making love was one way to rid our bodies of the residual tension we both brought home from the embassy. The closeness also made it easier to talk about the move to San Francisco, as well as my public relations business, the one I would start when we were settled in our new post. Patrick surprised me with ideas for advertising and other start-up details. It was so good to talk to him about it, hear his ideas without triggering an argument. We were looking forward together, in sync. Team Byron and McGhee. It was a good omen for the New Year.

It was these very tangible preparations that added buoyancy to my renewed commitment to relish every moment in South Africa, savor the extraordinary opportunity I had been given. That morning in bed, Patrick and I decided we would immerse ourselves in all things African, including the music. Prince and Luther Vandross were pushed aside. One of our favorite South African musicians was Johnny Clegg (white Zulu) & Savuka. I had listened to their music before moving to Cape Town, but

I had turned to my American artists to soothe the homesickness that had taken so long to shake.

Things between me and Patrick were on a high note now that I was on board with the new post, music bringing an atmosphere of optimism about our future. I was young again, young and in love—this time not just the knowledge of love I had clung to during our distant interludes, but the *feeling*, the powerful energy love brings that feels like all is right with the world.

That winter we would attend a Johnny Clegg & Savuka concert in an auditorium filled with blacks, whites, coloreds—all of us rocking out together. These talented musicians were part of the movement to unify South Africa, a joyful message of hope that resonated like a pulse through their music.

Nelson Mandela loved to dance. At large appearances a band would set the festive mood. Then the future president would come out in his colorful African shirts, hips swaying, arms waving. "Where there is music and dancing, that makes me at peace with the world...and at peace with myself..."

I've been around a lot of celebrities in my life, before and after Cape Town. None came close to the overwhelming reception that followed this man wherever he went.

The new Constitution of the Republic of South Africa Act was passed on January 25, 1994. Tentative excitement about the election grew bolder every day, especially among blacks. At the embassy we shared that excitement; outside the embassy, not so much. Afrikaners still resented Americans. Impact from our economic sanctions continued to ripple through the economy in everyday life—replacement car parts were hard to get, people could wait months for a light bulb. I think we all felt the resentment but tried to stay focused.

Voting preparation made it seem real. Ambassador Lyman had been working with the U.N. for over a year on the logistics of Election Day. An international election committee would take over that role with U.S. financial assistance.

The committee would coordinate the activities of all official election observers who would be flooding the country—assign them to districts, explain the need to work with their South African counterparts.

In a country where literally millions who had never voted would be queuing up to put their "X" on the line next to the African National Congress—or one of nineteen other political parties—voter education was paramount. Rather than voting for an individual, in the system of Proportional Representation, voters chose a party. The commission had less than four months to organize the election, a massive undertaking.

By the time they began work that January, the country was on a knife's edge. The committee was ill-prepared for some of the tasks—choosing suitable polling sites, assuring the parties' access to all parts of the country to run their campaigns, supplying polling stations with adequate materials, counting the country's vote. It was a difficult task, given the geography of warring parties.

In the meantime, the seismic shift taking place was beginning to crack the surface. Whites became edgy at the very real possibility of black majority rule. Blacks became become ecstatic. All except Chief Buthelezi, who still refused to participate in the election, holding to his demand for a separate nation in KwaZulu Natal homeland.

As if that weren't enough, vigilante activity continued in the townships. The right wing radical group AWB (Terry Blanche's white supremacists) had adopted terror tactics with the express purpose of obstructing the election. They used commercial explosives to bomb targets such as ANC offices, taxi ranks and civilian high traffic areas. Increased vigilante violence required significant effort to keep the mission, the American community safe. Patrick had his informants on the street as well as electronic surveillance to respond to, if not to prevent the attacks, but disaster could occur at any time.

At the embassy we struggled to keep up morale. All of our nerves were raw, including Patrick's. Ambassador Lyman encouraged him to take at least one weekend day off. He needed to pace himself. Security issues would increase as Election Day approached. He took the ambassador's advice.

The exodus had started months earlier as whites fled the country in droves over fear of a black government that would confiscate their homes and property. No one was certain how this new democracy would work—blacks and whites making up Parliament in a shared government. Thousands of white South Africans ditched their possessions and got out anyway they could, as fast as they could, with the election a mere four months away. They called it White Flight.

I heard stories of people pulling money from banks and selling their heirloom furniture and jewels to auction houses when they were short on cash or couldn't get their belongings out of the country. A friend told us about one family who sold everything they owned and loaded their yacht with money, sewing hundreds of Kruger rand, each one ounce of gold, into the bottoms of their drapes, like fabric weights. It was a clever idea. But it didn't work. By law, they could take only so much out of the country. Whites were stopped or turned back by the South African Navy, which came on board to search.

The surplus of goods left behind created a shopper's paradise. Patrick and I hadn't brought much furniture with us to Cape Town. My small apartment in Minneapolis with Debbie had been furnished. When I moved in with him, Patrick was single and traveled a lot. Except for a few pieces, we sold or donated what furniture we had. That left us with a State Department moving budget with little to move.

Auction houses were bursting at the seams as they took advantage of their increased inventory. Friends recommended several reputable houses in the industrial area of Cape Town. One Saturday morning we took the main road in Woodstock, checking out one store after another. Saturday shoppers stared as we parked. It gave us pause until we put two and two together—our left-hand-drive Honda Accord gave us away as Americans, not Afrikaners. It was just after lunch when we spotted a beautiful storefront with heirloom pieces near the entrance. The display drew our attention.

The auction houses reminded me of the antique shopping I had done with my mom. My uncle lived in Red Wing, a town in southern Minnesota, which became our base. Mom scoured the shops for teacups to add to her collection. Her brother was drawn to large pieces. He and Mom would speculate endlessly about the best way to restore them.

Patrick shared that love of beautifully crafted wood and the challenge of restoration. During the visit home to meet my parents, he and Mom bonded over conversations about varnish and stain. Before his commercial salmon fishing days in law school, Patrick had earned money for college working at the local antique shop on Gaylord Street in Denver. That job at Morrie's had given him a real hands-on education and an eye for quality furniture.

I pointed to a sign above the auction house advertising a live auction the next day. It couldn't hurt to preview the booty. My eyes had to adjust to the dark inside. Row upon row of huge furniture pieces transformed the aisles into narrow tunnels blocked by light. Single file, we wound our way down one aisle into another. I had never seen so many elegant pieces in one place.

Patrick stopped in front of one, an armoire. He stroked the wood as if he were petting a beloved dog, his fingers tracing the intricate detail, the layers woodcut, the weight of the ornamental brass hardware. "This is a beauty, very good oak, well-made...notice the carved scallop design." When was the last time he looked at me that way? Next to it stood a matching chest of drawers. Our eyes met. I knew that look, the same one he'd had when he saw Namutoni, our six-foot wooden giraffe.

A salesman approached. I got the sense he had been watching since we stepped in the door. Patrick's lovesick expression was a dead giveaway. We introduced ourselves, careful to not give too much information. He caught the American accent that belied our Afrikaner looks and opened with the familiar question: "Are you on holiday?" The next one was equally familiar: "Where are you from?" He took a step closer, drawing Patrick into conversation.

I slipped away but stayed within earshot.

My husband questioned the salesman in the manner of a prospective buyer assessing the armoire's pedigree—how old was it? (over 100 years); where was it from? (France); who was the original owner? (some uncle in the royal family); how did it come to be in his store? (wealthy Afrikaners leaving for Europe). It turns out owning antique furniture is akin to owning work by a known artist—you trace ownership not only for legal issues of provenance prior to sale, but also to learn the backstory you'll share with future admirers.

Age and pedigree are what separate antiques from other furniture, the rich story, the personal connection you feel. Watching Patrick, I promised myself to bring it up next time he teased me about Mom's old pots and pans. They weren't over a hundred years old, but they were a connection to my family. The backstory Patrick listened to would connect him with the previous owner, the previous time in history. Context gave the furniture life. Like my pots and pans.

The two men chatted away. The salesman and his brother ran the family-owned business. Patrick accepted the schedule he handed him for the next auction.

Later that day we stumbled into an excellent shop about to hold a live auction. Neither of us was familiar with bidding. Once was all it took. Vying to win ownership of an item brought the adrenaline rush of risking real money. It was addictive. Nervous, giggling with excitement, we moved on to another house, then another, and another, at each one placing a bid on some item. Luckily we were outbid. It was a great way to get our live-bidding feet wet. The next day we would be ready to win Patrick's armoire. And it *would* be his.

That Saturday was the first of many days we shopped at the auction houses. Some days business was light, the bids lower with the strength of U.S. currency a game changer. In one store, we got a sewing machine; in another, a side table. Another armoire. Our State Department moving budget would not go to waste. Neither of us said it out loud, but it was in my head— antiques are not something you ship from one post to the next.

Hefty furniture says one thing: permanence. Someday Patrick and I might have a gloriously ordinary life.

Four weeks, four armoires and three sewing machines later, the bidding stopped. As it was, we ended up with dozens of pieces, large and small, which would be stored in our Cape Town garage until we could send it to an address in San Francisco. Had we kept bidding, our next residence would have had to be a barn, an unlikely property in the pricy city.

Trips to the auction houses had a serendipitous effect. For the first time, I was excited about our as-yet-unknown home. Heirlooms would always remind us of our time in South Africa—the crumbling of apartheid, the long negotiation process, anticipation of the election, Nelson Mandela sworn in as president. If we could get to the election. This history would be our story—the antique furniture a talisman forever linking us to this watershed moment. And long after we were gone, the story would still be part of the furniture when another couple fell as much in love with it as we had.

By early spring, Chief Buthelezi had met with negotiators for the first time since December 1993 to discuss the ANC's proposals, among them a provision for each province to determine its own government. That should have thrilled Buthelezi. Mandela and President de Klerk accommodated his four conditions regarding government of the homelands. But the Zulu chief rejected the proposal as utter hypocrisy. Buthelezi could not be won over. Mandela was furious. He considered tribalism backward—a separate Zulu nation was counter to the greater good of the people. One month before the first nonracial election in three hundred years, the line of contention between the two black leaders held firm.

The Inkatha Freedom Party rejected participating in the election. Buthelezi took it farther. He and his followers began a campaign of opposing the interim constitution and the upcoming election. The chief stated they would fight the ANC "to the finish" unless the election was postponed. With that declaration, violence erupted across the land.

A bomb exploded at the offices of the National Party, Shell House, in the right-wing town of Ventersdorp. The home of ANC regional premier candidate Jacob Zuma was torched by a mob from KwaZulu-Natal. In Johannesburg more than thirty people were killed and hundreds injured in battles when tens of thousands of Zulus converged on the city centre.

President de Klerk declared a state of emergency across eleven magisterial districts in the East Rand, as well as the whole of the Kwazulu-Natal province. Buthelezi accused Mandela of stoking violence by forcing those in the homelands to choose allegiance between a tribal homeland or a united country.

As much as we tried to stay optimistic at the embassy, the touch-and-go nature of the situation got to all of us. South Africa had so much at stake. Our mission had so much at stake. The U.S. had put more than twenty-five million dollars into the election in multiple areas, from providing experts as consultants during negotiations to voter education. Backing came from both sides of the aisle, including the National Democratic Institute and the International Republican Institute.

No matter the outcome—civil war or unification—Patrick and I would leave South Africa. We would be okay. The same could not be said if the worst horror came to fruition. It was as if this opportunity would never come again. If Nelson Mandela couldn't win majority rule, there was no man alive who could— that was the consensus whether spoken or not.

As a way to cope with apprehension, I tried to focus on the next two years. Re-entry to the States would be difficult, I knew that. Patrick had told me about feeling discombobulated after his return from a dangerous post earlier in his career. In the States he stepped into an alien world, the mundane concerns of those around him at odds with the life and death situations he encountered on assignment.

At Kathy's wedding I had felt the same thing. No one asked me about South Africa. U.S. news had coverage—complete with images of bloodshed. But apparently no one wanted a first-hand account. Of course, that had been at a wedding, not everyday life. Still, on reentry, we were to face more of the same disinterest, especially after worldwide coverage of the election. Our sojourn in South Africa would stay buried, kept alive in me and Patrick alone. If anyone did ask, we would share the joy of success, the outcome of our mission. The harrowing details of what we had gone through to get there would remain tucked away as a private story, my story.

And so it did, for twenty-five years.

The deeper we got into spring, the more it became apparent that the International Election Committee had its hands full. Logistics were a nightmare. The commission not only had to establish and staff regional hubs, ensure registration, and educate voters, they had to recruit, train and mobilize thousands of international Election Observers. These volunteers would literally watch the vote take place.

The Electoral Commission believed the presence of neutral outsiders to witness the process—the voting itself, counting ballots, determining results—would tell the world the election was transparent, free and fair. Organizers also believed the presence of observers would have a stabilizing effect on would-be troublemakers and ensure that everyone concerned would be on their best behavior.

What an honor it was when Patrick and I were selected as observers. At the time, I wasn't sure what it meant, just that it was an honor. The weeks leading up to the big day turned into a crash course in Voting 101. For a college-educated woman who had almost a decade-long track record voting in elections back home, that wasn't so hard. What *was* hard was trying to imagine twenty-two million newly enfranchised voters learning how to cast a ballot, an adult population that was mostly illiterate. It was a huge concern for organizers.

Voting sites were another issue, the number and location. If voting stations in rural areas were inaccessible—a very real possibility given distances in the homelands and lack of transportation—the fact that a voter had learned how to cast his or her ballot would be of no consequence. And if there were too few voting stations in urban areas, it would be physically impossible to accommodate all those eligible to vote in the time allotted.

The International Election Committee projected approximately nine thousand voting stations to accommodate twenty-two million potential voters. That meant each polling station would have to handle an average of twenty-five hundred voters. Any malfunction in the process could result in hundreds of people being excluded when the polls closed.

At the embassy, we had more frequent briefings and updates on the situation in the Western Cape. My old rally mate, Political Officer Charles, was our go-to person for all matters pertaining to Election Day. He presented the plan for official observers, the process and polling areas. Charles also assigned designated teams.

For our assignment, Patrick and I would monitor three locations in the Western Cape. I was relieved we would be together. It couldn't hurt being with the top security guy. Our job was to keep our eyes open, report any unfair activity or obstruction to voting, like voter intimidation. Charles distributed blue armbands and logoed-hats to be worn as IEC identification. Each of us was given a Manual for Official Election Observers to study. As giddy as I was inside at being selected, the flip side was a visceral anxiety at the mention of potential violence on Election Day. We would be out in the field, the townships.

In the weeks leading up to the big day, lots of moving parts had to be reconfigured every day. My background helping organize congressional delegation visits with all the changes in schedules and meeting sites as security dictated was good training for the early chaos of the election plans.

Polling booths popped up in new places, some moved because of threats of violence. I tried to remember that all I had to do was watch, report. It seemed like a passive role, but given the volatile situation, I compared it to standing on a street corner at night in a big city back home. Alone I would feel scared. Standing with thousands I wouldn't.

Long days at the embassy flew by with preparation details—security, the daily program, official functions. Patrick had to be fully prepared. I watched as he came and went from his security meetings with South African counterparts to his site visits—reconnaissance missions to scope out main and alternate routes in case of disaster, access points to and from election sites, such as schools, public buildings, churches and makeshift sites to add on the maps. If my husband was anything in planning, it was thorough.

In addition to preparations for our official duties on Election Day, we also had to deal with Bill Clinton's presidential delegation visit, which was scheduled to arrive after the election, for the inauguration—assuming we made it that far, which is no doubt why the visit was scheduled for the inauguration rather than the election itself. President Clinton's Election Day delegation would be led by civil rights activist Reverend Jesse Jackson, with whom I was familiar by now, accompanied by congressmen, a few cabinet members, and former New York Mayor Dinkins and other notable Americans.

They would arrive days ahead at the Mount Nelson Hotel. As embassy officials and observers, our job was to accompany them on Election Day, travel in a secure bus from one polling station to the next along routes designated by Patrick. Part of the time he would be in the vehicle, part of the time not, but he would have briefed the local South African Police on our routes and destinations.

It was all-hands-on-deck with every staff person involved to some degree. Patrick rarely got home before ten. It was as if the earth might crack and open beneath us.

Any small act of violence could be the flashpoint for a riot, from there into a skirmish and on to outright war. We had lived it already. During the four months from January to April, eighty bomb attacks were recorded, half of which occurred in the last couple of weeks. Several of these were massive bombs. The murderous intent was evident—two bombs in public places the previous week killed nineteen people at random.

Cape Town was edgier than ever. Casual acquaintances who found out I worked at the embassy suddenly wanted to be my best friend. It was White Flight all over again, the crush for visas to leave the country. At that time the election hadn't been imminent. Now it was. If anyone was under the illusion that I could provide special access or expedite a visa, he was wrong. Those who stayed in Cape Town, like our friends the Donovans, prepared for the worst. Patrick had prepared as well. Store shelves soon emptied of tuna fish, cases of water, dog food, and dry goods.

In the eleventh hour, Buthelezi finally agreed to participate in the election. Clearly concessions Mandela had made for the Zulu chief's role in the future government convinced him after all. The Inkatha Freedom Party name had not been listed on the official ballot. By the time Buthelezi agreed to participate, it was almost too late to print extras, to say nothing of staffing polling stations in Kwazulu Natal. As it turned out, there were not enough ballots, driving the election committee to include an additional day of voting.

It was a Sunday, countdown to Election Day the following Wednesday. Three embassy friends and I needed time away from clocks that had become ticking time bombs. Plenty of radicals on both sides still opposed the new order. Anything could happen. For one day, we chose to rise above the stress, literally.

A favorite with locals, Table Mountain offered the best view of Cape Town. By ten o'clock Sunday morning, the four of us trailed up the face. Our chatting centered on the usual—work, marriage, kids, a smattering of office gossip.

It was good to talk freely. Government goons couldn't bug the wilderness. Conversation gave way to physical effort as we gained elevation. The world fell silent. All I heard was the sound of my own breathing. Forest shade added intimacy, shielding us from other trekkers as if we were alone. Wind rustled through the trees. Bright, colorful birds chirped. Merging into single file to climb the narrow trail, we focused on our ascent, the embassy and city below distant planets in our now-peaceful universe.

Trees thinned the higher we got, with shards of sunlight piercing the shade. Table Mountain was a huge tourist draw, so trails were well maintained. Even so, parts were steep, loose rocks slippery. Hiking boots were a drastic transition from my workday pumps. Two hours into the trek, a blister on my big toe screamed for attention. I waved the others on. Bev was still behind me. A squared-off boulder made the perfect place to rest to tend the toe.

Armed with moleskin from my pack, I gazed over the massive Cape Flats with their sprawling townships, a desolate wasteland ending at the lush properties of Camps Bay. Robben Island, Mandela's prison home, stood in stark isolation encircled by the Atlantic. The colors were brilliant—the dry township flats, barren but for bright blue plastic roof tarps visible even up high; the green foliage of landscaped lawns and tropical flowers in Cape Town; the ocean sparkling, alive under the African sun. High above the turmoil you could see the grandeur of it all. Helen said it best about those of us under Cape Town's spell: *Nature has blessed this part of the country by surrounding it with two oceans and magnificent mountains, a world of its own.* That's how I described the place in my letters home, like the billboard I had seen that first day in Johannesburg, A *World within One Country.*

My heart ached. Even if the election happened, even if Mandela won, how long would it take to bridge the fissure created by apartheid, a breach so wide maybe no one could close it. Not even Mandela. As much as I tried to remain optimistic, my faith floundered.

"I hope you're deep in thought about which candy bar to give me." Bev appeared, bedraggled but grinning. I scooted over.

"Litchi, plum, or…let's see…apple." I held them out. She smirked. We sat in silence for a moment. "It's pretty unbelievable how far we've come."

"Yeah, whose idea was this hike?"

I scoffed. "In three days, millions of South Africans will vote for the first time in three hundred years. And we'll be there to witness it."

"Don't get euphoric yet." Bev handed me a chunk of cheese. "That bomb in Johannesburg made the *Guinness Book of Records*. But if they think scare tactics will stop this election, they're wrong. Blacks won't allow this kind of oppression ever again. Even if the election doesn't come off, there's no turning back." She tossed her litchi pit. "Hey, we could just sit here, catch them on the return trip."

"And you with the '*I am Woman, Hear me Roar,*' sticker on your car. C'mon, let's go."

Twenty
Countdown to the Election

Election Week: Monday, April 25, 1994.

The next few days I barely saw Patrick. He started the morning running with an early meeting with staff to go over the final timeline for the presidential detail with Jesse Jackson. The plan was in place—transportation, polling stations selected, security, access, back-up routes. Patrick with his local South African security team had the latest alerts. That afternoon he met with diplomatic secret agents from Washington, D.C. on arrival at Cape Town's D.F. Malan Airport. From there he went straight to all sites the POTUS/Jackson delegation would visit in the next forty hours.

Tuesday, April 26th

Patrick and Consul General Myrick went together to the airport at ten o'clock to meet the Jackson delegation. I joined them at Bismarck's home for the briefing while the Reverend Jackson was taken to the Mount Nelson Hotel. Later that afternoon Patrick and the Jackson entourage attended a Peace Rally at Victoria and Albert Waterfront. After that they headed to Groote Schuur Hospital to attend early voting for prisoners and the infirm, then on to Hout Bay—Mandela Park—to tour the informal settlement.

Patrick was with the reverend for his media interviews at SABC broadcast station in Sea Point, then back to the Mount Nelson Hotel. Jesse Jackson wanted it all, embraced the frenzy of anticipation in the last remaining days before the birth of a New South Africa.

Our final event of the day was a small reception that evening at Consul General Bismarck Myrick's home in Bishopscourt for Jackson, U.S. officials, embassy officials and Election Observers. Patrick and I finally got home around ten-thirty. Though it was reasonably early, but both of us were too excited to sleep. I laid my head on Patrick's chest, listening to his heartbeat. He stroked my hair absentmindedly.

"Well, Mary, this is it. When we wake up, it will be the beginning of a new South Africa."

"It feels surreal after all this time, especially these final weeks with everyone holding their breath. Now the entire civilized world will watch it on TV."

"Yeah. Ya know, it's hard to imagine being part of something this important ever again in my ca—"

I popped my head up. "Maybe you should retire. We'll start a whole new life."

He tweaked my nose. "What I was *going* to say is that this is exactly why I committed my life to Foreign Service…to be part of real change that would improve life for millions."

My voice was a whisper. "I know."

Sensing dejection, he squeezed my shoulder. "In case I haven't mentioned it, you've been amazing, Mary. I see you at the embassy, in meetings with delegates, helping organize everything, planning diplomatic events, seen you with Princeton and Helen, with township clients, locals, all of it. I know it hasn't been easy, but you've been a real trooper. Remember how Helen told you she could never see herself representing the U.S. as a diplomat? I know you felt the same way. But that's exactly who you've become—a capable emissary. Right before your eyes."

"Hon, what a nice thing to say."

"I mean it. We did this incredible thing together, Team Byron and McGhee. Always and Forever. And this is just the beginning."

My eyes moist, I kept them downcast. How could he be so certain about our future? I wasn't. But in that moment I loved Patrick with all my heart. Had I not felt that spark the afternoon when he stepped out of the limo in Minneapolis, I wouldn't be about to witness history as a diplomatic spouse at my husband's side, as a Foreign Service Officer in my own right. Whatever else happened in our marriage, our post here would bind us for the rest of our lives.

Wrapped in each other's arms, we fell asleep, waiting for dawn.

Election Day: Wednesday, April 27, 1994

BUZZZZ. I jumped up. Why is it deep sleep comes in the wee hours right when you have to get up? Patrick had already left for his security briefing. In the kitchen Mr. Potato Head stood next to the coffee pot, arms pointed toward the sky, a big smile on his potato face. The Post-It read: *This is the Day! xo Moi (stay safe)*. Next to the note, spread out on the counter was the front page of the *Argus,* headline covering the top half of page in five-inch letters—*V-DAY*.

The night before, I had gone over my To-Do list, then spent half an hour choosing an outfit—dark pants, a thick sweater, wind jacket, sunglasses. The clothes were laid out over the bedroom chair; on the table beside it, the blue and white IEC wristband. My dad's lucky Twins baseball cap that had brought me good luck in Khayelitsha was next to that, along with the logoed IEC cap. The warm memory came back of my first visit to Mrs. Tambala in Khayelitsha, my first visit to a township. What must Mrs. Tambala be feeling today? What I would give to watch her mark the box next to Nelson Mandela. The warm image was followed by the jarring memory of barely escaping alive, which triggered the memory of Amy Biehl's murder in Guguletu Township. Guguletu was our first stop. Instead of succumbing to fear, I dedicated my work to her memory, as if my presence would represent her as well.

Eating Styrofoam would've been easier than the bran muffin I forced down. My stomach could take only half. Adrenaline fueled me even without my usual two cups of coffee. Dressed in layers to stay warm, the can of mace and the emergency whistle went in my sling bag. Then I put on the IEC armband and hat. Snacks for the day were already in my tote. Just in case, I wrapped the other half of the muffin.

Bev picked me up. At the embassy I would go with our logistics team via bus to the Mount Nelson Hotel to pick up Jesse Jackson and the delegation. It was barely light. On the bus everyone was quiet.

It might have been the early hour, but I suspect it was the significance of what was about to take place that rendered us speechless as we headed to St. Gabriel's Catholic Church in Guguletu.

Dismay, if not downright shock, registered on some of the delegates' faces as we wound our way through the narrow makeshift alleys of the slum. The streets were deserted in the early morning. I hoped our bus plodding through potholes didn't wake the neighborhood. A few minutes later the oppressive density of Guguletu shanties gave way to a wide expanse of undeveloped countryside. Our driver slowed to a crawl. We pressed our faces against the window, straining to make sense of what we saw in the distance.

A dark line at least a mile long formed a zigzag pattern across the field ending at a small church. It took a moment to register what we were seeing—people in line waiting to vote. No wonder the township had been deserted. Bundled in warm clothes, they must have been out there before dawn to get a place in the queue. As we watched, mouths open, the procession shuffled a few steps at a time toward the distant polling station.

My heart stuck in my throat. No one in the bus spoke. No words could express the feeling at such a profound sight. Without benefit of mentorship or training from the apartheid regime, it was anyone's guess how many would actually show up. But show up they did—old, young, disabled, robust, poor, uneducated, gangs, workers—in long zigzag lines rather than one straight one just to get closer.

Two young men lifted an elderly man each time the line moved. He was crying. The men were crying too, laughing and crying. Some cooked on makeshift *braais*, others sat on the ground eating breakfast. Women braided each other's hair. Young people danced the Toyi-Toyi. Tears pooled in my eyes at the knowledge that blacks, coloreds, Indians, Cape Malayans replicated this scene in every homeland and township across the land to cast their first vote.

The bus stopped near the entrance. Audible euphoria filled the air in a low hum of excitement. I made my way inside the church, signed in, took my place as Official Observer. My knees went weak. It was impossible to fully grasp the moment. One at a time, each resident stepped up to the ballot box. To a person, each one paused, as if making an indelible memory. I looked in their eyes, full of pride, hope. My own eyes blurred with tears.

It was almost an out-of-body experience watching history in the making—centuries of oppression at the hands of colonial rule wiped out—one vote at a time.

Officials checked identification cards in line. Passbooks were no longer required by law, but voters used them to show valid I.D., one of the issues worked out by the IEC. Once identification was verified, their fingers were checked for the spray applied after voting that showed up in ultraviolet light as a way to make sure they hadn't voted already. Then they were handed a ballot.

Some voters looked confused. Where's Mandela they wanted to know. In representational voting, parliament seats are based on number of party votes, people voted for a party, not a person. Familiar symbols were on the ballot for each party along with a picture of the candidate affiliated with it. Voters need not write a name.

A black woman leaned over and quietly asked my assistance in marking the ballot for her. I explained that I was not allowed to do that. An Electoral Commission official stood a few feet away. I waved him over to help her. The ballot for block voting may have been simple but the weight of the moment was not, the impact reflected on every person who stood before the ballot box to have their say.

After Guguletu, the delegation and I boarded the bus again for the ride to Christ the Mediator Anglican church in Mitchell's Plain, a largely colored township. Throngs like the one we saw in Gugulethu were also at this church.

Nelson Mandela chose to cast his vote in Chief Buthelezi's homeland of KwaZulu Natal. News reported people had shown up in extraordinary numbers that morning to wait for the polls to open so they could vote where Mandela cast his historic ballot. The international press was also there in droves. Mr. Mandela proceeded quite casually. First his voting documents were verified, followed by the dramatic secret marking of the ballot while the press waited outside. Not one to pass up a dramatic moment, before dropping the ballot he held it two inches above the box as a poignant gesture of significance at such an act. After the ballot dropped into the box, he looked around with the triumphant smile that had warmed a nation.

The deed completed, Mandela did oblige the press—reportedly frustrated over not being allowed to witness and photograph the actual casting—with a photo-op reenactment.

Once my duties ended accompanying the presidential delegation, I joined other staff to observe at polling areas in the Cape. I was fortunate to observe black, colored and white townships. Time had no meaning that day, as if we were suspended in the bubble of A Momentous Moment in History. Time melted away, just as it had on the set of *Woman of Desire*. No hunger, no full bladder, my entire physical and mental being focused solely on the moment. By the end of the day, I was back in the real world with real hunger pangs. Hours after observing voters around the Cape, we gathered at our "go-to" waterfront restaurant.

Relief was the overriding emotion for the first several toasts. At least in Cape Town, the election had come off without violence or tampering. Exhausted, exhilarated, we refused to let go of the moment, vying for turns sharing stories about what we had seen, how we had felt, incidents that could have derailed the elections. A bomb exploded at the airport in Johannesburg early in the morning just as the polls opened, along with other outbreaks of resistant aggression, but they were dealt with speedily and quietly by security.

Late evening, Patrick wrapped up his duties with the Jackson delegation and joined us for fish and chips. A fluid orange sun hung over the Atlantic, Table Mountain and Lion's Head aglow in triumph over Cape Town.

Participating in the election as an Official Observer was a powerfully moving occurrence. All this time at the embassy when we talked about everything going on outside its walls, it had been from a distance, one step removed—reaction to news clips on TV, reports of riots, police brutality, peaceful rallies. We weren't really part of it, not in the moment. But the sight of those long lines—voters changing the course of history in one day, my being there to witness the oppressed making their voices heard—was overwhelming. At each of three polling stations, with each new voter, I knew it was a high point in my life. The memory still sends shivers down my spine twenty-five years later. The election—deemed fair and open— was one of the most widely covered in the world. Nelson Mandela won sixty-two percent of the vote, just short of the two-thirds majority required to unilaterally amend the Interim Constitution. As required by that document, the ANC formed a Government of National Unity with the two other parties that won more than twenty seats in the National Assembly, one of which was F.W. de Klerk's National Party. The other was Chief Buthelezi's Inkatha Freedom Party. It seemed only fitting.

The first action by the new assembly was to elect Nelson Mandela president, the country's first black chief executive. Freedom Day, 27 April, is now a public holiday in South Africa.

May 1994

Prince Philip, Duke of Edinburgh, stopped at a bakery in Crossroads, the township next to Khayelitsha. Yasser Arafat, leader of the Palestine Liberation Organization, emerged from the VIP lounge at Jan Smuts Airport to give a press interview.

Hillary Clinton and delegation arrived on Air Force One. Coretta Scott King flew in with her delegation.

Representatives from the international community—politicians and dignitaries from one hundred and forty countries across the globe—showed up to witness the inauguration of South Africa's first black man, many making a stop in Cape Town before boarding the two-hour flight to Pretoria for the ceremony.

President Nelson Mandela was poised to take the stage for his speech in the amphitheater of the Union Building. Two weeks earlier these very grounds had been off limits to blacks. One of Mandela's special guests, his friend and former jailer James Gregory sat in the VIP section, testament to the extraordinary relationship that had developed between inmate and jailer over a quarter of a century.

A trip to Pretoria wasn't an option for those of us at the embassy. But we would not be denied the moment. Consul General Bismarck Myrick hosted an inaugural party at his home. Officers and families were invited to watch President Mandela's speech on big screen TVs, along with the attendant festivities.

Silence fell over the room when the ceremony began. Just like Mandela's speech at the convention center in Washington D.C. two years earlier, I knew the crowd feeling that followed. As President Mandela, flanked by First Deputy President Thabo Mbeki and Second Deputy President F.W. de Klerk, appeared on Botha Lawn beneath the Union Building, the place erupted with thunderous applause, shouts and cheers. The ecstatic crowd carried on for several minutes, Mandela, watched with his trademark big grin, while a restrained smile appeared on now-Deputy President F.W. de Klerk's face.

Mandela seemed to relish the moment; Mr. de Klerk looked respectfully contrite at the spectacle of triumph before him. After several minutes President Mandela finally succeeded in calming the crowd.

He addressed the masses, those in Pretoria and those of us watching in Cape Town, in big cities and small towns, rural villages and remote outposts around the world. Watching on TV at Bismarck's, none of us bothered hiding our tears. Joy. Pride. Relief. Humility. All of these emotions jockeyed for position behind a banner of collective astonishment. Chaos and violence had not been able to quell the fight for freedom. The miracle had taken place. Mandela tapped into authentic emotions as he spoke:

"We saw our country tear itself apart in terrible conflict. The time for healing of wounds has come... Never, never again will this beautiful land experience the oppression of one by another." Urging forgiveness, he said in Afrikaans, *"Wat is verby, is verby."* ("What is past is past.")

After all that had gone on, it boggled me then, as it does today, that he was able to move beyond it.

The ceremony ended. The celebration didn't. More than a hundred thousand jubilant South African men, women and children of all races poured into the streets of Pretoria. They sang. They danced. They hugged and cried. Traffic had been closed off, but the president's motorcade inched along at five mph through streets packed with throngs of well-wishers flocking around his car, Mandela at the window, grinning, waving, and soaking in the adoration. His beloved people. His beloved country. Thirty years later, the passbook-burning, forty-four year-old anti-apartheid activist who spoke at his sentencing about an ideal worth dying for had realized his dream—an equal voice for all South Africans.

At Bismarck's home we couldn't take our eyes off the TV. Camera crews trailed the procession on foot. Like the ecstatic mass they filmed, we, too, hugged and cried and toasted the extraordinary man who had given his life's energy to end legalized racism. Watching the scene, even from afar on TV, was the fitting culmination of our mission. We still had ends to tie-up. But we would hold on to this glorious moment until we could hold on no longer.

Reconciliation became his key priority once President Mandela took office. Wise man that he is, Mandela retained the services of the white heads of the police and the central bank. South Africa could ill-afford a mass exodus of knowledgeable staff with the skills needed to run the country.

The biggest relief for most people was what didn't happen. Because of Mandela's reconciliation and inclusion of long term white staffers in government, the violence and flight of capital and talent that many believed would happen post-election, didn't. Nelson Mandela kept his promises—white rule came to an end without retribution against the white minority, without the wholesale redistribution of white-owned land to a landless black majority. Mandela's efforts, including his support of the national Afrikaner sport—rugby— helped overcome the mistrust many white Africans intrinsically felt toward black people.

The dark heavy cloud of uncertainty that had hovered over the country the last two years dissipated. That's not to say peace and love reigned, but the terrible tension lifted.

At last.

Twenty-one
Bittersweet Parting

July 1994

They say the hardest part of a post is packing out at the end of it. When we arrived, everything had been new, the unfamiliar a novelty. So much had happened since then. Nostalgia always made me uncomfortable—looking backward, a process freeze-wrapped in loss. I didn't want to feel it. Leaving Cape Town would be hard enough. Focus on the future helped, but it also brought more conflict about leaving.

    Grateful to be alone in my office at the embassy in those final days of our mission, I set about the task of packing. The office was a veritable time capsule of my tenure. As Community Liaison, I'd been in various roles. As Mary McGhee, I had added those that came naturally. One was growing our embassy library. When I started work, *Prince of Tides* and *Patriot Games* were the best we had to offer staff. For a difficult and dangerous post in a pre-internet age, reading was a much sought-after diversion.

    Now the bookshelf against the wall had titles of fiction classics and nonfiction—biographies the most popular—as well as what would come to be known as "chick lit." The informal quarterly clothes drives for charity Bev and I organized had come with a serendipitous benefit—now the boxes included books they didn't want to ship back to the States.

    My file cabinets were stuffed with notes on every occasion and event I had organized, from baby showers to Fourth of July celebrations. That explained the stacks of paper on the floor. Several rolled-up posters made a pile on my desk, some from local artists, some from charity events, wall art accrued over two years that transformed the utilitarian State Department office into more of a hip lounge.

    A low narrow table displayed curios from home, alongside mementos from my work. I picked up the card from Mrs. Tambala, blowing off dust. How often had I glanced at the card, remembering our visit, the feeling of inclusion with the women of Khayelitsha. Through moist eyes, I reread her note of thanks for my work on her USAID project.

Mrs. Tambala would never know the huge impact she had on my life, the warmth running through me when she and the other women included me in the circle as we swayed and sang for the baby's future, for the future of South Africa. Baby Mandisa would be part of what was being called The Mandela Generation—babies born into freedom.

"Hey, there."

I jumped. Consul General Myrick popped his head in the door. "You look buried."

"Yes. Please rescue me." I got up from the floor.

"The fun part of the post, huh?" He scanned the pile of folders on the floor. "Sorry to add to your work. You might want to file this."

I took the card. He smiled and left me alone. The stationery had the official embossed insignia of the embassy. I opened it.

> *Please join us for a farewell celebration in honor of*
> *Mary Byron McGhee and Patrick McGhee...*

"Mary Byron McGhee" My lip quivered. Such a small gesture, but it struck me. This was Bismarck's doing. He had always known how hard it was for me to be Mrs. McGhee. For nearly two years, my name had not appeared on any official records. How beautiful it looked on paper. Now everyone would know. Thank you, Bismarck. I will miss you.

The next morning, my office was a hollow shell, a sad space devoid of life. What a transformation a few posters and curios had made, a desk with an overflowing inbox, a cup of half-drunk coffee. My first task that final day was to get the last embassy newsletter published. My heart was bursting to write about what these last two years had meant to me, all that we had shared—the congressional delegation visits, the Wheels-Up parties that followed, the violence, the drills, the tension, and the great sense of triumph seeing Nelson Mandela elected.

But no. It couldn't be about me. Besides, I had the perfect headline:

ROBBEN ISLAND OPEN TO THE PUBLIC FOR TOURS

Mandela would smile. It seemed a lifetime ago that Jane and I had sat on our deck looking at the famous prison where the future president fought apartheid from his cell. Now that cell was a tourist draw. What an amazing feat of determination and sacrifice.

The newsletter finished, the office packed, I took one last look before closing the door. As I walked down the hall, I smiled, thinking about my interview for the job, Officer Brown and the others expressionless as they peppered me with questions, most of which I was sure I had blown. *My foreign policy knowledge? Are you kidding? Two months ago I knew zilch about South Africa! My understanding of other cultures? Of course! The King of Norway stayed at our hotel.* But I had nailed the most important question—the one about the mission, the goal of democracy for South Africa.

My God. Had I known then what it would be like, would I have taken the job? With the last box of office belongings in my arms I shoved open the double doors of the building with a nod to the marine. Alone in the parking lot I broke into laughter.

Would I have taken the job? What an incredible ride it had been, what an honor and privilege to have been part of it! As long as I lived, this time in my life would be unparalleled.

Ages ago the Donovans had recommended a great place to hike. We had been so immersed in work before the election, now was our chance to explore this beautiful, diverse land. With no reservations, we took a chance. Saturday morning, backpacks ready alongside a small cooler, we headed out on a road trip to hike our favorite Garden Route in Tsitsikamma Forest.

A protected area on the Garden Route of the Western Cape, Tsitsikamma Forest is named in an African language that means "clear water" for the river by the same name in a thickly wooded area with rivers and canyons that stretches east from the coast. When we arrived, it was a bit chilly, windy, as it would be in winter in this half of the hemisphere. It didn't matter.

We stopped to shop for yellowwood trinkets to bring home before continuing west to the shore. As luck would have it, a small rustic lodge had a vacancy. It was low season, but the place was popular among locals and tourists alike. After getting settled, we sat with our cooler of juices and deli meats and local cheeses, the perfect picnic for our farewell journey to the South African coast.

The shore was desolate. We walked in silence for a while. It wasn't until that silent moment that I realized how loud life had been in Cape Town, not with city sounds, but the unpredictable sounds of civil unrest, the constant hum of tension like permanent white noise in the background. A mile into our walk, we found a fish restaurant.

At a fireside table near the window, we warmed ourselves over a drink. Patrick looked relaxed, youthful again. Chatting easily, the conversation no longer centered on Cape Town or the embassy or even the successful election. Patrick had a new post waiting. I had my public relations firm to start. We had family to reconnect with and a home to find. For the first time since we arrived, the thought of going home wasn't entangled with relief of escaping danger, but with excitement for what lay ahead.

At home family and friends were a short drive or flight away. That closed the gap between here and there. We would rediscover home. Patrick adored his Grandma McGhee, a solid, nurturing woman, and she him. Grandma would be the first visit on our list when we got to California.

One more party was on our schedule. The July Fourth Independence Day celebration would be our final bash with embassy friends, our last chance to say goodbye to Cape Town officials and local Americans. The traditional celebration with all-American fare would add sentiment to an already sentimental occasion—the Marine Honor Guard in all its traditional finery, a repeat of last year with a few new faces. This time I would take my camera, snap as many photos as possible, including one of the ambassador and his wife, my dear friend Helen. This really would be goodbye.

It was a cold, windy day, which should have made packing easier. I sat on the floor of the living room, half-packed boxes around me. Moving always made me sad, as if we were caught between two worlds, no longer part of either. How I would cherish my memories of the one we were leaving—that first day we walked into the flat with Jody and Henry; our reaction as we took in the Ethan Allen furniture, big windows, French doors, the wrap-around deck, the view—the vast Atlantic Ocean right outside our flat. I never did tire of it. But I'll never forget seeing it that very first time.

Now an echo bounced off the walls. Boxes grouped by colored dot told their own stories—green for household affects that would arrive soon after we did; red for storage; yellow for items to transport with us by plane. Thanks to the overflowing auction houses, we'd accumulated more than we thought we would. Each piece of furniture, artwork and curio needed a dot. The government allowed a budget based on family size and poundage, which we had taken into account with every purchase. Even armoires. Especially armoires.

The furniture didn't use up the whole budget. Cases of wine stacked against the wall would balance the scales, our favorites from Franschhoek and Stellenbosch wineries, including Shiraz and Pinotage, South Africa's signature varietal. What a big hit the wineries had been with visiting congressional delegations. As hosts, we had created our own tour that included Delheim, Boschendal and Meerlust.

Such outings were always a good way to end official visits on a high note, offered by bottled Cape Province bounty.

A gust of wind slammed the deck umbrella to the ground. I went outside to secure it. Whitecaps peaked on the water, chaos driven by the famous Cape winds. Lounge cushions would have to go downstairs to the storage locker. A throw pillow fell to the ground, triggering the memory. We hadn't been here a month. I sat on the lounge opposite Patrick at the table, his feet on the deck rail. The ambassador had arrived in Cape Town from Pretoria. Patrick told me it would be more important to meet Helen Lyman than Nelson Mandela so she could show me the ropes. I had tossed the pillow at him, nudged his sandal over the rail. How playful he had been back then, how young. Both of us. So much had happened.

A blast of cold air pushed me off kilter. I went back inside. Winter made it easier to leave. As I looked around the room, memories came flooding back. Tears came. Not tears of sadness, but those borne of the heavy feeling in my chest, the part of me that was anchored in South Africa, would always be anchored in South Africa.

Black liquid eyes stared back at me from one corner. Namutoni, that's what we named him. The six-foot giraffe had been carved by an artisan in Namibia where we visited before things got bad, before Chris Hani's assassination. Patrick had fallen in love with the wooden sculpture, insisting we could get it home in the Honda. For two days on the road, Namutoni's head stuck out one back window, his feet out another, his tail pointed up like a flagpole over the roof, us giggling as people stared when we stopped for petrol.

On the wall next to Namutoni there hung an election poster with a beaming Nelson Mandela. Next to that a framed shadow box of our special items from Election Day—two ballots, our armbands as Official International Election Committee Observers, and the *Argus* front page announcing Mandela's win in five-inch letters. These would have a place of honor in our next home.

I ran my hand along the couch, recalling our first night when we fell asleep on it, listening to the crash of waves; the night we made love on the floor after I told Patrick all about the Cape Town rally, his listening to every word. The wing chair had its own memories—Patrick collapsing with fever after his secret mission to Somalia; Peter groaning with joint pain as he sank into it the night he picked me up for the *Woman of Desire* wrap party, his arthritis erasing Patrick's jealousy.

We had struggled finding our way. I thought about the night of our terrible argument after the welcome dinner at the ambassador's home when Patrick told me that if I couldn't blend in I should go back to the States; finding him in the morning asleep on the couch; his surprise apology in the kitchen; the first of countless follow-up conversations that never happened; conversations that did happen on the deck, our designated meeting place once he told me about the surveillance; the argument on the beach that preceded it.

The safe room brought memories—sleeping in there for ten nights while Patrick was deathly ill after Somalia; the break-in New Year's Eve; *Father of the Bride*. In the kitchen I looked at the counter where Patrick always left Mr. Potato Head in various configurations to express emotions he couldn't; the table where I converted measurements in *The Joy of Cooking*, where Patrick ate countless dinners kept warm in the oven on late nights; the nook where I ironed his shirts in fear I'd become my mother.

The Donovans with Richard barbequing. Would Patrick and I ever see another barbeque without thinking of our secret meetings on the beach—his call to meet for lunch, being sure to bring the barbeque sauce, code for destroying sensitive material. So many memories poured into my brain—The McGhee special sandwich; Bev, our Sundowners with her favorite Chenin Blanc; Girl's Night Out; tennis with Helen; Patrick and I on the dance floor surrounded by onlookers at diplomatic events.

I smiled at the memory of Kruger Park— the joy of tracking wildlife; the utterly profound feeling of looking into the eyes of a lion, or watching elephants frolic like pups; the total contentment of sitting with Patrick in the Range Rover; the way we found each other; the moonlit night when I was at one with part of South Africa.

Painful memories came too—Amy Biehl's murder; the afternoon of the memorial when I sat on the couch sobbing for her, for all South Africans who had lost a loved one to violence, finally allowing myself to imagine the loss; the day I understood the old Afrikaner's reference to "our wretched ways"; the increasing tension between races as the election drew near; standing face-to-face with Chief Buthelezi in Ambassador Lyman's living room.

Had it not been for our post, I would have gone a whole lifetime not fully understanding the impact of oppression— Azisa's understanding that poverty was as simple as children not having shoes for the snow; slum living conditions I witnessed in Khayelitsha, Gugulethu, and other townships. I would not have believed the hatred, fear, and misunderstanding among races that resulted in so many thousands of deaths. Nor would I have basked in exuberance dancing the Toyi-Toyi in a crowd of thousands cheering for freedom.

I would never have known the satisfaction of work as a Foreign Service officer helping women achieve some degree of financial independence; would not have witnessed the power of one man's belief that life must be good, not just for a few but for all, or watched him go from prisoner for life to the zenith of his dream for a nation as its president.

Only for the great good fortune of falling in love with Patrick had I been part of it all—seen the human cost of apartheid rule; reveled in the joy of pushing toward democracy; stood filled with pride and humility at a polling site as an International Observer; watched the unshackling of three centuries of oppression unfold in long zigzag lines of voters waiting to cast their first ballot.

How small my world might have remained without those two years. As Mrs. McGhee, I had lost my identity. What I found was not the Mrs. McGhee who stepped off the plane in Johannesburg that August afternoon of 1992. But it wasn't the old Mary Byron, either. That Mary was a pale version of who I had become—the woman I might never have become had we not lived in South Africa where every feeling, every experience shaped me into the woman I am today.

In South Africa I had become a better Mary Byron. And a better Mrs. McGhee.

In the Foreign Service, part of leaving a post includes reaching out to the next family who will take your place. Patrick and I would be flying out of Johannesburg August 28th. New residents would move into our flat September 1st, a young couple from Kansas City.

From the dining room table, I gazed at the sea. What could I tell Katie about the life waiting for her in Cape Town? I chuckled, thinking about the letter I had gotten before we left D.C. from the diplomatic spouse who lived in our flat. She had painted a rosy picture of life in Cape Town—she made no mention of surveillance by government goons listening to the most intimate aspects of your life, or State Department protocol that imposed frustrating restriction. Things would be different for Katie.

Violence had abated, but pockets of unrest still smoldered in Johannesburg, as well as the townships, as people figured out the new constitution. As for Sea Point, the coastal neighborhood had reclaimed its status as Cape Town's gem, an idyllic vacation spot.

Dear Katie,

I am sure you're excited about your new life in South Africa. There might not be a lovelier city in the whole world.

On a separate page, I have included helpful information on the weather, local and westernized groceries stores (where I found peanut butter), churches, schools, how to handle the banking transaction - dollar to rand, names of people who can recommend vetted domestic workers, including child care and maids. In the flat, I will leave you our brochures from wildlife tours in Kruger Park, Robben Island, the wine country, the Garden Route and Table Mountain. There are amazing hikes to enjoy right in your new backyard.

On a personal note, my husband told me before we arrived that I was going to love South Africa. He was right, though not in the way I expected. As long as you keep an open mind, your experience will be very special. Two years from now I hope you leave South Africa with as much love in your heart as I have in mine.

Sincerely, Mary Byron McGhee

The sun was high when we boarded our South African Airways flight to the United States. It was my first time at the airport that I wasn't standing with embassy staff to wave off a congressional delegation. Now it was me and Patrick. Our dear friends the Donovans gave us a tearful send-off with promises to stay in touch. Just as boarding the British Airways flight from Washington D.C. to London for our honeymoon had been leaving everything familiar behind, so, too, did leaving Cape Town for San Francisco. I was leaving home.

As the plane taxied down the runway, I pressed my nose against the window for a final view, the same way I had two years earlier when Patrick whispered, *"You're going to love South Africa."*

A kiss on my neck startled me back to the present.

"Mary, just wait…you're going to love San Francisco."

~

PHOTO GALLERY

1992-1994

Just married, Mary Byron & Patrick McGhee, 1992

Arrival in Cape Town - Mary, Patrick and the iconic Table Mountain.

PHOTO GALLERY

U.S. Embassy July Fourth Celebration with Ambassador Princeton and Helen Lyman, Mary Byron and Patrick McGhee, Cape Town, 1993.

U.S. Marine Corps, U.S. Embassy

PHOTO GALLERY

President Nelson Mandela meets with U.S. Trade Delegation led by Commerce Secretary Ron Brown, Ambassador Lyman, Mary Byron and U.S. Congress representatives, 1993.

U.S. Trade and Congressional Delegation, Commerce Secretary Ron Brown thanks the embassy staff and community.

PHOTO GALLERY

On the set of "Woman of Desire" film with actress Bo Derek and actor Steve Bauer, Mary Byron shown with cast members, Cape Town, 1992.

Activist and actor, Danny Glover at U.S. Embassy reception, with Mary and Patrick.

PHOTO GALLERY

Mary's work included the USAID Project in Khayelitsha Township, near Cape Town, 1993.

USAID Project in central South Africa, Grasheprophidisa. Program Managers and Mary Byron, Self-help Manager, 1993.

PHOTO GALLERY

Activist and boxing legend Mohammed Ali visits U.S. Embassy with Patrick McGhee and Mary Byron.

South African Archbishop Desmond Tutu, Chairman of the Truth and Reconciliation Commission and Mary Byron, after the historic first democratic elections.

PHOTO GALLERY

Diplomatic Events

Mary and Patrick at the Marine Corps Ball with Richard and Michele Donovan and other friends, 1992.

Celebrating with friends at the U.S. Embassy Marine Corps Ball, Cape Town, South Africa, 1993.

PHOTO GALLERY

At the first Democratic Elections with Presidential Delegation, Rev. Jesse Jackson, Ambassador Princeton Lyman, Consul General (Amb.) Bismarck Myrick, Patrick and Mary.

Bidding farewell after the elections to the Presidential Delegation, led by Rev. Jesse Jackson. Consul General (Amb.) Bismarck Myrick shown here along with Mary Byron.

PHOTO GALLERY

First Democratic Elections

A Miracle of Apartheid's End and a New South Africa

PHOTO GALLERY

Mary and Patrick boating over to Robben Island, Cape Town.

Girl time with college friend Jane, at Cape Agulhas, the southernmost point in Africa.

Tour of Robben Island (Afrikaans: *Robbeneiland,* Dutch for "seal island") Since the end of the 17th century, Robben Island has been used for the isolation of mainly political prisoners, including President Nelson Mandela. It is now a public museum. Our group toured in 1994.

PHOTO GALLERY

Southern Africa Travel

African sunset at Three Rondavels

While on a Safari at Kruger Park, we spotted herds of elephants, frolicking at a water hole.

Hiking at Blyde River Canyon, South Africa.

PHOTO GALLERY

Saving African Penguins after Oil Tanker Spill

Mary working with the South African Navy rescue mission where endangered penguins were cleaned, fed and rehabilitated after the worst oil spill in South Africa's history. In June 1994, the *Apollo Sea* sank in a catastrophic storm off the coast, impacting thousands of penguins at their breeding colony near Cape Town. Patrick and Mary joined other volunteers who saved thousands of birds and released them back to sea near their colony.

Rehabilitating the oil-drenched African "Jackass" Penguin was a difficult and time consuming process. Patrick and Mary assisted in nurturing the penguins until their successful release into the wild.

PHOTO GALLERY

Mary and Patrick receive U.S. Embassy Honors for participation as IEC Election Observers and mission work leading up to the first democratic elections. Shown here, with Consul General Bismarck Myrick.

The Nobel Peace Prize awarded to Nelson Mandela And F.W. de Klerk for their work for the peaceful termination of the apartheid regime, and for laying the foundations for a New Democratic South Africa.

BIOGRAPHIES

Mary Ann Byron

Mary Ann Byron specializes in public relations, which takes her all over the world. From 1992-1994 she worked as a Community Liaison Officer and USAID Project Coordinator at the U.S. Embassy in Cape Town while on assignment with her husband, a Special Agent with the U.S. State Department. While in South Africa her work encompassed USAID development projects, diplomatic events and programs leading up to the country's first democratic elections. Since her Foreign Service experience in South Africa, Mary has yearned to share her personal stories of this tumultuous and life-changing experience.

After her assignment in South Africa, Mary continued her work in public affairs and special events working with NGOs, International Olympics, corporate and non-profit organizations. With a passion for international travel and adventure, Mary has lived in a dozen locations around the world. Currently, she resides in Colorado with her husband Patrick and their adopted pets. Mary returns to South Africa often.

No Ordinary Life, Mary's debut publication, is the first in the trilogy.

Lori Windsor Mohr

A native Californian, Lori Windsor Mohr has a Master of Science degree in Nursing from the University of California, Los Angeles. After teaching public health in the California State University system for fourteen years, she turned to writing full time. A novelist and short story author of twenty years' experience, Lori has more than two dozen stories published in magazines and online journals. Her debut novel, *The Road at my Door,* published by Alfie Dog Fiction in the U.K., follows a young woman growing up in 1960's Southern California against the backdrop of the aerospace industry, sex, drugs, and rock 'n roll.

Lori lives in Ojai with her husband and three dogs.

ACKNOWLEDGEMENTS

The African proverb, *It Takes a Village to Raise a Child*, rings so true here—my child being this story, the village my friends, family, other supporters who provided encouragement that kept me writing. After twenty-five years of journaling and holding onto this story, it wasn't until my husband retired as a Special Agent from the U.S. Department of State that I decided to share it.

Thank you Lori Windsor Mohr for taking on this project with me. From the stories I gave, she recreated the world I lived in for two years. Lori's insights, perspective—and most of all, her writing—brought my story to life. Both Lori and I are grateful to our editor, Nancy Hutchins, for her sharp eye and excellent advice. Many thanks go to beta reader Linda Parker for her multiple readings and useful feedback in the early stages.

I am very grateful to my dear South African friends, Michele and Richard Donovan for their support and friendship from the time we first met in Cape Town. Their perceptive readings of the manuscript, extraordinary memories that added detail to it, and insightful comments have enriched it.

A special thank you goes to Linda Biehl for her kind words in support of passages about the death of her daughter Amy, who was very much a part of my story.

Thank you to my embassy friends Helen, Princeton, Bismarck, Charles and Beverly for their support during my first assignment at the U.S. Embassy in South Africa and all the years that have followed.

To my long-time girlfriends, the Bison Babes, Zumba, Bonnie Brae, Bay Area network and special events team, your support and years of enduring friendship have been a bedrock.

The greatest thanks goes to my mother Patricia and my dear late father, Maurice, both of whom have always supported my aspirations, and who instilled in me a love of adventure, travel, the beauty of nature, and who gave me the priceless gift of seven siblings.

This book is for all of you.

DISCUSSION QUESTIONS

What struck you most about this insightful two-year period in South Africa's history?

How did Mary's marriage change? Stronger? Weaker?

Did you empathize with her struggle? Which part?

What feelings did this story first evoke in you? Have you ever experienced a similar situation of feeling displaced?

How did Mary handle the stress on her marriage in the beginning?

What would you have done at age 29?

Could you imagine yourself in her shoes, living with violence and death?

How did you feel as Mary found her voice?

What did Mary learn about her identity in two years? How did it change her?

How do women maintain their own identity in a healthy marriage? What makes it hard?

Did the story change your perception of the historical events? In what way?

How is the story relevant today?

~

NoOrdinaryLifeMemoir.com

CPSIA information can be obtained
at www.ICGtesting.com
Printed in the USA
BVHW041500040319
541707BV00009B/212/P